Actual Innocence:
A True Story of American Injustice

Robert Blankenship

DISCLAIMER:
The thoughts, opinions, and expressions herein are those of the author and do not reflect those of Cadmus Publishing LLC. Any similarities to actual events or people are purely coincidental. Names and distinguishing characteristics may or may not have been changed to preserve identities of any individuals.

Copyright © 2024 Robert Blankenship

Published by Cadmus Publishing LLC
www.cadmuspublishing.com
Haledon, NJ

ISBN: 978-1-63751-457-3
Library of Congress Control Number: 2024902325
All rights reserved. Copyright under Berne Copyright Convention, Universal Copyright Convention, and Pan-American Copyright Convention. No part of this book may be reproduced, stored in a retrieval system, or transmitted in any form, or by any means, electronic, mechanical, photocopying, recording or otherwise, without prior permission of the author.

Cadmus Publishing
www.cadmuspublishing.com

ROBERT BLANKENSHIP

Foreword by George Kayer.

Oath Keepers: The Ego's and Evils of Police and Prosecutors.

Oh how I wish I could say it is only a few bad apples, how badly society wants, even needs to believe this lie, this illusion.
The truth is factual and the facts uncovered the last few decades have proven, very clearly: oath keepers cover up for fellow oath keepers. Doctors and nurses stay silent when they drop a slippery newborn on the floor, leaving the child with lifelong disabilities and then, let their lawyers lie as the mother suffers, wondering what she did wrong. It happen to my son. What kind of evil is that?

In the pursuit of injustice, our criminal justice systems rely heavily on the integrity, competence, and the sworn oath of police officers, prosecutors and judges. While advancements in forensic technologies, not just DNA but also the debunking of 'junk sciences' have played a pivotal role in exonerating the innocent, non DNA cases are still the domain of the oath keepers, the badge holders. There's no DNA here to uncover their lies and treachery. No DNA to threaten the loss of their position in the community. No DNA to bring them in front of a review board or to be caught in their lies on the witness stand.

The oath keepers cover up isn't just a few bad apples, I wish it was. No sir, it runs from the beat cop through the public defenders office the prosecutors office, the crime labs right up to the Attorney Generals who wants to be Governor. I state this based on the facts. The fact that even after it is made clear that a state government is holding an innocent citizen, these fake ass oath keepers will fight like hell to dispel the DNA evidence and facts of the case. And do so for three, five, even ten years in some cases: that's the ego and evil of conspiracy.
Each person evolved in the case has their own petty agendas, fear of breaking the oath of silence, losing their job, their certification, their next election or perhaps the state will have to pay millions of dollars to compensate for their evils, how embarrassing !!
So collectively, in silence, they cover up the truth, knowingly leaving innocent citizens in prisons in your state and states all across America

Actual Inncocence

ROBERT BLANKENSHIP

ACTUAL INNCOCENCE

This book is dedicated to Sarah Hale (call me Sally). She was my one true advocate, she was my greatest joy, and she was my saddest loss.

Parts of this book are waves to my friends who do American Eskimo dog rescue, Vorgoth says hello. Tell everyone to buy this book, it has Eskies in it.

ROBERT BLANKENSHIP

Prologue

"Why should I read your book when I have no interest in it or its topic?"

When I was first asked that question, I knew I had found the first line of this book because I was stumped. I had no ready, easy answer.

The answer is, "Because one day its topic may take an interest in you and then, by god, you will either be very glad you did or deeply regret you did not read this book."

I am in prison.

This book will skim my life from the beginning to eliminate suppositions and to clearly show how some circumstances came about. I will write about relationships including sex for a good reason, but I will write as PG-13 as possible. There will be profanity used to show actual words spoken or my thoughts.

This book will culminate in the events, focusing on the very real trial that led to my current situation. I will attempt to highlight the mistakes I made in the overall process, and I will attempt to provide information for people who may one day need it which, in fact, could be anyone at all.

I am writing this book for two main reasons. One, am I innocent? All I can say is, please read the whole book, look at the actual documents and then decide. I would ask that the book be read as if it was a spouse, a son, a daughter or some other loved one because one day it very well could be.

The second reason for this book is that I hope to instill enough fear to break the mental barriers of, "It could never happen to me," or, "If I never do anything wrong, I can never get in trouble."

No one ever believes they could be the witch until it's too late and they are. Even when people see questionable circumstances they justify it by thinking, "That happened to, or because it was, him. Had it been me it would have been different." An error in thinking many have learned the hard way.

This book is not about witches or witch trials, but there are some very obvious parallels. There is a book titled "The Salem Witch Trials: A Day-to-Day Chronicle of a Community Under Siege," by Marilynne K. Roach. I will not be quoting that book directly, but I will be referring to the events that took place during the Salem witch trials and that is an excellent book to study.

When I wrote, "I am in prison," I am sure it aroused visions of shower rapes or other sordid perversions. There won't be any of that in this book. This is not a book about being in prison, but I may include some side stories to simulate time passing or to make a point.

Most forms of mass media equate prison to sex, but in reality, sex or the lack thereof is rarely mentioned because the number one, never ending, topic of conversation is food. I hate it when I see someone on TV like Propaganda Princess, aka Nancy Grace, say things like, "He will go to prison and he will eat filet mignon," (her exact words). Then I get a food tray and on it there is a sour smelling, runny, lumpy brown substance that I believe is either dead human anal leakage or partially digested regurgitated emu meat, though I'm unsure what regurgitated it. Anyone who equates prison to sex instead of bad food is obviously very well fed and they are full of shit.

A real prison story would read," I am bored. I am hungry. I've read that book. Someone farted. The end," (a riveting tale, can't wait for the movie). In prison there are exaggeration artists who could turn that into a two-hour story of malice and mayhem. I am sure any stories I relate will be tame just as I am sure there are others who know (or have heard) much worse (and worse every time they tell it).

I listen to the song titled "Under and Over It" by Five Finger Death Punch every morning before I write because attitude or focus requires fuel and that is the perfect song. I am definitely under it, and I am nowhere near over it, so there may be some rants or outbursts that are less than politically correct. I am also prone to a dark sense of humor, but should anyone be offended please refer to my theme song titled, "Harder Faster" by W.A.S.P.

Parts of what I write are currently a sensitive topic so my dissenting views some may not like, may not agree with, or may even despise. I simply do not care. I am not writing to convince anyone of anything. What happened to me or what has happened to thousands of others can happen to anyone because no one, of any age, is exempt or immune. If it does happen there is information that needs to be known beforehand because going in blind or worse, going in trusting, can be a huge, painful, irreversible mistake.

Every day countless innocent people are cried witch. Their villages will give each of them the semblance of a fair trial after they chop, then stack, wood for the bonfire, and after the jury finishes making, then lighting, the torches.

Congratulations! You're next!

If I could step back in time to the 1690s, and if I could write a book to warn the people of Salem of the impending witch trials, trials that will be started by two girls ages nine and 11, what could I write?

Or as an accused witch, how could I present my book to people who have no interest in it or its topic?

2012 to 2023

Robert, or Vorgoth

"One never knows if one is paranoid or just painfully aware of the possibilities, or not paranoid enough." - Robert

"I am an accursed storyteller for I neither spell nor write in a manner that is proper." - Vorgoth

ROBERT BLANKENSHIP

✦ X ✦

Table of Contents

Chapter 1: Possible Pasts 1
Chapter 2: Arrest 5
Chapter 3: Foreplay 14
Chapter 4: The Trial. 47
Chapter 5: Boned 82
Chapter 6: Climax 137
Chapter 7: Transcript Wars 176
Chapter 8: Actual Innocence 206
Documents 218

CHAPTER 1

POSSIBLE PASTS

There is a song by Pink Floyd titled "Possible Pasts," and have noticed all the way back to grave sex girl on Jew have written, "possible past," many times. They do flu a person, but they are never out of mind.

When I had came back to my mom's from Tennessee, bought my car I went to visit Lisa's grave several times. It did n nightmares and it became a place of solace for me. I would pack of beer, I'd sit at her grave and I'd talk to her. One day I go see her mom, but she was gone, it was not just Lisa's mo gone, the house was gone, and the basement was gone. It wa grown and someone had logged the mountain behind where had sat so it was totally changed. No one standing there would a girl had lived, or died, there but she was remembered.

On the other side of morbid, in Richlands I'd go to a store one would be all, "Wow, it's you, I thought you were dead, h member that time…" Sadly, no. I did not remember the time remember the person asking. Way too much water under way bridges since way back whenever.

One experience that must be in the book to go full circle funny, to me. Richlands is a small town, my mom had gone to c ever, and she knew all kinds of people. Every time we went t

he would see two or 10 people she knew. One day at the store
aused to speak to a lady who was in a wheelchair. The lady was
, and she had to be around 400 pounds if not more. I did the
d-and-wait thing. When we moved on, I asked mom who that
y mom told me it was my first wife Kat. What the huh!
y went back to look but I honestly did not see it. We had been
 years, she was only six months older than me, but she looked
der and 300 pounds heavier. Kat must have thought I was an
 not speaking but she had become so fat I had not recognized
he ended up on oxygen I had no clue.
ink Floyd song Lisa would be the frightened and lost but there
c for fat as a house. Way back in time when I had punched her
in the face, I wrote that I should have shook his hand because
 a massive favor and there it was. If not for him it might have
eding that thing. Okay, yes, I know that was mean, petty and a
alled for thing to say. Fun, but uncalled for. If one isn't going
iething nice one shouldn't say anything at all. As an apology,
 and is dead, I've been in prison for quite a while, if I get out
k the fat off that thing since sex burns calories and someone
wasn't keeping up. Sally wouldn't want to be first anyway, she
Well, that is if COVID didn't take Kat out. For the record,
ote that, I was damn near 60 years old, I weighed 165 pounds,
10 sets of 25 jumping jacks and pushups anytime. I only weigh
ewrite.
 all of that, Sally and I still visited each other a lot and we often
ents. One thing that Sally and I both had was the DVD sets of
Bang Theory," which we both liked. We both had a bowl to put
 and on that show, they mention a brisket a lot, but I'd never
e. I found a recipe online that used beer so it would have to
 decided on a Sam Adam's summer ale. The plan was that I'd
e Fourth of July then we would watch the fireworks which we
om Sally's.
, 2012 I went down to Sally's. That day I made hamburgers, no
Sally's, and triple onion on mine. I had bought a brisket and it
inate.
 4th, 2012 I cooked the brisket, I made corn-brussels sprouts
tter sauce, I made deviled eggs because Sally loved my dev-
I made baked potato wedges and rolls. For dessert I made

alcohol-cinnamon peaches with strawberry-butter pecan ice cream. Sally loved it when I cooked but she always whined about the mess, especially bowls and spoons. Good food requires a mess, it's not a TV dinner to be eaten with a plastic spork. Of course, Sally only whined about the mess after dessert was finished. After dinner we had mixed drinks while watching the fireworks.

On July 5th, 2012 I was getting ready to go home when Sally called from the back bedroom that she needed a hand for a minute. (Who makes the bed when I'm not there.) When I got back to the bedroom Sally said, "I'm wearing pirate panties," and she attacked me. The good, get naked, do stuff, kind of attack.

When Sally and I had been married, one time I had had a rough day at work. I had to square up the ends on 1,000 20-foot 2x12s. I had to lift each one just to barely cut maybe one-32nd off each end and then lift it down again. By the time I got home most of my parts didn't want to move and the parts that did move hurt. It was only around 6:30 p.m., I was in the computer room about to fall out, so I went to bed. I was not aware that Sally had made plans for sex, special plans, but when she came back, I was crashed, and I had not said goodnight. I was usually up and gone before Sally even woke up, so I did not see her until the next evening. As soon as I came in, I knew that look. She was like a pressure cooker with a loose lid and one little poke would cause it to blow. I expected it to be something to do with the registry or police report but nope, Sally had planned on sex, but I'd ruined it.

One day at Wal-Mart we were in the panty isle and by luck they had a lot of pirate-themed panties, so we bought a bunch. If Sally mentioned pirates or if she had on pirate panties it was kind of a slap upside the head hint. The best pair of pirate panties were black with a see-through skull-and-crossbones on the front that would be flesh tone when she had them on, a very interesting flesh tone. Sally played games. She would send me emails or texts asking me if I liked pirates.

One day I came home and Sally had on an eye patch. First I said, "What happened!" Sally just sat there so I said, "Oh, got it." Sometimes all Sally had on was pirate panties and those were good hints.

On July 5th, 2012 Sally was not joking, she had on pirate panties at the start but we had rampage sex for over two hours. I don't know if it was fate or some other crazy cosmic force but before I left Sally had an email. I was almost out when Sally said there was a rescue at the Kingsport Animal Shelter that a rescue group needed pulled to meet up with a transport, but it had to be done on the sixth. I spent the night at Sally's. On the sixth I spent $42 at the Kingsport Animal Shelter, and I met the transport person.

And here ironically my story ends and the book really begins. A little twist that the day I met Sally we had done a shelter pull then had sex for a start. On July 6th, 2012 we had sex then did a shelter pull. It was an exit because it was the last time I'd see Sally in the flesh, alone.

This entire story has been written to get to this point, to explain the conditions that landed me in the crappy house with no floors. The stage is now set for the final act, but it's a long, hard road to get there.

I wrote a long story to get to this point but due to a death, finances and editing some back story had to be cut.

To set the stage around 2010 I lived in Grey, Tennessee with my wife Sarah Hale (call me Sally). We had 2 houses, 4 vehicles and 13 American Eskimo Dogs. When life was good I built both Sally and myself very high dollar computers.

I ended up at my mom's in Raven, Virginia. My mom had a brain aneurism, I made a rent to own deal on a very old house that had flooded a few times, the floors were never fixed so the subfloor rotted to dust, the floors collapsed in places. The walls and roof were good but the floors were gone, I owned a damn nice gaming rig computer. This is evidence (of nothing) so pay attention.

In the Pink Floyd Song, "Possible Pasts," heed, "a warning to anyone, still in command, of your possible futures, to take care."

"And now for something really completely different." Monty Python.

Chapter 2

Arrest

Sally was not the only woman that I saw, there were several I could write about but only one matters. There was a married woman in Raven with three kids, two younger twins and an older girl named Brandi Lee Short. Then at the start I also need to explain that Raven and Doran were the same place. My house was listed as Raven, but the Doran Grocery was a two-minute walk from my house.

The married woman in Raven would come by through the week and sometimes the kids would come over, so she'd get dressed in the bathroom to sneak out. Good thing my back door was in the bathroom. The twins walked my dogs out back when I went to Sally's and Brandi was learning guitar chords on my guitar.

On July 8th, 2012 the mom visited me and she borrowed my vacuum cleaner which was one of her excuses to come by. She told me she had a pug they needed to get into rescue, and they knew I did rescue work.

Then there is a minor fill-in here. I knew Brandi was wild, but I did not know how wild or insane. Brandi had a black-haired girlfriend she played with at my house if I was out with a married woman. I knew they took pictures of each other and Brandi took pictures of her little sister when she was asleep or in the tub at their house. One time Brandi was almost caught with the pictures of her sister, so she broke the camera. The mom should wonder how would I even know the camera was broken and what was really on it. Brandi would use my computer to burn pictures to CD or DVD for her girlfriend. I showed her how to use an external drive to keep questionable photos off my computer and she used an eraser delete program that was military-grade delete.

Having written, rewritten, altered, edited and added to this book, not to mention suggestions, corrections, reprimands, (threats) and annoyances by Sally, and friends, I was going to save this part for the end. The plot twist, the big reveal or the rabbit out of the hat surprise at the end, but the story becomes so convoluted the real story goes into a vacuum if it's not maintained. Hell, that don't make sense, even to me, at this point but it will. Call it a true crime test, my bank statement proves me innocent.

At the same time, I would hate to alienate even one person who has read this far, but one simply must separate the wheat from the chaff. Anyone who is too fucking stupid to know what a bank statement is, stop reading now! To the rest, continue on, we don't need their kind (morons). It's an inside joke that's not very goddamned funny.

To the true crime aficionados, those who want to figure it out, find the clues, spot the facts, mistakes or bullshit, I do apologize for the following spoiler, but pay close attention. In Documents I have included three pages of my bank statement. For the record, I have personally polled over 500 people and Sally has polled over 500 people and every person polled agreed that yes, it is a bank statement. It clearly says Statement Period at the top and it has cancelled checks. If we agree it is in fact a bank statement, then we can move beyond this point of question.

Please note on page 2 of 4:
7/10 200 ATM W/D 15:47 7-9-12
13250 Gov. Peery Hwy
Pounding Mill, VA
7/10 4.92 DBT CRD 16:09 7-9-12
Doran Grocery
Raven, VA

The math here is very simple, it doesn't matter if one uses 15:47 to 16:09 or 3:47 to 4:09 that is 22 minutes either way. A person's whole life can be defined in just 22 minutes. But that 22 minutes could become very important to anyone at all.

The addresses needed are the ATM 13250 Gov. Perry Hwy, the Wal-Mart 13200 Gov. Perry Hwy both at Pounding Mill, Virginia.

I have included a crude hand-drawn map, from the ATM to Doran Grocery is 8.8 miles, 13 minutes if one drives at speed nonstop and if one goes right at Claypool Hill. The directions start out, "head east on US-19N/460 E, make a u-turn after 338 feet." With a u-turn into traffic and five red lights, driving at speed point to point would not be very likely. Anyone can double check that on any map program.

Twenty-two minutes, everything relevant is irrelevant.

On July 9, 2012 Brandi's mom and little sister brought the dog over to my house. I took pictures of the dog then I made requests to join several pug rescue groups. I had to wait on approval to post. Brandi came in. I had to go to Wal-Mart to pay my water bill and car payment. Brandi asked if she could go and maybe drive at the school some. I had told Brandi I would buy her a guitar chord poster like I had on my wall. Brandi had drove at the school numerous times or on back roads with her family, an uncle.

We left my house, 247 Kirby Road, Raven, Virginia. I forgot my cigarettes, so I stopped at the Corner Mart. I bought a six-pack of beer, a pack of cigarettes, and because she asked, I bought Brandi an energy drink. I usually kept a pack of cigarettes above my visor so that's where I put them. Back on the four-lane I drove to the school. At the school my gas light came on, so I pulled over to a gas station and I put gas in my car. I drove to ATM at Claypool Hill. I pulled over to the Wal-Mart and we entered on the food side. I had my envelope but not my car payment so we went back to the posters but they were sold out of the guitar chord poster. We exited the food side. I drove back to Raven, going right at Claypool Hill. I stopped at Doran Grocery and I bought a five dollar, $4.92, heated personal pizza, then drove home. At the house I put my keys, my change and my wallet in my bowl. I gave Brandi half the pizza.

Brandi's sister came in, I went to the bathroom and they left. Brandi stole my wallet, then on the way out she also removed the cigarettes from my car.

Later I was at my computer and all hell broke loose with people attacking my house. Raven was full of pill heads, and I was on the registry, so I called the police.

Brandi had told her mom I had attempted to lift her shirt, so they attacked my house but when the police got there that went from I attempted to lift her shirt to attempted rape. When the cop came in, I was forced to sit on my couch and I was not allowed to move. The cops asked to search my house, the "sexual assault" was supposed to have happened in my house, so I told them to search all they wanted. Later a cop asked me if I left the house, and I said I went to Wal-Mart. Over an hour later I was asked if I had on underwear and I said, "I want a lawyer." I was held and I was grilled for over six hours and all I ever said was, "I want a lawyer."

After six hours I was detained and they were going to move me outside, I got my keys, but my wallet was gone so I told the cops my wallet was stolen. I was detained so I could not file a criminal complaint about the wallet. The cop went out and he came back with two receipts that had been in my wallet.

It took over six hours to finally work out the story. The sexual assault was moved from inside my house to Ray Road. The story once they worked it out, at Corner Mart without being asked at all, totally at random bought Brandi a pack of cigarettes so that was contributing. After Wal-Mart I drove down to Raven, then to Daw Road, then to Ray Road. I walked Brandi 195 yards up a dirt road. I took off my pants, I took off Brandi's shirt, and I took off her bra. I attempted to remove her pants but then I decided I was bored, or it just wasn't working for me, so I stopped, and we drove home. I put the actual criminal complaint in Documents but in case it's hard to read it says:

"Responded to 247 Kirby Road for dispute learned suspects were upset because accused attempted to rape 14 y.o. daughter Brandi (Lee) Short. I spoke with victim she advised that accused drove around with her going to Corner Mart in Richlands and bought her a drink and a pack of cigarettes which she provided to me. They then went to Wal-Mart and then to Daw Rd. to Ray Rd. where accused pulled off the road and walked victim 195 yards on a dirt road where he took off her shirt and bra, exposed himself by pulling off his pants and then tried to take her pants off. Victim began to scream and cry and accused stopped taking her back to his car making her drive home."

That was written July 9, 2012 at 10:27 p.m. That is the actual criminal complaint. I was charged with attempted rape, Actual Inncocence (yeah), assault and battery and contributing to the delinquency.

Then we have a supplement but here I need to state I can only add so many documents so on the supplement I put in page 3, 4, 5 and 5 but I am missing a page 5. (Confused? You won't be later.)

In the supplement page 4, I bought her a pack of Camel cigarettes because that's what she gave them, an energy drink and I bought a case of beer.

"She went on state that in Wal-Mart he found a pair of sunglasses and placed them on his head, SEE VIDEO, they then walked out without paying for them."

"The two left Wal-Mart and headed back to Raven where she states he made her drive to Daw Rd. where he took off her shirt and bra and he took off his pants, was not wearing underwear. She turned her head and then he tried to take her pants off but she began to scream for help. He then grabbed her around the neck and started to choke her until she began to cry when he then quit. He made her get into the car and drive them home..." Who drove?

In the criminal complaint it clearly says, "where accused pulled off the road," meaning I drove to Ray Road, but in the supplement she drove. I made her drive, but I pulled off the road. It's minor but still a thought. In the supplement she screamed and I choked her but once again I stopped.

Now in the supplement when the cops first came, I did say I did not know what was going on because I didn't which was why I called the cops to start with. I do feel pretty damn certain that had I just sexually assaulted someone in my house or anywhere else I damn sure would not have called the police. Then I told the cop I had been home all day when I said I'd gone to Wal-Mart. (But not really.)

"Blankenship gave permission to search the house and we did." The assault was on Ray Road, why search my house? Because she originally said it was in the house.

Ah yes, the infamous Janet Lester 276-345-4374. She was not in the first supplement, she was added later, but that's a whole other story for later. But we have a witness who saw us at Wal-Mart.

On page 4, last paragraph I advised I was not wearing underwear but, "He never acknowledged if he would speak to us." Then, out of my empty pockets, I gave them two receipts. So, my keys, my change, and everything went in my bowl, but I held the receipts in my pocket then without acknowledging if I would speak. I said I had not left the house all day but here are two receipts to prove I'm lying. I did speak, a lot, I said, "I want a lawyer," about 500 times over six or seven hours. Any question I was asked I said, "I want a lawyer."

Then we have Detective Lane, my favorite. In the supplement page 5:

"She explained that there were going to be 2 Budweiser cans that are red and white. We arrived in the area and found the cans."

Oh shit! They found the cans, I bought beer, they found the cans, oh woe is me, why oh why did my family have to raise a goddamned litter bug? I am a fucked puppy, my goose is cooked, they found the cans, case closed, I am doomed.

Twenty-two minutes, everything relevant is irrelevant.

Has anyone ever noticed that if someone is damn annoying or needling like saying a thousand times, "I want a lawyer," the one being annoyed can never resist a parting shot? On the supplement the cop wrote, "I did this and Blankenship advised that his lawyer explained to him to say no to all of our answers." I had been on my couch for six or seven hours, pretty damn sure there was no lawyer in the room. And I do believe he was so annoyed he wrote, "To all of our answers," when he meant, "To all of our questions." Yep, him was annoyed.

The second paragraph on page 5 Detective Lane, "Advised that he found video of the shoplifting at Wal-Mart and showed me two still photos of Blankenship selecting the glasses…" I was issued a summons for shoplifting.

Damn, attempted rape, Actual Inncocence, assault and battery and contributing, those were no big deal but my God, shoplifting, how could my soul bear that burden?

"You can get anything you want at Alice's Restaurant," but don't litter beer cans and then to my mortal shame, a litter bug and a shoplifter. It's a hell of a crime spree.

Page 5 ends: "Detective Lane is still assisting me with the investigation."

For God's sake, has anyone spotted the most ironic part of the tale? (You will later: hint: Evidence Sheet.)

Wait. I don't know if anyone else is like this, but my boss used to be up my ass if my paperwork wasn't in by 4:30 p.m. "We ain't on overtime 'round here." Check out the second page 5. The supplement by Ray Smith. I was arrested July 9, 2012 but Ray didn't do his paperwork until March 5, 2015. Damn, three years behind on our paperwork there, Ray. However, one does have to applaud the identic memory. None of the officers took any notes but he perfectly recalled all the details in the report. Imagine all the cases he must have handled over three years but to instantly recall, without notes, the details, wow, impressive, most impressive. But then, Mr. Smith recalled some very weird shit. Now, had he said Brandi's mom worked under me once in a while I could have gone along with that, but he wrote that I said her stepdad had been working for me. Where the hell did that come from because it's only mentioned once anywhere. Then to make it crazier he implies that I didn't know how to call 9-1-1, I asked someone else to do it online, but they had the recording of me calling 9-1-1. I do believe Mr. Smith had been sampling some stuff from evidence.

Did anyone else see the original movie titled "Heavy Metal"? That shoplifting summons was like the charges read on Captain Stern, "And one parking violation." They had video and stills of me shoplifting and no matter what do not forget they found the beer cans. They also had video of me buying gas.

"I.R. Definitely Arrested." Held without bail.

Damn it. All my proof or test readers are friends of Sally's and they are all females who are persnickety as hell which is damn annoying. Yes, in the movie "Heavy Metal" Captain Stern had one "moving" violation, not parking. There, are we all happy again? I just wrote the trauma of being arrested for attempted rape, Actual Inncocence, assault and battery, contributing and shoplifting, so excuse me if I misaligned an infinitesimal detail of a fictional character in an observation. It's a good thing Sally assured me all proofreading was done naked by the women or I would be upset.

Here's a detail. I was arrested July 9, 2012 but somehow I used my debit card 15:22 July 10, 2012 at Doran Grocery right where Brandi lives, then I used it at 22:10 July 10, 2012 at Cedar Bluff. Uh, yeah, neat trick from jail.

Can I just say for the record, July 9, 2012 I had my beer, I had a young girl, I drove (she drove) to a secluded location, 195 yards up a dirt road, I chill out having two beers, I remove her shirt, I remove her bra, I remove my pants, I try to remove her pants, she screams, I choke her out, then I stop and we drive home.

When Sally was 13 years old, she was in a pool when her top came off. She never got confused about it after 40-plus years. Think on that.

The very next day I had a visitor. Damn, that was quick. Oh, it was just a cop who was very concerned about my poor dogs and he would like me to sign so they would have my permission to enter my house to check on my dogs. How about fuck no! I had called my aunt who had called Sally. On the 11th Sally came very early and she took my dogs with her. On the 12th an investigator showed up and he said there were complaints about my dogs. If I didn't give them permission to enter my house, I would be charged.

I told him he was a lying son of a bitch, my dogs were in Johnson City, Tennessee, so they must be loud as hell to get complaints in Raven, Virginia. I told him he wanted permission to cover up breaking and entering to steal my computer which they had done on the 10th. The lying son of a bitch left, and no charges were filed.

Once upon a time the police broke into a home and they stole a computer. Somehow the geniuses unhooked and they left four external hard drives which may or may not have contained thousands of cracked games, cracked programs, music, movies, and two little folders named "Brandi's Pics," that one could only imagine what might have been in those. I would bet that Brandi was in fits if she thought the cops had her Christmas pictures. But if this tale is real, Brandi's girlfriend and Brandi's little sister would be relieved to know those four drives were drilled, crushed, then buried in a massive landfill 10 years ago as of 2022. The police have the computer but the only thing on it were pictures of Brandi's girlfriend with clothes on. Those were in a desktop folder, and they were part of her Christmas collection, not taken by me or at my house.

I should point out the real spoiler here is that now the reader has information I did not have. On July 9, 2012 I had the criminal complaint and I had the shoplifting summons so read the reports carefully. Of course, the police could just give Brandi and her sister a lie detector test about my stolen wallet. Then again, everyone could just consider, "they found those cans," case closed.

What I really want to push is, do not justify what is read because it's me; read as if the same thing happened to your child and study all evidence under that light.

The main thing here is the route I claim, write it down, Corner Mart, Valero, Bank at Claypool Hill and Doran Grocery which my bank statement shows.

Then, and more importantly, I would ask any female who ever lost a top in public to really read that on Ray Road Brandi said her shirt and bra were removed, she would have been a 14 year old girl, topless, outside in front of a man.

ROBERT BLANKENSHIP

For the record I never said I did not leave the house, I said I went to Wal-M art.

Arrested, held without bail; so, let's do jail stuff for the next few YEARS!.

Chapter 3

Foreplay

Yeah, yeah. Not a great idea to name a chapter Foreplay after the chapter titled Arrest because it could give the wrong impression unless one considers foreplay any action before one is truly boned, then by the end of this chapter it will seem appropriate.

But first, Sally was fond of bluegrass music, so to show I'm multitalented across many genres, one has to imagine up-tempo bluegrass music and know that Virginia is often referred to as Virginny. I done wrote this little bluegrass ditty for Sally.

"Virginny is for lovers
They put homo-sex-uals in jail
And even if you're not gay
They will put you there as well
Virginny doesn't give a damn
About your situ-a—tion
But the only way you're gonna leave here
Is to agree to probation
Virginny is a gon-oh-rhea
Virginny is a fly in your soup
Virginny is a big brown wet stain
You thought was just a poot
Come on to Virginia

You'll damn sure stay a while
Pretty soon the whole damn state
Will be renamed The Green Mile."

"And that was R. Blankenship's latest number one bluegrass hit titled, 'Plea Deal Insomnia.'" Well, number one among the currently incarcerated, that is.

To simulate some time passing and to settle into jail I thought I'd add a few tidbits plus a few stories I have collected. Time does pass, albeit slowly, in jail and some days are longer than others.

I was in Tazewell County Jail, Tazewell, Virginia. Jails have pods and the pods at Tazewell were small, only 12 cells that were originally designed for one person. Then they added a second bunk, but they are set too high with no way to step up or get on it. Nothing funnier than a fat dude hanging half off the top bunk, legs kicking but he can't get up or down. Then they use a stack-a-bunk to put a third person on the floor which barely leaves room to stand at the toilet. Sometimes they don't have a stack-a-bunk so a person gets two blankets on the floor next to a toilet people have to use. Three people are jammed in a space smaller than a trailer bathroom for 23 hours a day. They cram 36 people in a space made for 12. The pod has two showers that work most of the time and there are no cleaning supplies at all. These conditions go on for years, it's an insane asylum without the good medications. "Don't shit where you eat," just means not at the same time in jail.

For those who have never been arrested, there is a shock factor. I would suggest a person sit quietly at home seriously taking stock of what needs to be done in the next 10 minutes, the next hour, today, tomorrow, next week or next month. Kids to or from school, work, bills, sick parents, pets, a chicken thawing in the fridge. Think of every detail no matter how big or how small that is the entirety of a person's life. A person has obligations. Once arrested all those details, all those obligations, swirl around in a person's head nonstop. A lot of times a new person sees a guard on a round, a supposed figure of authority, and they try to explain that they have kids, they have a job, they have a cat, they have obligations. Then the guard politely tells the person their obligation is to get on a bunk and shut the fuck up, nobody cares. That little spark of hope dies.

The second shock comes when newbie gets a food tray and they say, "What the fuck is that!" It's brown or yellow, it's lumpy, it's runny and it smells worse going in than it will coming out, so it's best not to know what it was before they attempted to cook it. It won't be long until food becomes an obsessive thought.

I collected a lot of stories, and one story was my favorite because it's a good example. They put a man in my cell who had no clue what was going on. At 1:30 p.m. he was at work and just 17 minutes later he was in a cell with no idea why. This happens way more than people would expect. Most people believe they have a right to a phone call, and they do, unless the guards are busy, short-handed, or if it's tray time. When a guard comes by the person will ask about a phone call and the guard will say, "They are busy, so it'll be about 30 minutes," or, "I'll check on it," or "Remind me on the next round," or, or, or, or and so on. Then it's shift change so the man asks about a phone call, and he will be told he had a phone call when he came in. It all means, "Fuck you—no call." People get one hour out a day, if they miss that one hour then it's no call until the next day, maybe. So, people do have a right to a phone call—eventually.

The next day the man they put in my cell called home then he really went crazy. He had seven kids and one of his daughters was missing. His wife was in hysterics, the daughter had not come home from school, and he had gone missing from work. Of course, he had to try to tell the wife he did not know why he was in jail. From the next tone I expect she said, "Bullshit." "No, I really don't know!" Then the man tells a guard he needs to go, he has to find his daughter, only to be told no, he needs to go the fuck back in the cell.

Can I just say, it's very damn hard to read a book when some dude is in full-blown panic attack over a missing kid. Of course, it don't help when we explain he is in jail, missing daughter, and they don't care about guilt. They arrest whoever is handy so he shouldn't get more than two life sentences, unless they find the body. I usually find an open grave in a graveyard before they put the coffin in, dig down a few feet, put the body in. Once the coffin is set no one ever looks for a body under a coffin in a graveyard. The man really don't like hearing that once arrested he is guilty, so chill, read a book.

It was three days before the man found out what was going on. The man had bought some novelty finger tasers. The girl and her brother had been shocking each other. He accidentally got her on the side of her boob. At school she had told a friend her boob was sore from a taser. The friend told a teacher, the teacher called protective services, and they kidnapped the daughter then the dad was arrested. It took three days of the girl saying nothing happened before she was allowed to go home. The man was held on three charges. Then the prosecutor went after the girl, and he threatened to charge her if she continued to refuse to testify. The girl left to live with family out of state to escape the prosecutor. The sad part was, both the daughter and the son wrote him letters everyday apologizing, but none of his kids could visit. It took three months for him to be released, but he was fired for being a suspected molester.

Then there was one that should be a wake-up call or a warning. A man had two kids, a boy and a girl. His wife had been in North Carolina for three years, but she claimed the girl to get assistance even though the girl lived with her dad. The man filed for full custody and three days later he was arrested. This is where it gets odd. It was his mother-in-law that made the complaint from North Carolina who said the girl had told her on the phone that she had been touched. The girl wrote her dad, she said she never said that, and the girl had not even talked to the mother-in-law on the phone. One would think the girl said it never happened so it's over, but that is not the case at all. If looked into, most states have laxed the hearsay laws on sex charges. What a prosecutor would do would be to present the girl as so severely traumatized she can't tell the truth, so her saying nothing ever happened is actually worse than saying it did. Then the mother-in-law would testify, and a jury would bury him. Then a lawyer explains if he goes to a jury trial they will stack charges until he faces life in prison. The more the girl says nothing happened, the more traumatized she looks and the mother-in-law can say anything she wants. The man took a plea deal for seven years, the girl went to North Carolina, and the son went up for adoption.

In three years at Tazewell there were 45 cases where a man, or woman, filed for custody then was arrested for molestation. Keep in mind, folks, whoever files molestation first wins because the accused cannot counter-file any charges and molestation is a 100 percent win in a custody battle. The best part is, no evidence needed and if the kid says nothing happened it's even better for the case. Sally found well over 200 custody cases that ended in molestation charges. Be sure to file first. Just remember that there should be a third party for a witness but those are easy to find.(Ask Crystal Owens.)

The worst one I read was a woman who had three kids, her husband went to prison, and her mother-in-law filed for custody of the kids. The woman won the custody battle in court, then she was accused of molestation. The boy in question repeatedly said nothing happened. Then the woman went to a jury trial. She had been offered a five-year plea deal but in trial she received two life sentences, so the mother-in-law had custody.

One complaint I read was damn funny. A woman went to a man's house to buy some stuff then wouldn't leave. The complaint read he exposed his penis and told the woman, "Blow me." But what was funny was in the complaint she said when she went back the next day, he did it again. (Victim goes back for seconds?) His case was thrown out.

One of the craziest cases Sally found was a couple in their early 60s was arrested. What had happened was the couple were in their own living room having sex on their own couch. Sometimes shit happens on the couch. In this case, a little peeping Tom had watched them through a window, so the couple each had two counts of Actual Inncocence. They ended up on probation to avoid life in prison. They had kids and they had grandkids they were no longer allowed to see. One day they are fucking on the couch and the next they are both registered sex offenders.

Not all stories were sex related. One man they put in my cell was dope sick. When he got out, he called his wife and he told her where the pill stash was. "Now honey, don't eat them." He told her exactly who to take them to to sell them then put money on his books (jail account). The cops got his pill stash, and they arrested his wife to boot. He did not get any money on his account. Don't do drug deals on jail phones.

One of the worst dope sick people I saw laid in the cell for three days passed out. When a nurse finally checked, she asked why I hadn't helped. Hey, I did help, I ate his food trays so he could rest, or die. They rushed him to the hospital. Damn, there went my extra food.

Then, there is no experience like being in a cell with a dope sick person who is either shitting or throwing up for three or four days. "Not really hungry today, huh." (hehehe)

Well hell, down to business.

I was appointed Jim Shortt for a lawyer, no relation to Brandi Lee Short in the complaint, or one could hope so, anyway. The first time I saw him he did the "jury will fry you" blah, blah, blah, plea deal. He had a good plea deal. I could plead to attempted rape for three years. To the uninitiated there is a steep learning curve here.

False advertising, bait and switch, all of that is illegal if one is buying a sofa, but in the so-called justice system it's not only allowed, it's also the heart of the system. People are well-protected if they are buying a sofa, but when facing life in prison there is no protection. A lawyer has a workup sheet. The charge of attempted rape carries 10 years. The lawyer will say the guidelines on a guilty plea could be one year nine months to four years nine months with a midrange of three years, and a judge rarely goes over the suggested midrange. That is a blatant line of bullshit when someone sits in jail for a while. I've seen a man sign a plea deal for 40 years and receive 160 years. One man signed for 12 years, and he received 47 years.

My lawyer laid out the plea deal and I said, "Jury trial."

Let the fucking games begin!

Hurray, good news! Here's a fun little tidbit for all the true crime buffs who believe what they see on TV. I had been hit with a summons for shoplifting but when we went to trial the video actually showed Brandi entering Wal-Mart with the sunglasses on her hat, so I was found completely innocent of shoplifting. Yep, the video cleared me, justice hath prevailed. I am still a litter bug since they found the cans, but I was totally innocent of shoplifting. Attempted rape, Actual Inncocence, assault and battery and contributing, but it had been the shoplifting that had me worried.

I had refused a plea deal, so I had a trial date. Yep, gonna be rocking a jury trial very shortly. But then comes stage two of the game. A person has a trial date and all they can do is sit and wait with the stress of an impending trial. Then, at the last possible second, a lawyer will swoop in with a plea deal offer and if refused the court date is postponed, so the stress starts all over again.

There was one upside. The very first day I had called my aunt Mary who had called Sally. From day one Sally and I wrote each other three to five letters a week every week. I did not mess up, I made absolutely sure any piece of paper from the police report to any lawyer letter a copy was sent to Sally. I wrote to Sally four to five hours a day every single day. She knew every conversation I had with a lawyer as well as day-to-day jail crap. Sally lived the entire experience as it happened.

As for Sally, she wrote me mundane details so I knew when she washed or folded clothes, I knew when she saw a doctor, I knew what she bought at the store, I knew what she watched on TV, what she ate, who called or visited, so it was like I was there. Sally sent me pictures and she sent me legal information if I needed it. Sally found one-cent books at Amazon to have sent to me.

From July 9, 2012 to January 2013 I had several court dates. "Would you like a plea deal?" No. Postpone. "How about that plea deal?" No. Postpone. "Gotta plea deal for ya." No. Postpone. How about a plea deal now, now, now, now? No. Postpone. It's psychological torture over and over and a lot of people do break. They accept a plea deal just to get off the merry-go-round.

How about more truth in advertising.

It bothers me when I see on TV, "He was indicted on X number of charges by a grand jury." In January 2013 I was indicted on attempted rape, Actual Inncocence, assault and battery and contributing, but let's take a closer look under the hood of this so-called grand jury.

Ladies and gentlemen, may I present for your viewing pleasure the grand jury: Rod Cury, Jerry Turley, Avery Richardson, Chad Murray, Donna Kessler, and Jeffery M. Bailey. Just six people who handled 71, plus 37 sealed, indictments in under three hours. That means 108 people with multiple charges in less than three hours. Tazewell County, Virginia has a small population, so I can't imagine what it would look like in, say, New York City. I guess it would be less impressive for the prosecutors if the news had to say, "He was one of 2,000 indicted in four hours by a grand jury of five people." That would be too honest for the justice system. But I do call 108 people indicted in less than three hours pure bullshit. The so-called grand jury is PROSECUTORIAL propaganda.

Oddly enough, there were three Blankenships on the indictments: Amy Gail Blankenship, Kristen Renee Blankenship, and me, Robert Mckinley Blankenship.

Oh wait. To Amy and Kristen, I only wrote the names to prove I had seen the indictment sheet. Way back in Chapter 1 I wrote the whole, "Blankenship-alcoholic-son of a bitch," thing, but I feel sure we aren't related and you two are perfectly wonderful women caught up in a corrupt legal system. Have a wonderful day. (I don't need no crazy indicted chicks on my ass, so that should work.)(Reference removed in editing.)

Hey, I was indicted so did that mean all the prior court dates were just bullshit to try to force a plea deal? It took seven months to be indicted, as I was arrested July 9th and I count July. But then, I had a real court date set for March 2013 since I'd finally been indicted. This is it, to the front, damn the torpedoes, full speed ahead, by God it's on, here we go this time.

"Homegrown's alright with me

Homegrown is good thing
Plant that bail and let it reign"
No, that's not right. Just chillin' out waiting on a court date.

Twenty-two minutes, everything relevant is irrelevant. I thought I'd better toss in a reminder.

They decided to stop dicking around, it was time to haul out the big guns to put an end to me. I had a March court date but my lawyer came to see me in February so I knew that couldn't be good. No lawyer ever shows up to go over a case. He laid it out, accept a plea deal or I would be further charged with abduction with intent to defile that carries 20 to life in prison.

But it don't stop there because they have one more con job.

"A plea by which a defendant in a criminal case does not make a defense but does not admit guilt. Nolo contendere." The lawyer explains it as a person is saying he is not guilty, but the state may be able to make him look guilty. It's called no contest, sometimes alpha plea. Do not get confused, it's a guilty plea and it's treated the exact same as a guilty plea. The only place it means anything is in the head of the person who was tricked into a guilty plea. Countless times I saw someone plead no contest for probation, then they go to the probation where they were told to write down exactly what they did. They have to admit to everything on paper. When they explain they said they were not guilty in a no contest plea, they are violated for being in denial.

So, the lawyer explained I could take a plea where I was saying I was not guilty, but the state may be able to make me look guilty. But he really piled on that if I refused, I would be charged with abduction with intent to defile. That charge originated out of human trafficking, as in going to other countries to kidnap women then bring them back for prostitution. That's a hell of a rap for a trip to Wal-Mart.

Keep in mind here, arrested July 9, 2012, so July, August, September, October, November, December, January, then indicated, and there was no mention of any abduction anywhere. Then all of a sudden, it's sign this plea deal, no contest to attempted rape for three years, or for refusing a plea deal I would be charged with abduction so I would face life in prison and a jury would bury me.

I told the lawyer I needed two weeks to decide. I had to write Sally which was four days to get an answer back. But while I write Sally, let's pause.

You, your son, your daughter, your spouse, your parent is here. This is not a joke, not funny, not a game. It's very goddamned real. What would you do? What would you advise your loved one to do? Make no mistake, you can choose three years, or you will be charged with abduction simply for refusing a plea deal. So, Mr. or Miss I'd-Never-Take-A-Plea-Deal, what would you really do?

While one mulls over that, I wouldn't want anyone to think these are solely my opinions or that I hadn't actually done any research or that I am making crap up on my own.

There is an article titled "Stacking Charges Forces the Innocent to Plead Guilty" at www.citizensforcriminaljustice.net/stacking-charges-forces-the-innocent-to-plead-guilty that says:

"This case highlights a serious problem. I know from vast (over 500 trials) trial experience that there is a place and process to tell the truth. The place is a courtroom and the process is a trial. Before the war on drugs caused such a case overload and dysfunction in our courts, it worked quite well. Today, however, there are too many cases for anyone to do things right, so the prosecutors have learned to 'stack charges,' threatening the defendant with so much prison time (vastly disproportionate to the conduct involved, and a direct violation of ethics). A prosecutor should not institute, or cause to be instituted, or permit the continued pendency of criminal charges when the prosecutor knows that the charges are not supported by probable cause. The prosecutor should not bring or seek charges greater in number or degree than can be reasonably supported with evidence at trial or than necessary to reflect the gravity of the offense. (ABA Standard 3-3,9(f)).

"No prosecutorial action is more consequential than the decision to charge a person with a crime. Yet there are no direct mechanisms with which to hold prosecutors accountable… Conviction Integrity Units: Toward Prosecutorial Self-Regulation? In Wrongful Conviction and Criminal Justice Reform (2014). 37 Berger v. United States, 295 U.S. 78,88 (1935). 38 (ABA) Standard 3-3.9. 39 ABA Standard 3-3-9(f) that he/she is scared to death to take a chance on a trial perhaps knowing that the judges are in such a hurry to move things along—due to wildly unmanageable caseloads—that even a good lawyer may not get in the evidence needed. Even the innocent plead guilty! Outrageous!

"Therefore, today more than 95 percent of ALL felony cases end in a plea. Wham, bam! It's over in 20 minutes, and in over 90 percent of those cases there is no presentence investigation. (I spent at least one-half a day every week in the presentence investigator's office, advising as to sentencing), so the defendant is sentenced on the spot, with the judge knowing little or nothing about the defendant, the victim, the exact nature of the crime. Wildly unjust and crazy disparate sentences often are the result. Ending the failed 'war on drugs' is the only solution to this and so many other problems in the system."

That article was written by Ken Abraham on December 14, 2014 and was sent to me to be used in the book for a good reason. Most people feel if they have a good lawyer they are okay or it won't happen. This article started with a lawyer who was about to have charges stacked against him, a lawyer! He entered an Alford plea which is just another term for no contest, he plead to misdemeanor contributing otherwise he would have faced 40 years from charge stacking. I like how they word, "He had potentially faced more than 40 years." Yes, had he gone to trial not due to any crimes. The headline is: Morrissey, back in his office Saturday, vows revenge. It's from the Richmond Times Dispatch.

ABA Standard 3-3-9(f):

"The prosecutor should not bring or seek charges greater in number or degree than can be reasonably supported with evidence at trial or than necessary to fairly reflect the gravity of the offense."

For those who know the standard, "absolute power corrupts—absolutely," a prosecutor can do whatever he wants to anytime he wants to without any controls. The article did upset me a little because it left out that evidence can be fabricated as needed or imaginary evidence is okay.

Now on a personal observation, it's extremely hard for the average person to admit fear which becomes not only part of the problem, but it also covers the problem up. A thousand times I have heard a person in prison say, "Boy, my lawyer saved me, they were going to charge me with...," They absolutely will not admit they were scared. What a person needs to say is, the prosecutor threatened me with...and my cock sucking lawyer was in on the threats. In North Carolina my lawyer did not save me, I was threatened with life in prison, I was scared, and I took a plea deal. When, and only when, people begin to say I was threatened with... so I took a plea deal, will the real truth reach the public.

I was threatened with abduction with an intent to defile. Now, the prosecutor cannot say upon review, or any of that, in my police report, day one, on page five of the supplement..., "I then conferred with Dennis Lee Commonwealth Atty. who advised to place him under arrest for attempted rape." So, the prosecutor was right there on day one. Then eight months later he threatened me with abduction only if I refused a plea deal. There was absolutely nothing different to justify the charge other than the plea deal. (Retaliation is prosecutorial misconduct.)

I wrote to Sally. I explained exactly what I was going to do and she was definitely not in agreement but for once she said she would support me 100 percent.

Oh, woe is me, abduction with intent to defile, 20 to life in prison, knowing no matter what a jury would put me away, fear. "Did anyone play the computer game Fear with the damn scary little girl ghost." I took a plea deal. Please refer to the Documents, see Plea 3-11-13 and I circled the numbers one to four. On page three please note number two, the defendant will plea to no contest to the following charge, to wit: attempted rape. Then the prosecutor shall move to nolle prosequi, not prosecute the following charges which would be Actual Inncocence, assault and battery and the contributing.

Now, I've included page six which clearly shows this was accepted the 11th day of February 2013, signed by all parties and initialed by me, RMB. It's a done plea deal, no way to fight a plea deal and it was only for three years, no big deal.

WAIT!

Look at my page four. When one does a plea deal there is a long list of questions, and each question must be answered then initialed. Look at question 21: "Has anyone connected with your arrest and prosecution, such as the police or the Commonwealth's attorney, or any other person, threatened or in any manner attempted to force you to enter this plea of no contest?" I was supposed to say "no," I wrote "yes," then under that I wrote, "Yes, I'd face abduction and life in prison." Over to the side my lawyer drew an arrow like "don't look down, look over here." He tried to scribble in, "Advised may be charged with abduction." There was no "may," he said take a plea or be charged.

That's what I wrote Sally, I was going to put that I was threatened with abduction and life in prison on the plea deal to absolutely prove the threat to her and the whole damn world. I also told Sally when I did that I would be charged, and I would be in prison for life. I'd never see her outside of prison again. She was not happy about it, but she said she would stand behind me.

I would now reach out to people, keep in mind that 90 to 95 percent of all cases cave and take a plea deal so I would say, if you are in the 10 percent of holdouts, if they offer a plea deal and make threats of more charges, accept the plea deal then put the threats on it to prove they were in fact threats.

Some people may not realize it, but had I accepted the plea deal then no proof would ever exist of the threat because it's all done in secret out of the public's eye. I could say, "They threatened me with abduction," but no proof would exist. All the public would ever see was, "convicted of attempted rape," with no proof of any threat. If I flat refused the plea deal no one would ever know they offered me three years long before any abduction was ever charged. I had to prove that the plea deal was real, and I had to prove the threats are real.

Most of the time when a person takes a plea deal it takes two or three weeks to get back into the courtroom. I was in the courtroom in 12 minutes and the plea deal was thrown out. I can say that all parties involved were quite upset with me, they hate it when someone messes up the game.

So, first I drove a young girl to a secluded location to not rape her, then eight months later I abducted her to drive her to a secluded location to not rape her. We were not in the preliminary stage, I'd had a preliminary hearing July, 2012. All the so-called facts or evidence was collected, that's all there is. I was indicted and I had a solid jury trial date. So, what great revelation or new evidence came about? None. The only justification for the abduction was that I refused a plea deal.

But hey, I have a March trial date, the lawyer did scribble in, "May be charged," so maybe they won't charge me. Maybe we will go on to a jury trial.

The first time it took from July 2012 to January 2013 to indict me. The second time it took from February 2013 to March 2013, less than 30 days to indict me a second time. The second grand jury was CR-13-335, Melissa Anderson, Lynn Brown, Stephanie David, Ellis Cole and George Hayes, only five people. They handled 47 people plus 73 sealed. They handled multiple charges on 120 people in just over three hours. Talk about speed reading. On the second indictment I was the only Blankenship but the first and last person was named Lisa, "Bargo to Yost." I do feel justified in saying, once again, that the so-called grand jury is propaganda bullshit. Instead of working for the prosecution they should have to present exactly how many people are indicted in each session. "Indicted by grand jury on abduction," sounds good for prosecutors but, "One of 120 indicted on multiple charges in three hours," would be less of an impact, not to mention honest. I believe they should have to present the truth which should not be a bad thing from the justice system.

When I had been charged in North Carolina I was threatened with life in prison from charge stacking to force a plea deal. I was scared, I caved, and I took a plea deal. Then for three years I had tried to explain the threats to Sally but all she ever saw was, "Actual Inncocence that only carried two years—plea deal," so I had to hear over and over that she didn't see why an innocent person would accept a plea deal. I had no solid proof that any threats ever happened. I wrote to Sally and I told her that I had been threatened with the abduction charge. I told her I would write the threat on the plea deal. I would be charged and I would spend life in prison. Then I put copies of all the papers in her hands so there was no room for any doubt in her mind.

Welcome to phase two of the punishment or the retaliation for refusing a plea deal. I was postponed from March 2013 to September 2013. Don't want a plea, we'll just lock ya up until ya change your mind. That was a seven-month jail sentence for refusing a plea deal. "Let them stew in their own juices," but hey, we have seven whole months to prepare for a jury trial. It should be obvious that abduction—life in prison, did not scare me and I don't give a rosy-red rat's ass how many charges they stack.

May I now direct the attention to the Documents section, a letter dated August 7, 2013 from the Commonwealth attorney to my lawyer. I will go over the letter, but I'll say up front this is another stage of punishment or retaliation. Once a person refuses a plea deal, they up the charges on the plea deal offers.

"Dear Jim, (how cute)

As you are aware, we have a jury trial set on the above mentioned case in mid-September. I am writing to ascertain whether this will, for certain, be a jury trial. There are a number of witnesses and officers and I would like to advise them as soon as possible as to our status."

Damn, March, April, May, June, July, August. As soon as possible would have been to write the letter back in March instead of waiting six months, dipshit. Maybe someone should buy a calendar.

"As you recall at the preliminary hearing level the defendant agreed to waive and plead guilty to attempted rape. At his plea on February 11, 2013 the defendant backed out of his plea deal and we subsequently indicted him on what we otherwise would have charged him with: specifically; abduction with intent to defile, attempted rape, Actual Inncocence, as well as misdemeanors. He presently faces a maximum of life plus 22 years."

Now, I hate to call bullshit bullshit, but we were not in the preliminary hearing level. I'd had the preliminary, I'd been indicted, and I had a jury trial set for March. That alone is way beyond the preliminary hearing stage.

:A prosecutor should not institute, or cause to be instituted, or permit the continued pendency of criminal charges when the prosecutor knows that the charges are not supported by probable cause: ABA standard 3-3.9(f).

"I would offer at this time the following: the defendant (me) pleads to attempted rape and Actual Inncocence and the Commonwealth dismisses the abduction charge and the court sentences after a presentence report. I have included my estimate of the Virginia Sentencing Guidelines. I have also included guidelines for all three charges."

The guidelines are included in the Documents, one year nine months to four years nine months with a midpoint of three years. Odd, the guidelines for two charges were the same as they had been for one charge. By the way, the prosecutor was a lying son of a bitch on the guidelines but that comes up later. At this point one either spots the lie or they don't, but if it's their life or their loved one's life in the balance, they damn well better spot the lie. No lawyer will ever point out the lie.

"The fact he is a previously convicted sex offender will not sit well with the jury I suspect." Meaning I would be tried for the same crime twice.

"I expect we will try it on that on the September date."

It's only 2013. Poor Ray Smith don't even have his paperwork done yet.

Fear not, it was rather funny. Two days before my trial my lawyer called the jail. I was in the middle of booking on a recorded jail phone. My lawyer explained on the phone, "he" could get the abduction charge dismissed, I could plead guilty to attempted rape and Actual Inncocence, it would be three years, blah, blah, blah… he didn't want to submit the plea deal unless I stated I would accept it. I said, "Jury! Trial!" and I hung up, so my court date was postponed. The lawyer tried to pawn off what the prosecutor wrote as his idea. We are postponed, no one will believe what happened next. My attorney helped convict me.

Everyday Sally would write me a paragraph or four on her computer. When she had six pages, she would print then mail the letter to me. Sally went back to college which was fun to read about. In a poetry class there is a style of poetry where there are four lines. Lines three and four become lines one and two in the next four lines. I wrote about camping where wildflowers grow, and Sally had to read it in front of her class as a perfect example. Sally took a trip to Ireland, and she mailed me letters with pictures from her trip. She took a trip out west and I have pictures of Sally with six women standing on a corner in Winslow, Arizona.

Sally's apartment complex had a pool and she, uh, "worked" as a pool attendant if one considers laying around in a bikini reading a book, "work." Sally would write me very good descriptions of women at the pool, specifically one young lady in a flesh tone bikini. When the bikini was wet it would all but disappear. Having a lesbian girlfriend is a real plus when one is in jail. She knows what to write about.

There was one incident in jail that made the papers when Sally posted it online. It was hilarious. First, every day, twice a day on the food trays we received vanilla wafers as a dessert. I had a bowl with a lid, so I'd save the wafers, I'd put peanut butter between two, and I'd let them sit overnight. I'd have a bowl full of vanilla wafer-peanut butter sandwiches.

Out of nowhere I received a water bill for $970. What the fuck! Three separate times I had mailed a check only to have my water cut off then somehow they let it run up a two-year past due water bill (25 months). It even says right on the bill that failure to pay in a prompt manner would result in discontinued service, so how the hell was I allowed to run up a $970 bill? I once read somewhere that any true, legitimate offer to settle a debt must be accepted. I wrote the water department with a copy to Sally. I explained that at Tazewell County Jail one does not even wear their own underwear. I honestly owned, and my total self-worth of all assets was, a bowl of vanilla wafers of which I offer half in a true, legitimate attempt to settle the debt. The bill was lowered to $180 which made it even funnier. Sally had posted it online and it made several newspapers. On the Eskie groups over 100 people posted, "Vorgoth Lives," when they saw the story.

"Would you like a plea deal?" No. Postpone. "How about a plea deal today?" No. Postpone. "Got a plea deal for ya." No. Postpone. Yep, we played plea deal insomnia from August 2013 to May 2014. I will be honest here, what I am about to write is both very simple and it's extremely complicated at the same time. It will seem totally unbelievable, but it happened. I (and Sally) lived it.

It began with a letter from my lawyer that I put in Documents. The letter is dated May 20, 2014.

"…in which you would plead guilty to attempted rape and Actual Inncocence…"

I had not plead no contest to one charge, what the hell made them believe I'd plead guilty to two?

"You and I also reviewed the discretionary sentencing guidelines the attorney for the Commonwealth provided to me."

That's the one year nine months to four years nine months with a midrange of three years. That alone made both the prosecutor and my lawyer a lying son of a bitch. (I say that so often—where's my proof.)

"You advised you would reject same." (duh)

The end of the letter I made it very clear that I understood any jury would be biased with preconceived opinions of guilt in sex crimes or accusations. Hell, just in writing this one chapter I have counted 18 separate sex crimes in this news. So, I was under no delusion. I do not believe they ever fully grasp that in a war when there is one soldier left facing one thousand, he knows he will die so he charges. I knew when I went to trial any jury would bury me and I knew I would be in prison for life. A person in that position can't be scared or shocked into a plea deal. He is already dead.

But I would like to throw a rant to the prosecutor. You stupid son of a bitch, I never backed out of a plea deal. I used it to prove the threats are real. For the guidelines, all parties involved are lying son of a bitches which I'll prove—later.

I feel better. Yeah, I knew I was dead, I did not say I was happy about it.

"Now comes the unbelievable."

I had a lawyer visit, but it was not my lawyer, it was a senior partner in the law firm. Wow! Yep, they hauled out the all-knowing legal guru, the walking knowledge base of all things legal. Hell, I was almost impressed. Aren't we all just a wee bit in awe that little ol' me ranked a visit from a senior partner? Please pause while I genuflect in subjugation to this momentous occasion in a most appropriate manner.

Oh no! He has some bad news for me. Gee, I hope they didn't turn my water off, I was damn near out of vanilla wafers. The bad news couldn't be shoplifting, I'd been found innocent of that.

Damn, I bet my girlfriend was pregnant. I'd tell people my girlfriend was in college, and they be like, "What is she, 19, 20 years old, ya pervert!" (They were off by about 40 years.) But I knew it, date a woman in college, she out there flinging that pussy around, she gets pregnant, so they blame the boyfriend. Hey, July 2012 to May 2014 I'd been in jail, bitch be knocked up—N.M.P. (not my problem).

Abduction with intent to defile, attempted rape, Actual Inncocence, assault and battery and then contributing, I was sitting on life plus 22 years. I knew I was going to prison for life and yet, somehow, the senior partner felt he had bad news. Unless he had the death penalty in his pocket, I didn't really see myself being shocked.

Wow! It would seem the sweet little angel I was accused of sexually assaulting had landed on then violated not one but double probation. She had breaking and entering, destruction of property, and then she threatened much younger children at school with a rather large knife, so Brandi was in a juvenile detention center.

Uh, July 9, 2012 to May 20, 2014 my alibi was pretty solid, in jail, so I really failed to see how her crime spree was bad news for me. I leaned towards N.M.P. (not my problem). But at the same time, I felt the senior partner's bad news would end in a plea deal offer. Wanna bet a honey bun on it? (Honey buns are high dollar bets in jail.)

Throw on a double wow! My lawyer, acting purely in my best interest, had gone to the detention center to talk to Brandi. He not only talked to Brandi, but he also made a video.

The movie "Shrek" "ogres have layers like onions," this story has layers upon layers so I would suggest one smoke pot upfront.

The senior partner explained that Brandi went over her story numerous times, she was very precise, and she was very consistent. He could not stress strongly enough just how very consistent she was. The senior partner really pushed that if she testified like she did on the video a jury would bury me. Her story was bad, she was very consistent. In light of her story, in light of her being so very consistent, in light of the video, and in light of life in prison, it really would be in my best interest to accept the deal. (There it is, I knew it—who owes me a honey bun from the bet?) The senior partner explained the guidelines, what's three years when one is facing life. Yep, just three years and a judge rarely goes over the midrange on a plea deal. Then the senior partner went on to explain that there is a plea where I am saying I am not guilty, but the state may be able to make me look guilty.

Did anyone see on the TV show "Supernatural" when Crowly gave Sam and Dean the Colt to kill Lucifer, the line, "How about you don't bloody miss! Okay!"

"Defense: the arguments in behalf of the defendant in a law case."

I don't believe, even once, that it ever dawned on the senior partner that he sat there telling me that my "defense" attorney had went and he had not found, he had created, brand new evidence to help convict me. Well fuck me, someone tell the prosecutor he can sit this one out, the defense attorney will prosecute ME!.

Hey, if you find a very consistent witness how about you don't make a bloody video! Okay! (Crowly voice.)

Keep in mind I said layers, so creating evidence was not the way they meant for it to play out. The senior partner had meant to make it very serious. Brandi was very consistent; they made a video to show me just how very consistent she was. If a jury saw that, or her, like that it would mean life in prison for me. I could plead no contest, it was only three years, sign here and everyone, except me, is home in time for dinner.

So, Mr. Dumb Fuck senior partner could not even be bothered to skim over the case file or he would have seen that we already played nolo contendere, no contest, Alford plea, Alpha plea on the plea deal I had killed to prove that threats are very real. No matter the wording, never get confused, it's a guilty plea plain and simple. The only place that plea makes any difference is in the heads of the people they trick into believing it means anything other than guilty. To the world at large it is a guilty plea.

Do not get me wrong, the senior partner was very sincere in his whole presentation. Had he not been a lying son of a bitch on the guidelines it would have seemed he cared about my case or my future. He really should have at least skimmed the case file before he tried to run a con on me. (I keep saying every lawyer is a lying son of a bitch—where's my proof.) He had a first-rate act, and I would bet a good 80 percent of the time it would have worked. His act was almost flawless.

I don't think he liked when I told him he was a fucking moron, had he bothered to look at the case file, I already killed no contest on one charge so what the hell made them think I would plead shit to two charges? I told him point blank that I was going to a jury trial no matter what and if just one of the son of a bitches put even half the effort into a trial as they did goddamned plea deals I would never accept, it would be over by now. I said, "JURY! Fucking! Trial!"

Ya know, out in the world, and in prison, they have anger management or some other cock-n-bull shit that try to tell people don't be upset, that's not positive. Well, fuck that, my defense attorney created brand new evidence to convict me, I would say anger is damn well justified. And I am not joking, evidence created solely by a defense attorney helped convict me. (But he was not alone.)

At the same time, every single plea deal, and there were dozens, the whole case was built on I said I never left the house, I bought Brandi cigarettes, they had video at the gas station, they had video at Wal-Mart, they found the beer cans. That was done over and over and over then on top of all that they had brand new evidence created by a defense attorney.

Thank the fucking gods! It's time for a huge hallelujah happy dance. My one real bright spot was that Sally began to lose her law-and-order-itis. There's some shit one never sees on "Law and Order" or true crime. "Your honor, at this time we would like to present a video the defense attorney made to help convict the defendant." (Huh?)

When one writes on legal pads or letter pads, when the paper is gone there is a glue strip left and I mailed Sally every glue strip which she saved. She sent me a picture of a massive pile of glue strips. I literally wrote Sally four-plus hours every single day and people often commented they had no idea how we could write so much, but I wrote Sally every single detail. With crap like a defense attorney out to convict me, I never ran out of topics.

Speaking of pictures, next to the glue strips one can see a "tax jar." Most people in jail are very worried about the spouse having sex, which they are. I told Sally to put in a pussy usage tax jar. If she got laid, he (or she) had to put ten bucks in the tax jar. Sally gets laid and I get coffee, or a honey bun, everybody's happy. I don't know if she got laid, but I never ran out of coffee.

Then, on a note here, I was quite impressed with Brandi. Even in my wildest younger days I never ranked double probation. Had she not stolen my wallet then lied about sexual assault I would have been proud of her. She's the daughter I never had. Oh yeah, I forgot, girls never lie about sexual assault--hold that thought.

Crap, I got distracted, life plus 22 years in prison. I have an actual court date and I have to review a video that my defense attorney made to help convict me. Okay, writing that annoys the hell out of me. Can anyone imagine that their son or daughter is accused then the defense attorney creates brand new evidence to help convict them? I am a discordian, I love Monty Python, but I have read thousands of books and I have never read any fiction where the defense attorney helps convict the accused.

But let's review the case up to this point. I was at Corner Mart, so they had a receipt. I bought gas so they had the video. They had the Wal-Mart video. I (she) drove from Wal-Mart to Daw Road to Ray Road. I walk 195 yards up a dirt road. I enjoyed two beers—they found the cans. I removed her shirt and bra. I took off my pants. I checked her out then I stopped, and we drove home. That is in the police report and the supplement that was written the day of the supposed incident.

Twenty-two minutes, everything relevant is irrelevant.

My lawyer-prosecutor came to see me. Hey, what the hell is the legal term for a defense attorney who is also the prosecutor? I have looked, Sally has looked, but we can't find it. "Prosdef" maybe? Uh, "D-cutor." Damn! First I'd point out the letter from my lawyer was dated May 20, 2014.

In the Documents section I have included the actual transcript from the video that Jim Short made of Brandi Lee Short at the detention center. I need to state emphatically that the entire thing is video—note that for later. Look at the date at the top of page one, May 21, 2014. So, he mailed me a plea deal offer or the letter then the very next day he goes to create brand new evidence to force a plea deal.

At the bottom of page one Brandi makes up a whole new detail. I hired two kids to clean my house, a house with no floors to clean, and I would pay them $30 each, completely made up by Brandi.

On page two she don't think we ever went to any bank at all. At the Corner Mart we only bought cigarettes, she completely forgot the beer cans or any beer. Then she drove from the school to Wal-Mart.

On page three she still claims I stole sunglasses. I guess they forgot to tell her the video showed her walking in with sunglasses on her hat. I was found innocent of shoplifting.

Then I made her drive back down to Raven, to Daw Road, then to Ray Road.

"And when we got there he walked…there was a piece of a chimney…so after that he started taking his clothes off and I told him no because I already knew what he was going to do…he didn't listen, he kept taking them off…he came after me, picked my feet up off the ground, put me on the ground and was on top of me with his hand around my neck and he was trying to take my clothes off with his other hand and I started screaming telling him to stop, please, and taking my hands, moving his hand away from my clothes and finally stopped and put his clothes on and made me get back in the vehicle and drive from there to his house and then I went home…do you need to know what my mom did."

There are a few mistakes in the above, but this thing is 13 pages. On pages three and four we still have Janet Lester in the loop.

Do I really need to point out here, I was on the phone with the police, my door was never opened, and I believe had I been punched in the face I would have said so on the phone, so why would Brandi make up such a lie on her own mom?

Why was Neal Reedy in jail, was Brandi involved? That's page five.

Then on page six we get down to it. But keep in mind that from the get-go I was told Brandi had been very consistent several times.

"Did he take all of his clothes off?"

"Yes."

On page seven she didn't run because I was buck naked, but I may have a weapon.

"Okay, did he remove any of your clothing?"

"No."

"Did you, what kind of markings did you have from this incident?"

"It didn't leave no markings because he didn't push down enough."

So, on page eight now she claims I am buck naked, I pick her up, slam her to the ground, I jump on top of her, one hand is around her throat, one hand is trying to remove her clothes which, since I did not push down on her throat so my full weight would have been on her. All of that and there was not one mark or any dirt.

"Okay, so after he got off of top of you, he was still fully nude, right, and you had all your clothes on?"

"Yes."

"He put his clothes on and told me to take him to his house and he made me drive from there."

"What were you doing while he was putting his clothes on?"

"Walking to the vehicle."

"Okay, alright, and you do not want to testify in court, right?"

"No."

On page eight Brandi was in detention for knives but on page nine she took a knife to school and she would be released on Sunday.

Page seven:

"Okay, did he ever remove any of your clothing?"

"No."

On page 10 Brandi mentions she had anger management without any details which becomes a point much later.

I do like on page 12 when she says she only lied when younger, shirt-bra off, no clothes removed, one of those (or both) is a lie.

For those who have read this tragic tale from the start, I had been with one or two, uh, okay, a few women in my time. I know how to take a lady's clothes off and it can't be done the way Brandi described. But one must test any theory. Sally got on her bed, not a dirt road, she'd get her hair dirty, but Sally's female friend got on top of her with one hand on her throat without pressing down and Sally's friend could not remove her clothes. In fact, Sally and friend found that there was no way to put the hand on her throat without raising up one arm. If she laid flat out to lightly grasp Sally's throat her friend's hand had to be backwards. Either way, it was fun to read about that experiment.

"Okay, did he ever remove any of your clothing?"

"No."

I wanted to go over the 13 pages, peel down a few layers. When my lawyer had came in to set up the video, he laid out a plea deal on the table like, "I'll just leave this out to consider as we see how bad, and consistent, she is." I scared the crap out of my lawyer. During the video I busted out laughing like a maniac which startled him because he didn't get the joke. (Son of a bitch…what the hell!) My goddamned so-called "defense" attorney had never read the police report. He had no clue there were huge, massive discrepancies in the whole damn thing.

Again, Sally was 13 when she lost her bikini top and after 40 years she never forgot it. I drove to a secluded location, I removed Brandi's shirt and bra, she was half-naked outside in front of a man but: "Did he ever remove any of your clothing?" "No."

But the discrepancies were only part of the problem with the video. In the whole video Brandi describes the whole attack like someone watching paint dry. She has no emotion of any kind. She is 100 percent bored in the whole video.

Keep in mind, my defense attorney supposedly made the video completely as a fluke. It was meant to show me how bad her story was to scare me into a plea deal. He had no idea it would flip the script and work in my favor. The video was made May 21, 2014, we viewed the video May 22, 2014. Then it got stupid or stupider because for all of one day my lawyer got excited about a trial which was set for June 4, 2014. Look at the Subpoena Proof in Documents. My lawyer filed a subpoena on both of Brandi's probation officers, Robbie Davis-Tazewell, Brad Goff-Lebanon. Then my lawyer filed to review Brandi's probation records. Keep in mind my witnesses on the subpoena.

I do have to admit that had I not read the police report that video did sound bad, so in reality my defense attorney did make a video to burn me, but then he wants to go to trial.

"Homegrown's alright with me
Homegrown is the way it should be."

Oh, sorry. I blew a mental fuse there for a second, had to put my head back right.

I do love "Monty Python" and as a discordian I thrive on the ironic or the absurd. Cue the "Monty Python" theme song as this is about to go beyond silly.

My defense attorney creates brand new evidence that describes a much worse attack, slammed to the ground, jumped on naked. Hell, play that for a jury and call it a day. On May 23rd, 2014 my lawyer is very excited about a trial. The probation records were never reviewed. The defense attorney made a video that would fry me.

See motion to seal video filed not by my lawyer but by the prosecutor. (I need a drink—maybe some pot.) The defense attorney makes a video where a young girl is slammed to the ground and a naked man jumps on her and the prosecutor moves to seal the video to protect the accused. Suddenly my knight in shining armor is the prosecutor.

Do I really need to point out that that is shit no one will ever see on "Law and Order?" "Defense attorney wants to convict accused with a video he created but prosecutor moves to save the day."

It did not end there. When the motion to seal failed the prosecutor then made a Virginia State Bar ethics complaint to remove my lawyer and to remove the video. When that failed he, the prosecutor, made eight separate attempts to seal or remove the video. He was desperate that no jury ever see the video.

If anyone is confused, don't be because there are still layers to the video which I will now fully explain so it all drops into place. Time to put it all into a neat perspective. The whole story is on page eight of the Jim Shortt video transcript. Brandi refused to testify, and she did not want to testify.

Look at item 4 on the motion to seal. The prosecutor, Officer Caldwell and what they call a victim-witness coordinator all showed up at the detention center. Why? July 9, 2012 Officer Caldwell filed his report so his job as a police officer was done, it was a matter for the courts. What crime required the presence of a police officer, "at a detention center."

From the top, Brandi did not want to testify. The prosecutor violated her probation and he put her in detention. Then he told her if she made the video she would be out in 10 days or she could rot in detention. The parties present were the prosecutor, the arresting officer, the witness coach, the probation officer and my lawyer. They told Brandi if she made the video it would prompt me to accept a plea deal and she'd be out of detention and she would not have to testify in court. The actual check-in sheet showed all parties there at the same time and it explains the presence of Officer Caldwell to help the story. He was not needed for any other reason. The witness coach actually teaches people how to testify on cue with the prosecutor.

Or one can believe that my lawyer, who had not even read the police report in damn near two years, just randomly happened by a detention center, where Brandi just happened to be, where he just happened to be set up for video, where he just happened to find a very consistent witness which he thought he better record for a jury and whose senior partner just happened to pop by with the bad news. All of that in just a 10-day window.

The only hilarious part was, out of all those people no one thought to double check Brandi's story or to maybe bring a police report. They expected Brandi to at least tell the same lie and she royally screwed them.

Why else would a prosecutor move to seal a much worse attack? A jury could not see that video. Which he did just six days later May 27, 2014.

Well hell, we have a June 4, 2014 court date, read the police report, play the video, Brandi lied and we all go home. Oh, not so fast. We can use the video but my lawyer has to recuse himself so he can be a witness for the defense. That meant we had to postpone. And that is how Jim Shortt the defense attorney turned prosecutor turned witness for the defense.

Lawyer creates video to convict, prosecutor moves to block video, then lawyer becomes witness. Have they done that one on "Law and Order?" I was then appointed Mike Dennis as a lawyer. He is the actual third prosecutor in my trial. What, y'all think I'm joking?

"Would you like a plea deal?" No. Postpone. "How about a plea deal?" No. Postpone. "Gotta plea deal for ya." No. Postpone. Hey, I know this song, God knows I've heard it enough. The same damn plea deal, plead to attempted rape, Actual Inncocence and it would be three years which made Mike Dennis a lying son of a bitch right along with the rest. (Hell, they all can't be liars, can they?) That sucked, my aunt Mary used to babysit Mike's kids. Mike was a nice guy, but he was still a lying son of a bitch for a lawyer.

I did warn Sally that this part would be in the book and as typist, editor and proofreader she damn well better leave it alone. For years I had listened to Miss Holier-Than-Thou, Sally, say over and over how she didn't understand why an innocent person would accept a plea deal. Several times we had an actual trial date, three separate times Sally drove to Tazewell only for it to be postponed the very morning of the trial. Sally had copies of every plea deal offer or letter I received. In one letter it really pushed the three years, and it said after all I was almost three years in so take a plea deal, then ride it out a few months then get out.

Sally and I spoke on the phone maybe twice a month because jail calls were expensive. Sally had the letter that said I was close to three years and Sally said that maybe I should just accept the plea deal. Did I not say I burnt her ass on all points?

Whoa! Talk about an in-your-fucking-face moment! She broke, she, Miss I don't see why an innocent person would take a plea deal, broke, she caved, epic fail, ass burned. She told an innocent person to take a plea deal. I won! I won! I won! Winner—me! Sally was cured of her law-and-order-itis. Okay, three years in jail, life in prison, that may be a bit much to make a point or win an argument, but by God, I won.

Oh, I did so very much want to rub that in her face. I wanted to slam Sally for the three years of her holding it over my head, but Sally bought me coffee so I told her I revoked her three points. In one of our many debates on Virginia grammar verses Tennessee math, we set up the same IQ test on both computers and she beat me by three points. So, then I revoked her three points because she really messed up.

The funny part was, the very next morning Mike Dennis just happened to pop by with a plea deal. After all, my girlfriend thought it was a good idea.

At the very start I wrote that there are things a person had better know ahead of time and the next part is deadly serious. If someone refuses a plea deal and they are hell bent for a jury trial, be very damn careful at all times.

A good example was when a man named Jim was in my cell. They put a new guy in the cell. The new guy had coffee, he played cards and he seemed okay, talkative, joking around. At one point the guy jokingly asked if he should remove Jim's wife and Jim said, "Yeah, kill her and toss her in the pond." The next day he was offered a plea deal for three years or he would have four charges along the lines of conspiracy to commit murder. The new guy had been on a wire. Jim was in his sixties and his wife put $20 a month on his jail account. He could barely buy a honey bun and he'd been married over 30 years, so I highly doubt he was capable of conspiracy to do anything, but he took a plea deal.

Of course, if one listens to Propaganda Princess Nancy Grace, in one breath she will say everyone in prison is a liar, but with the same conviction she will exclaim, "You won't believe what another inmate said." The witnesses for the state are not liars.

A few things to watch for, if one ends up in a cell alone, be damn careful of the next one in. A person on a wire can be very friendly, they share coffee or commissary, they remove their shirts, they joke around, they may have tobacco or pot, but be damn careful. Any mention of remove the problem, remove a witness, make the problem go away, there are a lot of wordings, and all it takes is one slip.

Over almost three years I had 12 separate people on a wire put in my cell, that is, 12 that I knew of. One person asked me if I needed a witness removed and I said God no, there were four bodies under my house already, I couldn't risk any suspicion. That guy was suddenly needed in booking in under 10 minutes. I don't know if they dug under my house, but I guess they didn't find any bodies.

One guy they put in my cell asked me if I needed Brandi taken care of. Whoops, he made a boo-boo. Where did he get that name from? He was definitely on a wire, so I told him no, when the child porn she forced her sister into came out it would be a shocker.

The one that counts was a guy asked me if I needed a witness removed, so I made up a line of crap about Brandi offered me sex for money. The prosecutor used it in trial, but no one ever testified to any of that.

One day they put a guy in my cell, but he was too fast. He said for $1,000 he made problems go away. When a guard made a sound, I yelled out the door, "Guy on a wire in here," and the pod exploded with people raising hell. A lot of people in jail are there due to some asshole on a wire, so when they catch one it is not pretty.

One guy didn't even make it into the pod. As soon as he came in people were yelling, "Snitch-bitch on a wire," "Hit that muthafucker," "kill that son of a bitch," "Snitches need stitches at autopsy," and others, so the guards took him right back out.

The lesson here is damn simple. Any person anyone meets at any time could be on a wire.

"Would you like a plea deal?" No. Postpone. "How about a plea deal?" No. Postpone. "Gotta plea deal for ya." No. Postpone. Of course, once again I had to hear over and over that they had the receipt, they had the gas station video, they had the Wal-Mart video, and they found the beer cans. Then they had the video the defense attorney made to help convict me.

We had a court date in 2015 and my lawyer came to see me for the next stage of the game, "time served." Won't accept a plea deal, we will just hold ya in jail three, four or five years then offer time served. They offer to let a person out if they accept a plea deal and a lot of people do fold at this point. Just once had my lawyer came with a legitimate offer,

I may have considered it, but he wanted to play the lying son of a bitch game.

Two terms one needs to be aware of would be dispositional and nondispositional. It's easy, nondispositional means set in stone. If a person signs for three years and then a judge goes over that, the deal is off. If it's dispositional, a judge can do whatever he wants. My lawyer really pushed "time served" so I asked point blank if he could get it in writing and it had to be nondispositional. The lawyer said no, but a judge rarely goes over the midpoint.

Now I will explain what Sally did not know and what no lawyer ever said. A second conviction of Actual Inncocence has a sentence of a mandatory minimum of 10 years. Look in the Documents at the letters written by the prosecutor and by Jim Shortt. One year nine months to four years nine months with a midpoint of three years, but not one mention of a mandatory minimum of 10 years.

I told my lawyer that a second conviction of Actual Inncocence carried a 10-year mandatory minimum, so he either didn't know which made him an incompetent son of a bitch, or he knew but didn't say so he was a lying son of a bitch. If I signed for three years, time served, I would have received 20 years.

The way they fuck people, each one stipulates, "sentenced after a presentence report." I would have signed for three then they would have acted like oh, look what we found on the presentence report. We had no idea about a 10-year mandatory minimum. Sucks to be you, sorry about the 20 years, bye-bye. So, the letters, the guidelines and time served, every one of them was in fact a lying son of a bitch, now proven.

"What, you lying son of bitches think I can't read!"

I said, "Jury! Fucking! Trial!"

Wow, I need a cool down.

My ass got fat. When I'd been married to Kat, I had weighed 147 pounds. When I'd been married to Sally, I weighed 149 pounds and nowhere in between had I ever went over 151 pounds no matter what I ate. Stuck in a cell 23 hours a day, reading books and eating Moon Pies I blew up to 230 pounds. Sally had seen me put down six eggs with gravy and biscuits and not gain weight, so she was shocked.

Wait! Hell's bells! I have a court date. I told my lawyer no more goddamned postponements for any reason. Don't even think plea deal in my general direction. I would never accept any plea deal and I did not want him to fuck with me until we were actually going to trial. No postponement. I would not agree, and no goddamned plea deal offers of any kind. God knows I'd played plea deal insomnia for three years, I was done. I went on a rant that I would not agree to any postponements for any reason, and I would not discuss a plea deal.

The very morning of my trial I was up at 4 a.m. I was jacked up on coffee and I wrote Sally my final thoughts before we went to the front lines, or before I met the firing squad.

Holy Hell! Goddamn it, I knew it, I just fucking knew it! My lawyer came very early, I could almost smell the shit stink of "plea deal—postpone" all over the jail. So, what fresh level of Hell had they come up with this time? I could not imagine anything worse than what they already had tried. By the pricking of my thumb something stupid this way comes, probably.

"Trial: the act or process of trying, testing or putting to the proof test." (jury trial)

"Trial: a hardship, suffering, etc. that tries one's endurance." (jail trial)

"Trial: a person or thing that is a source of annoyance or irritation." (fucking lawyer)

So, I was facing a trial by jury having suffered the trial of three years in jail without taking a plea deal. Endurance, then one minute before trial I had the trial of an annoyance or irritation of a person called a lawyer. I do believe I had more than expanded my understanding of the word "trial."

Uh, yes I am stalling because I am having trouble trying to decide exactly how to present this part. I thought Jim Shortt fucked me over when he went and he created brand new evidence but he wasn't even close to the worst.

July 9, 2012 I was arrested and I was appointed Jim Shortt who did a motion of discovery.

June 2015, damn near three years later, after I had thrown a bitch fit saying I would not agree to a postponement for any reason no matter what, one hour before we are set to walk into the courtroom for a jury trial my lawyer tells me "they," at the very, absolute, last possible second, they found a completely innocent, inconsequential, really insignificant, wouldn't mean anything really, a tiny statement where Brandi Lee Short may have threatened to lie about sexual assault. The statement really wouldn't change anything at all, and worst, to use it we would have to postpone to subpoena other people.

Three years! Three goddamned years, the prosecutor, Jim Short, the senior partner and then Mike Dennis had buried that Brandi had threatened to lie about sexual assault. Then my lawyer, at the very last possible second, tried his best to get me to play it off as nothing at all. He expected, since I had thrown a fit, that I'd say screw it then, go to trial, but I said hell yeah, postpone.

Do I, a person that Brandi Lee Short lied about sexual assault on, want to overlook a statement where Brandi Lee Short threatened to lie about sexual abuse? What in the blue bloody hell would make a "defense" attorney even ask such a question?

Please look in Documents: Redacted Statement-1: for Brandi's statement, "mom suspects drug use, Brandi curses, screams, threatens to say she is sexually and physically abused, kicks things when she doesn't get her way, per mom's report. Recently Brandi was charged…"

That is a redacted statement that my lawyer had in his hand. See, nothing really, near totally inconsequential. It's from a psych report on Brandi, so that tiny little statement was all we could see. "Uh, there may have been another mention of the same incident somewhere in the report," he wasn't sure.

Does anyone else wonder how the motion of discovery was done in 2012 but somehow that little tidbit never came up until 2015? And just how did that information suddenly pop up at the very last second?

I do believe from Jim Shortt's letter that failed to mention a 10-year mandatory minimum to the current lawyer who had sat on those statements for over a year, I do believe I lack representation and I did from day one. Someone threatening to lie about sexual abuse is a pretty goddamned huge detail to bury in a sexual assault case or I would expect.

Then I was hit with a new twist. They would introduce the plea deal from 16 years ago so I'd be tried for two sexual assaults instead of one.

At the same time, the current plea deal from 2014 was sealed and it was blocked from trial. There was a gag order on the plea deal. They could use a 16-year-old plea deal, but I could not use a one-year-old plea deal that was actually concerning the present case.

The reality was the prosecutor presented that I was investigated and charged with abduction in July 2012, so the plea deal didn't match his version of events. Get used to that.

So, this little side note is to all the hardcore, adamant people who say, I'd never take a plea deal. My case is not unique. In fact, it's very common. When I was put in jail more than a few had been held for two-plus years without a trial while hundreds caved and they took a plea deal. Lawyers lie out their ass and they do anything to make a plea deal happen.

Remember, guilt or innocence was irrelevant at this point. The abduction charge was a threat, and it was charge stacking to force a plea deal. Three separate times I filed for a fast and speedy trial, but the filings were destroyed in the court.

There was some back story removed so I will sumize.

In 1997 I lived in Hickory, North Carolina. I drove a little girl named Ashley Renee Bradshaw to school a total of two times. Ashley only lived with her mom part time. What I did not know was that twice prior to me Ashley had been separated from her mother, twice she made masturbation accusations where she said be beats it in the middle, I was the third person she used the exact same words on and was back with her mom full time.

At that time I was charged with one count of Actual Inncocence. I was appointed a cop in law school who worked out of his car for a lawyer.

What I write in this book, when I say going in blind, stupid or trusting is a mistake, I knew as I did not know anything in this book.

At that time I was told Ashely said it was one time and she did not see if my pants were unzipped. Then I was slammed, I'd never been in serious trouble and I was 38 years old. The lawyer made it out like no big deal, I could accept a plea deal for 12 months probation, no prison time and I'd be on the sex offender registry for 5 years. OR! I could choose a jury trial but they would "stack" charges so I'd face two life sentences, and on any sex charge a jury would bury me.

I was scared, I was a moron and I took the deal. But the biggest mistake I made, I did not read the police report. It was sealed. First I found out the registry was for life not 5 years.

I won't write the ordeal here but people I thought were my good friends turned on me like a dog. One woman I used to watch her kids if she had to work Saturdays, she knew me for 2 years but would not speak to me.

Then I had to see a shrink and he told me to write down what I did. I told him point blank, I did not do a damn thing, I took a plea deal to avoid life in prison. We fell out quick so I told him he could accept the truth or he could go outside and play hide and go fuck himself.

Around 2003 I met and I married Sally Hale. Almost the day we were married she had emails from so called watchdog groups warning Sally I tricked young women into marriage, Sally was 13 years older than me. The emails said I'd molest her kids, Sally has one son who is a submarine commander, not a good idea to molest someone who literally has a boatload of nukes.

For 3 years, not constantly, but over, over, over and over some stress would come up over the registry. The day I met Sally I went to adopt an American Eskimo Dog with Sally. Now, incase Sally's family reads this I will write as delicately as I can, due to North Carolina I'd been locked up for 18 months, Sally hadn't had sex in 6 months so we ended up on her floor, she rode me like a jackhammer in a box of chashews, then asked me to spend the night.

That night Sally cooked Keibasa and rice and asked me how I liked it. At that second I was thinking one night of sex so I loved the food. I lied, rice is nasty. We ended up together so I had to admit I hate rice.

But, Sally and I had a lot of stress. Emails or something would come up and Sally would say, "what does the police report say," when I said I never read it it sounded like a lie after all I'd lied about the damn rice.

Sally had law-and-order-it is, all she saw was, one count of Actual Inncocence that only carried 2 years and plea deal. A thousand times I had to hear, "what does the police report say," "I don't see why an innocent person would take a plea deal," and "what does Actual Inncocence even mean." One time we blew 300 dollars on back-ground checks but there was nothing prior to North Carolina.

Then I was laid off, on an internet dog rescue group I wrote I was off work. The lady who ran the registry was an internet stalker, I went to buy hotdogs and Sally had a full on swat raid. I was arrested for failure to register, I made bail and was back home. They didn't have rules for laid off so it was lowered to misdemeanor attempt.

We tried every way hell to get the N.C. police report, we even called the cop who wrote it and said without names just tell Sally what it said, it was no, record sealed, an act of God would not unseal the police report. At one point I told Sally if I had that goddamn report I'd tattoo it on her ass and buy her a mirror to squat over.

It was a problem, I had no proof they threatened me with more charges to force a plea deal so to Sally I was lying like I had about the damn rice.

Of course, when Sally caved and she told an innocent person to take a plea deal, she broke and that was all that mattered. She saw the threat's were real, ass burned.

"Jury! Fucking! Trial!

Chapter 4

The Trial

In the song "The Trial" from Pink Floyd's "The Wall," the judge is a huge ass, literally, which I feel is most apt. I would love to write the lyrics but as I am in prison, I could not get permission, but the lyrics are perfect.

In my trial the evidence was not so much incontrovertible as it was imaginary, fabricated, or just implied. Let's don't present any evidence, let's get a bunch of people to say what the evidence would look like if we had any evidence. There really was no need for the jury to retire since they would only be allowed to deliberate for one hour anyway. And the judge had definitely never heard before of someone more deserving the full penalty of law—for refusing a plea deal.

I have had more trouble writing this part than any of the others even though I had a perfect guide. The problem was that I have the advantage of hindsight, so it's hard to write everything in the way it unfolded without revealing too much too soon. My trial and all of the events afterward were like being wrung out then kicked in the head. All I would suggest is for anyone reading this to consider what if it was their child on the stand or chopping block. Every word spoken in that courtroom, every action could mean life in prison, and it should all be viewed under that light.

I did have helpers. Sally and her friends and two of her friends did not like me at all which made things fun but annoying. Together we decided it would be best to just go through the trial transcript, but I would try not to be clinical or boring. Parts of what I write people may not believe or they may doubt the transcript in the book. By all means, feel free to order a transcript from the court. At first, I was only going to add certain pages of the transcript to the book but then people could say, "Oh, what's in the missing pages," so I requested the entire transcript be typed into the book.

I do feel that from July 9, 2012 to 2022 everyone else has had their say, so now I will have my say, but in having my say a few people may be offended. To them I would say, if ya don't want to be called a lying son of a bitch—don't be one!

I believe most people have a concept that when an accusation is made, the police investigate, they collect evidence, if it is warranted, they make an arrest. At trial the evidence is presented to a jury, then the jury decides if a person is guilty or not. That's how they do it on TV, but that concept is pure bullshit. In the real world the police arrest, charge stacking is used to force a plea deal, then if needed they will simply fabricate whatever evidence they need, or they eliminate evidence that would win a trial. The ultimate point of a jury trial should be to examine all evidence, not simply winning a conviction at any cost to punish those who refuse a plea deal.

My trial was set for July 21, 2015, over three years after my arrest which was actually fast and speedy for anyone who refuses a plea deal. But only having a paltry three years to prepare, there was some very last second motions they had to rush in at the last second. Well, first there were two more plea deal offers of time served but I was innocent, so I prefer life in prison.

Nothing is ever simple so why in the world would my transcript be? I have requested the transcript be typed into the book, but I do not know how they will deal with the page numbers. Do not look at me like that, I didn't do it. It should be simple, right; one, two, three, four and so on. Page one is page one, page two is page two. The first transcript is Motions done on July 20, 2015 and the pages are 1 (378) to 16 (393). Then the trial transcript has page 1 (394) and so on. I will attempt to roughly explain what happened, but it won't make a damn bit of sense at this point.

Spoiler alert, I was sentenced in November 2015 and as I am in prison it's quite obvious I did not win. In December 2015 a transcript was made.

Sally ordered the transcript, and I filed a habeas. That transcript was immediately removed, it was sealed, and it now resides in the office of the Attorney General where no one can read it.

In February 2016 a new day one and day two were created, but then day two was removed, so the transcript I have is day one from transcript two and day two from the third transcript that was made in May 2016, but it wasn't until 2017 that I had the last three pages. On the pages there is a darker, bolder number one with a smaller 378 in the corner, so I'll refer to the raised dark 1-16 numbers. I will explain the mess at the end.

This is kind of hard to explain but I will do my best. I did not have a defense lawyer and he repeatedly conspired to convict me intentionally which I will prove beyond any doubt.

To start with, Brandi was on probation and a psychological report was prepared for probation so there is no question on the report's source, it's a court document. I was all set to go to a jury trial, but my lawyer waited until 30 minutes before my trial to say that in that file the court found one or two little statements where Brandi may have threatened to lie about sexual assault. He made them sound trivial and wanted to go to trial without them, but I postponed.

This is so convoluted it's crazy. First, my attorney tried to remove the statements to help convict me, but it didn't work. The report they "suddenly found" had been filed July 17, 2012 so they had sat on that file for three years. But that is a secret so don't tell anyone. That report was filed just eight days after my arrest.

Again, anyone reading this book has way more information than I had when I started but it is my hope to write things just as they unfolded at trial. I may seem to make some points stand out that seem silly, but they won't be silly at the end. I did not have a jury trial I had a carefully choreographed stage production displayed by a lynch mob. It will be fun for any of the jurors who read the book. Now they can see all the stuff they missed.

There is a massive oddity here that is very ironic. The report that was prepared for probation and was filed with courts to keep tabs on the criminal Brandi, the prosecutor who would not hesitate to use that file to burn Brandi in her trial made a motion to quash said file because it went against him in my case. He was arguing for the court not to use a file that was turned over to the court for the court to use against Brandi. (huh.) There was a bunch of quashing around my case all from the prosecution.

In the transcript for motions July 20, 2015 on page three the prosecutor says:

"The Commonwealth may have had a misperception as to what exactly was being requested and if what is being requested is the two or three lines the court pointed out in review of the file...I don't think there would be a problem with that..."

In reading this it is obvious that the court reviewed the file, and it pulled what the prosecutor calls two or three lines, and the prosecutor is saying, "What is being requested." The two statements are the redacted statements in Documents which I will write.

"...mom suspects drug use, Brandi curses, screams, threatens to say she is sexually abused, kicks, hits things when she doesn't get her way, per mom's report Brandi was charged..."

"CPS has been called, Brandi will be yelling, screaming, cursing, demanding cigarettes, beating a mailbox, threatening to say her stepdad raped her though she denies sexual abuse..."

Those are the statements the court provided to the defense which turned out to be a complete sham. But on page four the defense steps up:

"The court in reviewing that file found certain information that pertained to the complaining witness in this matter and possible issues may go to her credibility in the allegations she made against Mr. Blankenship. We are asking the court to release ANY information that may pertain to her credibility and issues that would undermine her credibility or attack her credibility..."

All of that seems very clear to me and I do not see any way to misinterpret what is being requested. We want any information that may be used to attack her credibility in any of her accusations against me. Key words: ANY INFORMATION!

Now, if one reads from page four into page five the defense claims, "I am aware of two notations within the file," (This Way to the Great Egress) the defense (prosecutor) is lying. That file was turned over to Jim Shortt on August 5, 2013 and it went to Mike Dennis when he was appointed as the case file but let's all pretend he is only aware of the two redacted statements.

If one reads page five at this point my so-called lawyer states he has not read or reviewed that report, and he would trust the court if the court reviewed the file. Then I get lost on the bottom of page five going into page six. Before my previous trial date the court reviewed the file and then provided two statements but then the court says it thinks the court had reviewed the file:

"Which I think the court had previously reviewed which was exculpatory and was provided…"

"Obviously how that gets back to the alleged victim is a question obviously because it was both."

Say-huh! I have read that sentence over numerous times, and I have no fucking idea what it means, he is babbling.

The real meat on page six is when the judge rules:

"Anything that might be exculpatory WOULD be able to come out for the defense."

"Exculpatory: to free from blame, declare or prove blameless.…"

"What is the defense requesting? Any information that would attack Brandi's credibility. Any exculpatory information would be able to come out for the defense."

All of that seems very clear, very straightforward—simple. Every damn word was a pile of lying bullshit. But we don't know that yet, do we. To Judge Patterson, Dennis Lee and Mike Dennis—guess what Robert has!

Wow, talk about backed up. The report was filed July 17, 2012, the motions were July 20, 2015, so three years and the poor overworked judge has to work through lunch to review the file they just found three years ago.

There are other motions to get to and the first I believe violates the right to a "jury" trial. I believe when a jury is formed, they literally hold a person's life in their hands, and they should be very aware of that fact. The jury should look at every piece of evidence, or complete lack of evidence, under the weight of a person's life. The jury cannot be told what a person faces or that Virginia has no parole at all.

I do like on page seven when the prosecutor says:

"Apparently the defendant feels that numerous plea agreements have been offered…"

Gee there, Mr. Prosecutor, Sally posted 50 of your letters online and I believe the book more than proves there were hundreds of offers. What you are saying is it would not do if the jury knew "you" offered three years on one charge long before the abduction charge, but they can see the truth now. I could have been out seven years ago.

Then the funny part. I am not allowed to mention a two-year-old plea deal offer because I would look innocent, but we can enter a 16-year-old plea deal that makes me look guilty.

Once again, we wade into the waters of "This Way to the Great Egress!" By that I mean concerning my prior conviction there is a statute they wrote so that a person can be tried for the same crime twice to circumvent the Constitution. But they pretend under that statute they can enter the final order meaning they can state the charge, the date and the place, which is in Actual Inncocence, 1999, North Carolina. What they cannot do is use any evidence from a previous trial and in this case, there are only two things from North Carolina. One is the plea deal and the other is, yes, police report blues take two. The goddamned police report makes yet another appearance. This turns out to be very bad and the best thing ever. Ironic. Wait for it.

On page 12 the prosecutor says:

"We'll (well) introduce the order but not any of the facts or any of the material that was filed in the motion itself…"

He is saying he will enter the plea deal but not the police report. Then on page 13 the court rules or says:

"The court is NOT going to allow the additional information…"

Meaning the court will not allow the N.C. police report to be used. Uh yeah, good job, Clem!

Now I need to clear this up. Cumberland Mountain Community Services are a shrink hut, but they generated the psych report for the probation office on Brandi which I will refer to as Brandi's probation report to keep it simple.

There are hundreds of little, I am not sure if "nuances" or "subtle twists" is the better term or maybe subtle nuances that no one would ever in a million years be able to spot unless they had the overall view. On pages 14 and 15, look at the bottom of 14.

"mother—it"

In my transcripts there are a lot of N and M dashes. These are cut lines where items are removed or altered. The prosecutor claimed the motion to quash was made on behalf of the mother, on the bottom of page 14, "I believe the mother--," then it says, "it is Tiny Looney."

I never understood this at first because the defense, not the prosecution, asks that the mother be present for the trial. Why? But what got me was Tiny Reedy was not in that room that's why it would make a killer stage show. There are only four people in a side courtroom, the judge, the prosecutor, the defense and myself. I completely missed this at first:

"Mr. Lee: Yes sir she is a witness."

Then the Court seems to be speaking to Ms. Reedy but he says, "You will be a witness for the Commonwealth…" Well of course she'd be a witness for the Commonwealth. Now go back to "mother—it" and alter all of that. All that was said was, "I believe the mother will be present." Lee: "Yes, she will be a witness," then the rest filled in later. That was a stage show to completely mislead the truth.

I know it seems I am being overly nit-picky, but everything just spoken sets a precedence that it was the defense who requested Brandi's mother be present. Why the hell would I want her there? It's the victim's mother—not listed among my best friends to be sure but then, and I did not catch it, the prosecutor says she is a witness. The judge says for the Commonwealth. "This Way to the Great Egress."

Huh! From them there court shows I do believe the prosecution calls a witness then when done the defense cross examines so I would assume at some point she would have to finish her testimony, but it is curious wording. What was just read I sat through. It was a pure con, but I missed it and it cost me, bad. Later I will set that record straight. Everything in those motions turned out to be bullshit, a hoax. Still, only having three years, working through lunch, we never got back to the Brandi probation report. But there ends the motions for that day.

I don't think I ever pointed out that way back in 2012-13 the idea for this book was born. I would send Sally copies of every scrap of paper, and I would write her letters of every tiny detail. I wrote letters three, four or more hours every day. She literally lived every second. At my trial I filled legal pads full of notes of every little detail. When one sees a person sign a plea deal for 25 years and receive 125 years more people should write books, but it's not easy.

I only point that out because the trial transcript has been altered all to hell so some things I cannot prove but I can ask a person to read to the end to then decide what is more probable.

Please keep in mind as this is read, I did not have the transcript, I did not have a lot of the documents in this book so I may go forward then come back later to some points. In many places the transcript is a mess. But I can only go on what I have.

Day one, July 21, 2015, starts with page 1(394) up to 255(648). I cannot explain this phenomenon because the total transcript is 515 pages and none of them add up to 394, there is an offset of 133 pages—do I really need to lob a complaint that this transcript is altered all to hell. But what I do have makes a good book. This will be real true crime, not some bogus re-enactment. I will refer to pages one to 256. Please take a gander at page three for future reference and see how smart the true crime gurus are. There is a ton of information on page three that only the most astute will notice. (The page pisses me off.)(See page 3 Exhibits in Documents).

Right out of the gate we have a boo-boo. These things happen when one rushes to trial in just a measly three years. The court reads the charges, but he only has the January 2013 indictments, the one before I was threatened with the abduction charge, so the judge missed it. That's okay. On page five the prosecutor jumps in to add the abduction. I hate to be persnickety but if one reads between four to six, I never enter a plea. I am never asked how do I plead, or there are about two pages missing. The court comes in on page six saying before he accepts a plea I never made.

I cannot explain this but there is a lady named Cheryl A. Clayton at the probation office. Can someone send her the book so she can see page six? I say I have two years of electronics—do not misread that then call me a liar. (inside joke)

There is a bunch of blah-blah-blah in the transcript so I am only going to point out a few pages as I go, but the curious can read all of it if they want to. The next step in the defense attorney acting as the prosecutor is right on page eight. The defense attorney, first he points out that Sarah Hale or Sally is in the courtroom—he is aiding the prosecution.

This is why lawyers are lying son of a bitches. When the court asks if I gave the names of my witnesses to my lawyer, yes, I did, but the son of a bitch did not subpoena them and then the defense points out that Sally is in the courtroom—only Sally is in the courtroom, period. Keep in mind that in the Jim Shortt video Brandi said that she was thrown on the ground, that none of her clothes were ever removed, that a naked man was on top of her for over two minutes, meaning she would be dirty. My car had black cloth seats and Sally was the next person in my car and my car was clean. The ONLY person I ever told that was Mike Dennis.

On page 10 the prosecutor jumps in calling the Rule to remove Sarah Hale but what neither he nor my so-called defense attorney ever say is—oh, we have a fabricated recording that would discredit Sarah Hale if she attempts to testify. My so-called defense attorney conspired to discredit my witness then withheld that information. Why, you ask? The prosecutor made a deal with Brandi that no one would be present if she would testify but he did so without a mention in the court. My lawyer then conspired to help prosecute me. The minute Brandi was done my lawyer brought out the recording, so Sally came in. Keep that recording in mind because it violated the motion for discovery. Which my entire trial was a violation of the motion for discovery. On page 10 the court accepts the plea of not guilty I never made. On page 11 they kick Sally out for no reason.

I am going to state for the record that Mr. Robert Mckinley Blankenship NEVER!! Requested that Brandi's mother be present! That line was only added to the transcript, it was never stated in my trial. Hey, I sexually assaulted a young girl, let's put HER MOTHER on the stand. What a great, wonderful idea! Fucking moron. Brandi's mother was a witness for the Commonwealth that my lawyer conspired to put on the stand and I will prove that beyond any doubt. I did want the sister, but my lawyer refused to subpoena her, and she was not in the hallway. Lying son of a bitch.

Okay, I'm back.

I did not get page 12 at first that Mr. Dennis wanted it on the record about the witnesses, but I was slammed over the head with that one later.

Finally, at the bottom of page 12 into page 13 we are back to the Brandi probation report where on page 13 the court claims that it pulled all relevant documents, meaning the court pulled all the information that would be exculpatory which would be "just" the two redacted statements. Then I ran into a hell of a confusion.

The day before on the 20th the defense said it was unaware of the contents of that file, but it would trust the court to review it. Then on the 21st suddenly the report is made part of the case file for both sides to review.

On page 13 going into 14 my lawyer claims some silly shit but it's hard to read. On page 13 he is speaking to the court saying that any further information the court found was cumulative or more reports of one incident. "Additional report of the same information, then the defense stated."

"…and there was no additional information that pertained to Mr. Blankenship's case."

The reason I say it's hard to read is because—did he or did he not review the file? The way it reads the defense is saying he was going by what the court provided and that the court, and the court alone, was responsible for the information pulled even though the court just said it made that report part of the case file.

Y'all may think I am being a bit overboard on the whole Brandi psych report but I'll tell y'all what, when your ass faces life plus 22 years and y'all find out the defense lied his balls off to gain a conviction—THE DEFENSE gained a conviction—it does cause one to look at things closely.

My ultimate goal here is that thousands are about to be or are arrested, to the guilty ones—fuck it, plea deal and go home. But to the innocent who chose to go not guilty no matter what—you're walking on eggshells in a nest of deadly vipers. No one is your friend. No one is your advocate. Any judge, any lawyer will fuck you over seven ways to Hell and throw you under a bus. Every action, every word spoken, every sealed record, gag order, every breath is not to provide justice but to net a conviction at any cost. Personally read every document!

Ah yes, welcome to rule 2:403 that's the Virginia Rules of Evidence. Basically rule 2:403 says that relevant evidence can be excluded if it causes prejudice, is confusing or misleads a jury. Ah, but what is "relevant evidence?" Look it up, I don't have time at the moment. I could save a lot of time here. There should have just been just one motion—anything the prosecution wants to use is great with the judge. At this point if the prosecutor pulled out an ax I used to cut Brandi's head off before it grew back it would be allowed. My lawyer would object but only to the time of day I cut her head off not to the ax. And any "exculpatory" evidence would NOT be permitted. And that covers all the motions. The prosecution has open leeway but the defendant is tied neck-and-heel. "Y'all done be thinkin' I'm joking—huh."

Hurrah, on page 17 we be in the lynch mob, part two (except for one person). Twenty-five people came in and they are a prime group. Anyone who wants to can read all the blah-blah-blah.

I do apologize, I have been most remiss in the introductions. For the prosecution we have Dennis Lee and his second Ms. Menefee. For the defense we have Mike Dennis and co-counsel Mike Letson. Everyone keep an eye on Mr. Letson. He was appointed as co-counsel to handle my appeal should we lose (hehehe) because Mr. Mike Dennis had to assume his new duties as attorney for the Commonwealth—yep, my defense attorney was the new prosecutor for Tazewell County—a round of applause, please. He was a damn good prosecutor—at least at my trial he was—not so great at the defense thing though. But it only looks good on the surface because Mr. Letson was not appointed co-counsel for the appeal, but I can't spoil the surprise.

Here is a neat little side story the average person don't know. I didn't, but Sally found it online. There is a jury selection 101 online where the prosecutor will mention "law and order" while a spotter watches for positive, or negative, reactions. On page 36 Menefee says, "From all of OUR 'Law and Order' episodes," almost word for word in over 400 jury trials which I meant to put in the book but couldn't. I lost access to some information. But yep, good old Menefee made a hook up, gonna fry a pervert like they do 20 times a day on TV, now it's OUR turn.

It can't be read in any transcript but on page 51 I asked my lawyer, "What the fuck, dude!" A goddamn member of a police force on my jury. A police dispatch, a person who for over two, almost three, years was continuously exposed to criminally intense situations, every manner of crime. She was at the forefront, domestic assaults, rapes, sexual assaults, over and over and over for years. Then not just a severely psychologically compromised person but a female on a sexual assault case. That alone was grounds for a mistrial, ineffective counsel and prejudice. I even wrote in my court notes, "Yeah…make this bitch foreperson find me guilty and call it a day why bother with a trial!"

I did skip over one. Ladies and gentlemen please allow me to introduce a Ms. Connie Bailey from pages 48, 49, and 50.

Dennis: "Would the fact if he chose not to testify or not to present any evidence…"

Ms. Bailey: "I just don't understand the—he doesn't have to present any evidence."

Goddamn, that is just wrong on so many levels. It's sad to the point of tragedy but it's also hilarious in a Monty Python sort of way. The first question, Ms. Bailey, would be—would you know evidence if it was or was not presented? I do hope someone gets Ms. Bailey a copy of this book. I speak to her often. To you, Ms. Bailey, while I would very much love to show you some "real" evidence, I would love to have shown you some evidence, but it was not allowed. If Ms. Bailey reads this book, she will see that she, as a juror, missed half the trial and she missed two-thirds of the evidence she never knew existed. But now Ms. Bailey can see what "evidence" looks like. Page 50:

Ms. Bailey: "No, no when you watch it on TV..."

Well Ms. Bailey, I do believe it would be safe to say what is in this book will never be seen on TV. I did not have a trial—I had a lynch mob of prosecutors.

On the jury was a Ms. Maynard who was the only honest person. Too bad it was only one out of 13.

And the jury is:
Melissa Buchanan
Bridget Quesenberry
Bradley Rhody
Jonathan Mitchell
Kayla Nelson (cop!) (pig girl)
Nellie Maynard – my favorite
Christopher Wimmer
Connie Bailey (evidence lady)
Lisa Graham
Roma Matney
Connie West
Thomas McClain
Dreema Pruett

The first real trial point came on page 69. Anyone who is curious what it is exactly can look up, "Motion for Discovery" in a jury trial. The defense files a motion for discovery which specifically requests the prosecution turn over the evidence it will use at trial. This includes:

Any and all exculpatory evidence
All documentary, photograph, recorded audio.

Both of those seem very clear to me. I do have the motion for discovery but only one copy but the prosecutor, Lee, responds it is unaware of any items as requested. There is an explanation for this but again, why spoil yet another surprise?

On page 67, oh look, the prosecution just after jury selection suddenly found some "surprise" evidence it conveniently forgot to mention on the motion for discovery a whole 20 pictures. If one steps back and watches, Ms. Bailey, my entire trial they do not present one piece of real evidence.

They have pictures and someone to describe what evidence would look like if there was any evidence. (Violation: 19.2-187, 19.2-187.01)

Actually, the case is simple, too simple. First, they lie saying, "He said he never left the house," then the entire trial does not prove I was ever on Ray Road, they just prove I left the house, but the trial is ludicrous. The photos are needlessly cumulative, completely irrelevant, not relevant evidence and a violation of the motion for discovery. It's what a defense lawyer would have said but to help the prosecution he just objects to the time of year which don't even make sense.

Now I have to call on Ms. Bailey if she would care to tell the truth. On page 69 do you recall the "I.T. stuff" when the prosecutor put up a photo for the entire trial? It's the Wal-Mart photo in the book Documents. It's supposed to be me holding Brandi and proof of the theft of sunglasses. Look closely at the photo, Ms. Bailey, then tell me what is so wrong with that photo. It proves that is not me--do you see it? I will prove beyond any doubt that that photo is not me at all.

There is a running joke in my trial but it's a very long running joke. It took six years to get the punch line. On page 70 the prosecutor says, "This barely-14-year-old girl." Oh yeah, she's just a precious little sweetheart who never done no wrong, a little angel to be sure.

In the Documents I put the Jim Shortt video which started yet another running joke, but it still depicts how completely stupid my trial was. On page one of the Jim Shortt video Brandi says, "He'd pay them 30 bucks apiece for cleaning house, or he said he would pay them." On page 69 we go into opening statements and logic takes a holiday. On page 71, and I do wish the prosecutor had have put in a time, but he testifies "that morning" I go get a couple of 12-year-olds who I intend to pay $60 to clean a house that has no floors. Brandi made that detail up in the Jim Shortt video, so in fact the so-called defense attorney made brand new evidence to help convict me. First lawyer turns rogue investigator.

So, Ms. Bailey did it ever occur to you as a jury member that in this version I nabbed a couple of 12-year-olds, all alone, all day, in a house, with me. And they cleaned all day long, nothing in the world like a clean house, super-duper clean.

I hate to do this—page 72:
"CIGARETTES!" "CIGARETTES!"
"He buys a package of cigarettes."
"He gives the cigarettes to Brandi."

Does EVERYONE see that right there on page 72 the word "CIGARETTES" is in the transcript—twice just on that page.

Cigarette: "A slender roll of cut tobacco enclosed in paper for smoking."

My thesaurus does not list any other word for cigarette. I could delve into slang, stogy, fag, cancer stick, but is there any doubt first on what a cigarette is and second that cigarettes "would pertain to my case?" There was exactly one piece of evidence at my trial—a pack of cigarettes. So, from that I would say that cigarettes are the only thing that pertains to my trial.

I would almost suggest someone take separate notes because this gets so twisted up or so convoluted that, I was there, and I could barely follow it. This becomes a spider web that all leads to one thing, "This Way to the Great Egress!"

At the bottom of page 72 the prosecutor testifies that I do something strange, "He asks Brandi." Fuck, that's not sinister so he changes up to, "He tells Brandi to drive." Yeah, that's better, more menacing. "Drive my (brand new very nice Toyota Corolla) wench, to, uh, the bank!" Let's all pretend that I put a little girl behind the wheel of my very nice low mileage ride, who would drive all over the place, but my insurance would not cover.

This is only opening testimony by the prosecutor but in this version I drive to Corner Mart, I run in the store, I, without being asked, totally at random just buy someone a pack of cigarettes. Oh sure, I do that all the time, doesn't everyone do that? But then I force Brandi to drive to…the wrong bank, then…oh crap.

Since this confused the shit out of Sally's friend, I will fix it now. The Valero is at the Taco Bell so the words Valero and Taco Bell mean the same place. We did not go to Taco Bell before or after Valero, we bought gas at the Taco Bell/Valero.

In this version the sequence is Corner Mart, bank, Valero and then Wal-Mart. It should not be hard at all to keep up with but somehow this became the entire trial or the most fucked up series of argued irrelevant crap in existence. This alone would make one hell of a stage play or a damn good Monty Python skit. I could easily rival "Who's on First" with this one. If I seem to make fun of some parts, remember I have had LOTS of time to process and some of it is worthy of just making fun of.

I did however receive a bad shock at this point. I steal sunglasses at Wal-Mart. On page 74 it's yet another mess going into 75. The prosecutor says:

"And you will see—you will see."

They edited that part because he got very flustered.

"You will see—video."

"You will see video stills."

"You will see stills from the footage."

There is a good reason he became so flustered but ya simply must be in the know. I can however provide a hint: police report transcript page three. "All will be revealed." I am not a judge. I don't need sealed records to cover my own ass. I say post ALL documents online. Oh wait, I did that already.

Our story so far according to the testimony from the prosecutor is I drove to Corner Mart, Brandi drove to the bank, to Valero, to Wal-Mart. Game over—fatality! He then claims we drove over Kent's Ridge Road. That would be Kent's Ridge Road, over Daw Road to Ray Road. I do so hate estimates but here I have no choice. How long would it take a person to get out of a car, walk 195 to 200 yards up a dirt road and then drink two beers?

Now on pages 76 and 77 the prosecutor spins a good yarn, but it will be up to the reader as to which version they prefer.

Police report:

"Where he took off her shirt and bra."

"Never on the ground."

Jim Shortt video page seven:

"Okay, did he EVER remove any of your clothing?"

"No."

At trial – third version

Only shirt removed.

Not that it matters because they both blew it. Okay, out of car, walk 200 yards, remove clothes, drink 2 beers, perform one of three assaults, get dressed, walk another 200 yards back…I'd call it 10 minutes at the least but not more than 15. Ten will do fine.

HEY, LOOK! Right there on page 78:

"He gives her the—CIGARETTES!"

He re-gives her the cigarettes? Uh, he gives her more cigarettes? Either way I regive Brandi the cigarettes I gave Brandi at the store. This bitch gotta learn to keep up with her own shit.

Thank you, Mr. Prosecutor for page 78. You completely blew it later, but it starts on that page—major mistake. I do agree one can't keep track of little nuances but that was a royal fuckup.

On page 79 the prosecutor makes a curious point in a very, very roundabout way. It's extremely subtle and unless one knows what he is doing it would not even be noticed.

"She is upset and she tells him as best she can what has occurred to her and she writes down a little statement."

The prosecutor at my trial is terrified of one thing—the police report. He is setting stage to attempt to discredit the report. The jury, at my jury trial, by consent and in conspiracy with the defense NEVER sees or hears the police report from the day of my arrest July 9, 2012. It's referred to numerous times but avoided by both sides. That alone proves ineffective counsel.

I still love the fact that in one breath I say nope haven't been out of the house all day and oh, here are these two receipts to prove I'm lying. Yep, totally lying, look at this receipt, see, I lied 'cause I did leave the house. So, right off the bat he is lying.

Then the prosecutor blows it, the first time, on page 80, "They pull the videos."

Anyone wanna hear a good joke, read page 81. "He picked a vulnerable 14-year-old girl..." I am sorry it takes six years to get the punchline but's a damn good joke.

"He groomed her by buying her things and stealing her trinkets." (Sunglasses)

On page 81 the defense testifies, and he could have defended me right there, but he chose to testify for the prosecution. There is a very curious point no one ever asks, not even Sally, and she was three points smarter than me. It's not what the defense says, it's what the defense don't say that people need to watch. Of course, there were some things the prosecutor did not say which were curious.

On page 83 the defense, testifying for the prosecution, says I hired two kids to come and clean my house. And one would think well first, no one ever testified to that, but it should be a simple little detail with no way to screw up, but they do.

Damn, where are my manners? Ms. Bailey, juror, please allow me to introduce Mr. Mike Letson, co-counsel, and Mr. Mike Letson, co-counsel, let me introduce Ms. Bailey, juror. Now Mr. Letson, do you have any little tidbit, any smidgen of information you'd like to impart? No. We will check back later.

On page 89 now we are into the meat of the action: Brandi Lee Short. What no one will ever see was that when Brandi entered, do you recall Ms. Bailey that a bailiff locked the door and he stood there? That violated the right to a public trial, but witches do not have any Constitutional rights. No Ms. Bailey, I would never ask you to speak up. No one will speak up when it's your innocent family member either.

"And you had a trespassing charge then a fight at school..."

Page 91, wow, can you believe anyone would press trespassing on a barely 14-year-old little angel? A fight at school? I bet she was defending the innocent. Gee, I really hope there isn't, oh, a sealed document that would disprove what a little angel Brandi is. They don't lock someone in detention for minor trespassing.

Jim Shortt video:
"He said he'd pay them 30 bucks."
Transcript page 93:
"He said he'd pay them 30 bucks."
Yep, so far so good on that point, and on page 94:
"They was over there finished cleaning up the house."

Damn it Sally, stop correcting me or that line in editing—I rewrote seven damn times—leave it alone!

Brandi! Tenth grade, really? The word "was" is first and third person singular. "I was," "he was." For plural or second person use the word "they were." See, they were over there finished cleaning up the house. You say it. Sally corrects me so let's all step it up a notch, okay?

But hey, Brandi came in around 3:30 p.m. so from morning to evening I have had two obviously hard-working helpers over cleaning up my tiny house, but it's 100 percent clean. Look my house up online next to Godliness it's so clean. My house is so clean it's the second stop on the rejected midget clean house bus tour. Gaze in awe upon the cleanliness. (Have I made a point yet? Two or three people...cleaning...all day.)

This is amusing on page 94:
Q. "Cleaning up whose house?"
A. "Robert Mckinley Blankenship."

Q. "And who is he?"
A. "Robert Mckinley Blankenship."

First, damn it Brandi, use "'s" on Robert McKinley Blankenship's if you mean it was my house. But hey, nice prep work on getting that in twice like that, hardly noticeable at all. I am the majestic Robert Mckinley Blankenship. Full name, two times. Whoo, whoo, great job, perfect coaching, got it right both times too.

On page 94, yep, Brandi went all the way to my couch to ask her mom if she could go with me. Again, I hate to nitpick, but it does make the book better. In the police report the aunt Janet called the mother from Wal-Mart but on page 95 the mother was on the phone with Janet. Long phone call. Well damn, on page 95 the illustrious Robert Mckinley Blankenship is back to just plain old Robert again. Oh, how fast the mighty fall. But it does save me writing out the full name. You try signing Robert Mckinley Blankenship on the tiny lines most forms (DMV) have.

Let the action begin!

Page 96 I drove to the Corner Mart:

"He ran in."

And there is that damn word again, "CIGARETTES."

Q. And had you asked him to get anything for you?
A. No.

So, I enter a store then without being asked at all, just randomly buy someone cigarettes. That sounds a wee bit illogical to me, but that's the claim. The reader should keep track of these facts, or not facts…versions. So, I bought cigarettes, I gave her cigarettes.

On page 97 things almost go sideways. This is only funny at the end.

Q. And what happened after that?
A. We went to Taco Bell.

Oh no, she done went and all kinds of fucked up. You do not contradict Mr. Prosecutor, he will attack—"No, you dumb bitch, you went to the bank!"

Q. "And did you stop at the bank?"

Uh, your honor, we could save time. Let the prosecutor testify then just tell Brandi to nod yes. Oh, we are doing that. Huh. It's only stupid when one knows Brandi told the truth but then the prosecutor corrected her, so she committed perjury. But for now, let's go with this version. Page 97 Brandi testifies she drove to the bank, TruPoint Bank in Richlands near the police station, and Brandi was driving. This actually becomes a song and dance routine or a rap song later. But right at this moment a whole lot of crazy shit happened that don't show up in the transcript.

A most fortuitous happenstance. To start, I did not catch this until the third time it happened, so I was slow. The prosecutor had an empty yellow folder (it was empty when I stole it). He would lift the folder and Brandi would need a break but in this instance it really helped. One half is in the transcript, one half is not. When Brandi ran out, I had my lawyer get Sally. This caused a hell of an argument later but that's a whole other story. Sally came in and I quickly filled out a Power of Attorney which my lawyer's assistant notarized. Brandi lied about the bank, so I sent Sally to get my bank statement. (If you are smart enough to know what a bank statement is.) Thanks to Brandi, I had overdrafts on my account that Sally had to pay 156 dollars to get my bank statement.

At the same time, Ms. Maynard came out to say she could not be objective because she knew that Brandi had threatened to lie about sexual assault, even rape, numerous times. If one reads from 96 to 105 it's only on 105 it comes out:

"It probably would because of the stuff that I've knowed that…"

Just to be very, very damn clear here, no one can read what she said after the "…that," because of one person, a lying bitch named Carla J. Faletti. There is about half a page of transcript missing all thanks to Carla J. Faletti. The book would have been better except for her. Ms. Maynard knew Brandi had threatened to lie about sexual assault numerous times.

If there ever was a stage show, Ms. Maynard nearly gave the prosecutor a heart attack. When the judge told her to step out the prosecutor grabbed her by the elbow saying:

"Your Honor, do you want her to step out this way or out this way?"

The prosecutor is damn near dragging the poor woman to the door farthest from the jury. God knows we can't have the jury hearing the truth. The truth in a court of law is never allowed. But for a play it would be funny. I do so love the wording on page 106. The prosecutor:

"…based on her personal I guess rumors…"

Oh yeah, all kinds of nasty rumors about our little angel Brandi flying around enough to make a female juror get up and walk out on a jury trial that a lot of, uh, rumors was it. Of course, the judge sides with the prosecution--why stop now? Once again, we have lying bitch Carla J. Faletti to thank for messing shit up. This mess started at 11:11 a.m. The jury entered at 11:23 a.m. There was a motion entered, that is, the prosecutor

sent a bailiff to make sure Ms. Maynard had left the building. Her kind-
-honest--ain't welcome 'round here. Then there was a gag order on anything Ms. Maynard may have said "or on her actions," meaning neither
I nor anyone could say why she left or what she said in the courtroom,
motion removed.

So, tell me Ms. Bailey, did you ever wonder where the other juror
went, or why?

On page 108 we are back to Brandi Lee Short. For a recap, I drove
to Corner Mart. She drove to the bank in Richlands, then on 109 she
continued to drive to Taco Bell to buy gas. Then (does anyone else see
how damn stupid this is) she drives to Wal-Mart where the sole purpose
was to enter, steal a cheap-ass pair of sunglasses, then walk right back out
again. This would have all worked out better if the prosecutor had have
picked one or the other. "Grooming" is when a person buys a young girl
or boy gifts to win them over for sexual favors. But if I am terrifying her
by dragging her around by the arm with the intent to drive her off and
rape her, grooming is irrelevant. At one time he argues one but at the
other he changes. Either way on page 110 I steal sunglasses.

I hope Brandi reads this because right there on page 111 is where she
blew it. It must really suck to know there were only two choices, A and B.
A is correct, B is incorrect, and she chose B.

Q. Was that on Kent's Ridge Road?

A. Yes.

So, we drove over Kent's Ridge Road, over Daw Road to Ray Road and
on page 112 I had two beers. Yep, there is them beer cans I littered that
the cops found. And on page 113 as soon as Brandi said I took her shirt
off, up goes the yellow folder and she ran out of the room. Excellent,
good show, perfect timing. Thank God she got a few points down on the
coaching side. That was at 11:29 just six minutes after the last break, but
we were back on 11:40 a.m. Uh, Ms. Maynard was a distraction, but Ms.
Bailey don't forget to look up at that Wal-Mart picture on the huge white
screen right in the jury's face. Have you, Ms. Bailey, figured out why that
picture is not me yet?

How about you, Mr. Letson? Any little thing burning at the old con-
science you'd like to share with the group? No? We will check back later.
Any second now Mr. Letson is going to expel a most shocking revelation.
After all, that's the defense's job isn't it, to defend the defendant? Yep,

Mr. Letson will come out with a surprise that will knock Ms. Bailey's socks off—later—uh—maybe.

On page 113 we are back at it at 11:40 a.m. with Brandi on Ray Road. I drink two beers, I get naked, I have her shirt off but from 114 to 115 why is the prosecutor asking the defense if he needs something repeated? I do not see interaction that would require cross communication other than they are working as a team. Had he been making a stronger point he would have turned to the co-prosecutor to maintain us verses them, but he turned to the actual second prosecutor—the so-called defense attorney. The only thing here is that only her shirt was removed. So, we go with the third version of her story.

In my previous summation I forgot the get naked thing, walk 200 yards, drink two beers, get naked, perform one of three assaults, get dressed, walk another 200 yards. I am leaning more on the 12 to 15 minute range. Would you say that's fair, Ms. Bailey? It don't really matter but I would like a fair estimate. So, to be easy let's say 12 minutes. That's to stop then to and from and back to the car, everyone call it 12 minutes.

Do I really need to say here that there is one very consistent point in every version that Brandi tells that has always annoyed me? I stopped—why? At one point she says she started crying. At another she was crying the whole time. At another she never cries, I just stop. There is a pondry, it's a shame I was never on Ray Road.

On pages 116 and 117 it must be hell when the witness just will not stick to the script—bad actor. When Brandi or we got back to my house she ran to her mom's, but the prosecutor said, "You dumb bitch, you forgot the cigarettes. Goddamn, get with program will ya!"

Q. Did you take anything with you?

Your honor, wouldn't it be easier to just have Brandi wait outside while the prosecutors testify? It would save time having to correct her all the time. But do please note in this version the CIGARETTES and the sunglasses were on the car seat. Does everyone see that once more there is cigarettes in the mix? It's a safe bet that cigarettes are 90 percent of the case. I believe I have damn good arguments that cigarettes are "relevant" and that cigarettes do "pertain" to my case.

A young girl, barely 14 years old, a little angel was driven to a secluded area, then she was sexually assaulted, then she is home, get away, run like hell…oh wait, don't forget the smokes, nothing like a good smoke after a sexual assault or lying about sexual assault and Brandi would be the one who would know.

Again, I do hate to be nitpicky but on page 117 there is another oddity. In the police report we have Janet Lester. In the Jim Shortt video, we have Janet Lester. For three years the police completely missed a second witness no one ever mentioned until Janet Lester refused to lie for Brandi. Then, wow, how very super convenient, exceptionally damn lucky, we just happen to have a second aunt who pops up out of nowhere. A spare witness, wow, imagine that. Oh yeah, nothing fishy about that at all. It's a damn shame Crystal Owens rode the short bus. They never put up signs for regular children at play but Crystal definitely had "Slow Children at Play" signs in her yard. She made the world's worst witness, but she was awesome for the book.

I really do hate to be too nitpicky, but it's kind of my job. In open statements the prosecutor testified on Ray Road that "I took Brandi," and "I put Brandi in the car." Yep, totally mean. But then on page 116 while I get dressed Brandi takes a nice little walk down to the car, so she wasn't exactly dragged down then crammed in.

I have never understood page 118. If my mom hit someone in the face, I would not see shit and I damn sure would not rat out my own mom under oath in a courtroom—that's cold.

Page 118 could confuse someone who tried to understand it unless they know what's going on. The prosecutor is moving to discredit a piece of evidence that was never entered, a most curious little piece of evidence. The evidence is referred to numerous times, but the prosecution is terrified of it. The one item he cannot allow in the jury trial is the police report from July 9, 2012. Yep, usually the police report would be front and center but in this trial the prosecutor won't allow it.

On page 118 he uses the words you were upset you wrote a brief (tiny) statement. What he is referring to is the criminal complaint which Brandi did not write but it explains his several mistakes. Now if I was the prosecutor one of my assistants would be fired for real.

"In your statement you didn't mention that you went to the bank."

If one reads the criminal complaint only then it only lists Corner Mart, Wal-Mart, then Ray Road, but had he bothered to read the supplement he would have adjusted his story to Corner Mart, Valero, Bank, then Wal-Mart. Brandi did say bank but only TruPoint Bank not which bank. Face it, the prosecutor is desperate to keep the police report out. I have the only trial in history where the prosecution spends 90 percent of its efforts removing evidence or concealing evidence. Either way Brandi committed perjury.

Everyone should look at page 119 very carefully because something damn odd happened. When the court says the record will reflect the witness identified…look at the next two questions, prosecutorial questions.

Q. And did you take the police that evening back up to where it happened at?

Q. And did you point out to them where he assaulted you?

Then Mr. Lee comes back so where I thought there were four prosecutors there were five because those questions are from the judge. It shows by Lee, Court and then Lee.

I do wish my lawyer had been a bit more clear here on page 120, but it becomes very obvious later.

Mr. Dennis: "There is something I need to review prior to doing that."

The series here is important to make my point. Brandi testified that she drove to the bank in Richlands which was perjury, so we sent Sally to the bank, and she obtained a bank statement which she gave to my lawyer. In that courtroom there were exactly two people who knew, "the bank at Claypool Hill," and that would be me and the defense lawyer. I told him the bank at Claypool Hill and my bank statement proved it—that is what he had to review. That may not sound like much, but it becomes a very huge deal, kind of like a disaster.

But then we broke for lunch so we were back on around 1:12 p.m. and on page 122 the cross examination begins, or it would be easier to write that Mike Dennis takes over as prosecutor.

On page 123 they cut out part of Brandi's answer, but I am not sure why other than it would spoil the prosecutor's claims.

"Yes, if I was with my brother and sister or my mom. That's usually…"

Brandi said that's usually where mom goes during the day. But if the mom visited me that would not match the prosecutor's claims.

I really hate to write this part because on one side it's funny in a Monty Python sort of way but mostly it's just sad.

Jim Shortt video:

"He said he'd pay them 30 bucks apiece."

Page 93 transcript:

"He said he would pay them 30 bucks apiece."

Page 126-27 transcript:

"Mommy told…now, this is what I heard. Mommy told me he was going to pay them 30 bucks apiece."

Uh, okay, so who told Brandi? On page 127, "But he didn't tell me exactly how much!"

It's really not apparent until one really looks at the question.

Q. "Did you hear Robert talk about what he was going to pay them or how much?"

The defense was helping the prosecution but then in a most unexpected turn, all Brandi had to say was, "He told me he would pay them 30 bucks apiece," but nope, she completely flipped the script. So, under that light the defense turned prosecutor actually turned defense because Brandi answered wrong. So, who if anyone ever said 30 bucks apiece, or no one?

Hello Ms. Bailey, how are you today? All comfy at home, are we? I do hope you're having a lovely day relaxing, reading a book maybe. Ms. Bailey, if you're reading this, may I direct your attention to pages eight and nine?

"He also requested the witness' younger sister be present. And I understand from Mr. Lee that she is present in the hall also."

That would be Shania Lyn Short or as she is currently referred to, "house cleaner." So now Ms. Bailey, as a juror, did you ever ask yourself why they made a huge deal about house cleaning, but they never once put one of the actual cleaners on the stand, even when one was just out in the hallway? Don't worry Ms. Bailey, Sarah Hale was in the hallway, and she made videos which are online. Shania was never present. Kind of curious that there were two so-called ground zero witnesses the prosecutor never called. This becomes more apparent later. He called the aunt and grilled the hell out of her for what she saw in June. Think on that.

Now someone please correct me if I am wrong, but when Brandi said—under oath—that, "He said he would pay them 30 bucks apiece," and, "He never said exactly how much," one of those is another case of perjury. Well, one or both are perjury because both cannot be true, contradictory hearsay.

But on page 126, "They was over there finished cleaning up the house." Yep, yes-siree-bob, my house is exceptionally clean. My house is so clean, "Robert's Clean House" is the 13th most-used blessing by the Pope. Raise thy hand and feel the universal cosmic forces that pulsate from how clean my house is. My house is so clean it repels microscopic dust to a radius of 100 miles. My house is so clean when females cross the threshold, they are reborn virgins in mind and body. (Okay, that one may be a little over the top.)

I'll say it flat out—if anyone loves Monty Python and smokes pot now would be a damn good time to burn one. Hell, burn two, one for me. Yes, most of the people reading this will notice that the defense is a master at irrelevant questions.

On page 127, it would be a safe bet that 100 percent of people exit a door to get in a car so, "Did you leave the house to get in the car?"

A. "Huh?"

Oh, I do so apologize for confusing you, but I understand leaving a house to get in a car is a totally new concept no other humans do, but if you could please walk us through this phenomenal concept. "You left the house?" Fuck no, we drove the house to the Corner Mart. Now wouldn't Mike Dennis shit if Brandi said that. Yep, we be all abby-normal, we exited by the front door. Good Lord, half a damn page just to exit a door of a house and we ain't even in the car yet.

Q. "Okay. And where did he drive to the first time?"

By page 128 we finally managed to exit a door to get in a car, then I drove to Corner Mart. She did not say one word all the way to Corner Mart. But then, opening statements. "I ran in the store." Brandi testified I ran in the store but then page 128 she ran in the store, or she went in the store, so one of those is perjury.

I apologize for what I am about to write. It's a slap in the face to any type of logic but I can assure anyone, it's the transcript, not me. From start to finish it just gets stupider and stupider.

But first...

Q. "And what did you see Robert buy in the store?"

On page 129, "CIGARETTES." Yep, here we go again, that damn word over and over and over. I am making an annoying point. HEY, Ms. Bailey, don't want you, a juror, to feel left out. Do you see cigarettes all over the transcript? In your professional (is jutorial a word? Fuck it, it is now) jutorial position would you, Ms. Bailey, say that in fact cigarettes would pertain to my case or be considered, "irrelevant."

Q. "And what did Robert give you when you got back in the car?"

Gee there Mr. Prosecutor, isn't that just a bit obvious? You should have just said he gave you cigarettes and let her agree. Defense turns prosecutor. The defensive question would have been, "What happened next?" But both the prosecutor-prosecutor and defense-prosecutor know that it's not safe to give Brandi an open question and hammer in cigarettes.

Oh crap! Here we go.

The bottom of page 130 or 129-30 when we came out of Corner Mart Brandi got in the passenger's side so the defense on page 130 asks how she got in the driver's seat to drive "to the next location," and she blows it because he, she, they forgot the bank.

Police Report: Corner Mart, Valero, Bank, Wal-Mart

Transcript-Prosecutor: Corner Mart, Bank, Valero, Wal-Mart

A. "To the next stop, Taco Bell."

Which as one recalls was exactly what she said the first time until the prosecutor corrected her, but the defense did not.

Q. "But did you drive to the Taco Bell?"

A. "No. He did."

"Oh lord, won't you buy me a color TV…" Sorry, brain slip due to "stupid overload."

Brandi just testified that she drove from the Corner Mart to the bank in Richlands, then she drove to Valero. Now she testifies I drove to the Corner Mart, then I drove to Valero. I leave it up to the reader who drove where by Brandi's testimony.

Then on page 131:

Q. "Did you stop anywhere before Taco Bell?"

A. "No."

Q. "Did you get out of the car at Taco Bell?"

A. "No."

Q. "Who drove from Taco Bell?"

A. "I did."

Q. "How did you get in the driver's side?"

A. "I'm confused."

Well hell, aren't we all! But if anyone makes a play out of this at this point when Brandi runs out to be coached both the prosecutor and the defense are out in the hall with Brandi. (You don't know what's going on, do you Ms. Bailey?)

Look on page 133 when they all come back:

"Again, you said you got out of the car at Taco Bell on the passenger side and went around to the driver's side."

Well now. What I read on page 131 was:

Q. "And did you get out of the car at Taco Bell?"
A. "No."

So, then the defense-prosecutor testifies for the prosecution in aiding the testimony of a witness to convict the defendant. Now you said you got out of the passenger side and got in the driver's side. That is not a question, that is a prosecutor leading a witness, but I did not have a defense lawyer to object.

So, now in this version at Corner Mart I not only forced her to drive but I also forced her to drive from the passenger side. Wow, I are evil! But just so we don't get confused, at Corner Mart I forced Brandi to drive to the bank, then Valero while I drove from the Corner Mart to Valero where she got in the driver's side. See, simple. "On the road again. I can't wait to get on the road again…" From Valero Brandi drove to the Wal-Mart. We seem to be missing a bank which would match the Jim Shortt video where Brandi said we never went to any bank.

There is one tiny little stipulation here that I would like to point out. At Wal-Mart we did park on the grocery side. We entered the grocery side and three to four minutes later we exited the grocery side. We were parked on the side, not in the parking lot. I would love to have a real photo to prove the door we used but I don't, it's not allowed. No, Ms. Bailey, the photo you stared at for the whole trial was not me. Did you spot the problem yet? It's very obvious once one sees it.

And here once again I stole sunglasses. Yep, bob-bastic-fantastic-criminal. I bet Ms. Bailey, juror, has not spotted a huge hole in this tale. Tell me Ms. Bailey, do you have brothers, sisters or kids? Keep that in mind. On page 140 she does say we were not in the parking lot but around the side.

Pardon me a second. Yo, Letson, dude, this is the defense cross examination. If you're going to do the surprise revelation any time now would be great. No? We will check back later.

On page 140 we went across Kent's Ridge Road to Daw Road to Ray Road. Page 141 she is sure, everyone is sure, we went across Kent's Ridge Road. Uh, Ms. Bailey, do you know the route of Kent's Ridge, Daw Road, River Road into Raven? By the way Ms. Bailey, did you know that Brandi went to the shrink—often—near the college where yes, she traveled that route both ways. That's why on 141 yep, she knew how to get there. But we don't know that yet, so keep it under your hat for now.

Oh, joy and elation! Praise the Lord we have deliverance, and a big ol' sloppy thank you to Brandi Lee Short.

Do you see page 142, Ms. Bailey, juror?

Q. "And you didn't go back by your house or by the house without stopping earlier before you went to Daw Road?"

A. "No."

No one, not me, not the prosecutor, not the defense, not Brandi, and not the jury would ever know how bad Brandi fucked up on that one line. At that time no, I did not know at all because I missed it, but now we are about to enter a shit storm. This is where we beat out "Who's on First."

Q. "When did you stop at the bank again?"

A. "On the way after we got done at Corner Mart."

Q. "I'm sorry, after you got done at Corner Mart?"

A. "Yes."

Q. "So, you went to the bank before you went to Taco Bell?"

A. "Yes."

On page 142, read it, she has now answered this question three times. She said after Corner Mart, before Taco Bell. I do not see any confusion or any misunderstanding. But he changes tactics.

Q. "Do you remember Caldwell?"

A. "Yes."

That line of questioning is completely outside the scope of the trial. Think where that question is coming from. Caldwell has not testified, and the police report was under gag order, so the jury had no basis for comparison, and she has clearly answered three times exactly like the prosecutor claimed.

Read page 143 very carefully because it's a trick question.

Q. "Do you remember telling him that you went to Valero before the bank? You went to the bank after Valero."

Both of those mean Valero then bank—a trick question. He is busting his balls to correct her to the right bank. But she says:

A. "I think so, I'm not sure."

All she had to say was "yes," but she did not pick up on it.

Q. "Do you remember if you went to the bank before Taco Bell or after Taco Bell?"

A. "Huh?"

Q. "Do you remember if you went to the bank before you went to Taco Bell or after you went to Taco Bell?"

A. "Before."
Q. "Before you went to Taco Bell?"
A. "Yes."

Good God! There is yet two more times she has answered the question. Uh, excuse me there Mr. Prosecutor, but the wicked defense-prosecutor is literally badgering the hell out of your star witness. Shouldn't you jump in with oh, an objection thingy at some point? "Your honor, I object—he's badgering the witness—she has clearly answered the question five times the same way!" There, see? Easy.

Q. "So, if you told Caldwell you went to the Taco Bell before the bank it wasn't correct?"
A. "No."
Q. "Is it possible you went to the bank at Claypool Hill or at Taco Bell TruPoint Bank?"
A. "I have no idea."

Okay Ms. Bailey, you read the criminal complaint, the supplement, the entire testimony of Brandi Lee Shortt and not once, anywhere, at any point does anyone other than my so-called defense attorney use the words Claypool Hill. I told my lawyer outside the courtroom at a holding cell that we went to the bank at Claypool Hill and that the witness committed perjury. And the son of a bitch conspires with the prosecutor to correct Brandi to the correct bank. He became so flustered. Corner Mart is in Richlands, Taco Bell is at Cedar Bluff, and the bank is at Claypool Hill, so where did Taco Bell TruPoint Bank come from? They are not even close. You, Ms. Bailey, should see that he badgers the hell out of Brandi to get her to commit perjury to the Claypool Hill bank and the prosecution never objects at all, not one word.

Once more, all Brandi had to say was "yes." Thank God she's a moron who isn't quick on the uptake. A: "I have no idea." Uh, you just said five times bank before Taco Bell, so ya kinda did have an idea, a bad one, but an idea. It's like watching two color-blind people play checkers.

Q. "Now you testified earlier you went to the one near the police station. Could it have been the one near the Taco Bell?"
A. "Huh-uh." (no)

Uh, Mr. Dennis, I hate to interrupt your most courageous attempt to correct Brandi to the right bank. I understand you're helping the prosecution convict me, but when this book comes out that will look silly. TruPoint is nowhere near Taco Bell at all, not even close. And you suck

ACTUAL INNCOCENCE

as a prosecutor—in this case, anyway. Let's look at the series shall we, just for fun.

1. Q: "When did you stop at the bank?"
   A: "After Corner Mart."
2. Q: "After Corner Mart?"
   A: "Yes."
3. Q: "So bank before Taco Bell?"
   A: "Yes."
4. Q: "Remember Caldwell?"
   A: "Yes."
5. Q: "Do you remember telling him bank after Valero?"
   A: "I think so, I'm not sure."
6. Q: "Do you remember bank before or after Taco Bell?"
   A: "Huh?"
7. Q: "Do you remember if you went to the bank before or after Taco Bell?"
   A: "Before."
8. Q: "Before you went to Taco Bell?"
   A: "Yes."
9. Q: "If you told Caldwell bank after Taco Bell it was incorrect?"
   A: "No, I was confused."
10. Q: "Is it possible bank at Claypool Hill?"
    A: "I have no idea."
11. Q: "Testified near police station could it have been near the Taco Bell?" (where there is no bank)
    A: "Huh-uh." (no)

Fuck it! Just go to Ray Road!

Watching all of that was painful. First, the defense attorney tries seven ways to hell to correct Brandi to the right bank, but she just don't pick up on it. He hammered the hell out of that question, he badgered her. Hell, he slammed her with that line. And yet, not a peep out of the prosecutor who allowed the badgering. Over and over he asks and she answers. Questions one, two, three, seven and eight are all the same question with the same answer. Now, I feel really bad that Mr. Dennis completely failed—epic fail-in correcting Brandi to help the prosecution which does constitute ineffective counsel with extreme prejudice, but here, let me give it a go:

"Brandi you brain-dead cunt, we have the goddamn bank statement that shows the fucking bank at Claypool Hill, so for fuck's sake would your moronic ass say Claypool Hill—JUST SAY YES. Might want to knock off the psych meds, dumb bitch!"

Well, I certainly feel better, and I didn't need 11 questions to fail. Sometimes with the…very…slow…ones a more direct approach is needed.

Having failed—epic fail—to correct the witness to convict the defendant, the pretend defense attorney, in frustration, moves on to the actual and only point in their play. With an exasperated sigh he must now, and forever, live with the failure.

Well hell, I do not like page 144 at all. "He was finishing his beer, he threw IT over in the weeds." What the hell! I like the other version where I had two beers. Who the fuck took my second beer?! Somebody owes me a beer. I shant forget this slight.

Okay, there are two ways to ever read the truth here on page 146. One way would be to get the first unaltered transcript from the office of the Attorney General. Good luck with that. Or call up a lying bitch named Carla J. Faletti and say hey, got that transcript yet, lying bitch, because until you do you are a lying bitch. "Thank you, drive through!"

There are about eight to 10 lines removed because Brandi was asked if I was circumcised, and she said she never saw anything and at two points she said he removed his underwear. I don't write a lot about Ray Road but:

Police Report:
Shirt and bra removed.
Jim Shortt video:
No clothes at all ever removed.
At trial, split the difference:
Only shirt removed.
Jim Shortt video:
Naked man on top of her on the ground.
Trial:
Knocked down and sprang back up.
Jim Shortt video:
No beer cans at all.
Trial:
One or two beer cans.

No one will believe me here, but this is pathetic. If one goes back to the very start of the opening statements then reads very damn carefully, especially where there is direct examination of Brandi Lee Shortt by the prosecutor, there is an item no one will find because it never existed before page 147. At the bottom of page 147 Brandi suddenly says he stretched my neck. At that point Menefee left the room. I am sorry, I do not have the page, it is online, or one could ask Mike Dennis or one of seven lawyers for it. There is a brand new page five to the criminal complaint supplement where an addendum was added July 21, 2015 at 2:17 p.m. which they added that a stretched shirt was observed. Three years later after page 147 they observed a stretched shirt. Brandi then, on page 148, claims she "was writing," but the prosecutor Lee in the motion for discovery said there were no written statements so one of those has to be a lie. And once again by page 150 I just stop. That annoys me. Especially on page 151, at every other point Brandi started crying so I stopped, but then she says she was crying the whole time.

I really don't know how to explain page 153:

Q. "So he never made any contact to you of any kind of sexual nature?"

A. "Not that I know of."

Uh, when someone asks a seven-year-old if someone touched them and they answer no, but then Brandi says she has no idea if she had sexual contact, that is odd.

Pages 154-55 are a bit of a mess, but I believe Dennis is confused as to where Ray Road is. In her story we went in using Kent's Ridge Road, Daw Road to Ray Road, but out it would be Daw Road to River Road then into Raven. The only key point is on page 156 because she never alters that we went in across Kent's Ridge Road. (See Hand-drawn Map)

Goddamn. I got the cigarettes...the sunglasses were on my hat. Well hell, she finally told the truth. She removed the cigarettes from the car, the sunglasses were on her hat. Before the sunglasses were on her seat, but then they were on her hat.

Now we have some curious questions. If one reads the Jim Shortt video transcript that is the only place the high school was mentioned. She never told the cops but in that version at Corner Mart only cigarettes were bought, no beer. She says we never went to any bank, I drove to the school, then she drove to Wal-Mart, then back to Valero, then Raven to Ray Road, but none of her clothes were removed.

On 156:

Q. "And why did you get the cigarettes out of the car when you got out?"

A. "I don't know."

Then we have a crazy part everyone brushed over. Brandi's brother and sister were still at my house according to her, but then they blink out of the story.

Pages 158 and 159 have another serious flaw. Keep this in mind for later because it's funny as hell. The defense attorney grills Brandi on what she said to her mother at home.

On page 162 the prosecutor still hammers away at that statement Brandi wrote out, but it's never been entered. It don't exist or he lied on the motion for discovery and either way he is not making a point or any sense. On pages 163-4 the bank is in the police report so either she wrote it or said it, but it was not left out. Yo, prosecutor, dude, read the supplement so you don't sound like a moron. Oh, too late. Where is this so-called statement she wrote down that on page 165 she claims is the truth? Well, we would all love to read that. Did that say shirt and bra removed truth, no clothes ever removed truth, or shirt only truth, or is there a whole new version of truth we haven't seen yet?

"We want the truth, nothing but the truth, objection overruled!"

Wow. That was one hell of a ride. On page 165 the witness left, thank God. Now is everyone perfectly clear on who drove where, when, and all that? (You're only reading it, I lived it!)

Twenty-two minutes: everything relevant is irrelevant.

It was pointed out by Mellow I did not explain this properly so, spoiler alert part two.

See Bank Statement, Hand-drawn Map and Google Map. The bank statement shows, ATM 3:47 and Doran Grocery 4:09 that is 22 minutes point to point. If one is at the ATM, pulls over to Wal-Mart, parks around the side; it to Sally 4 to 7 minutes. If I use 4, 22-4=18 minutes or less to be inside Doran Grocery.

At the Wal-Mart one cannot go left, they must turn right onto U.S. Route 19-460 then U-turn in 338 feet, see Google Map.

At the Claypool Hill redlight, less than one minute, there are two ways to get to Raven.

One way is to turn right onto Route460 and drive the 4-lane down to Richlands, Raven. That route 8.8 miles 13 minutes if driven non-stop at speed, not likely with one U-turn ahead and 5 redlights. With only 18 minutes left at Wal-Mart, the only route I could have driven was to go right at Claypool Hill.

The second route is, at the Claypool Hill redlight go straight on Route 19, then drive over Kent's Ridge Road, over Daw Road, over River Road into Raven. That route is 12.1 miles 22 minutes if drive at speed non-stop, there is one U-turn and 4 redlights. That is the route Brandi testified to with a 12 minute stop on Ray Roald, or she claimed a 34 minute drive when I only had 18 minutes or less at Wal-Mart. Brandi lied, but she did testify she was no in Raven before Daw Road. My bank statement proves me innocent we never went to Ray Road.

Hi Ms. Bailey, how are you. I know, I know, you wonder why that didn't come out at trial, it did, you missed it. But, boy, wouldn't it be a kick in the ass if, oh, say there was a legal Court document that irrevocably states, "Brandi lies," that had been concealed in violation of Due Process. That would explain her 3 version of an assault.

I am still annoyed that Counsel only asked Brandi hypothetical "did you say" questions. He never once put the police report out and directly say, "why did you say shirt bra removed," then say, "no clothes were ever removed," or, "why did you say slammed to the ground, naked man on top of you for over two minutes," then change a 3rd time to only shirt removed. She was never confronted directly so the Jury could see her lies.

And, Ms. Bailey, it was pointed out I asked if you had kids or siblings. Do you really believe I told Brandi's brother and sister "here's 30 for you, 30 for you but for Brandi a cheap-ass pair of sunglasses," she wouldn't be groomed, she'd be pissed. I had 3 younger brothers, any mom would know "siblings can fight over who gets more cereal, they know."

And to Cindy, "nude" proofreader, the reference was cut so I'll fix it.

P(hineas) T(aylor) "PT" Barnum had a sideshow tent of oddities, people would linger inside thus preventing more from entering. Inside the tent at one end he made an elaborate façade like an entrance to a new section with turns inside, he put a very fancy sign, "This Way To The Great Egress!" Most people, then could read a little but few had any idea what an "egress" was, when they went to see it they found themselves outside.

I use, "This way to the great egress," to depict deception by misdirection. Or, when one is almost, but not quite, entirely unlike being honest as Douglas Adams would say.

In it's simplest form my bank statement next to Brandi's route in the Google map proves me innocent. But let's see what happens next shall we. By the way Ms. Bailey, do not trust me, you go and you drive the route, it took Sally 47 minutes but by all means check it out.

Chapter 5

Boned

"The conceit of specter evidence allowed many to be arrested… those who confessed did so from fear and confusion."

"Specter: Something that seems to appear to the sight but has no physical form: an apparition or phantom."

"The defendants were as good as condemned before trial…"

"Confident that they understood events the magistrates (judges) disregarded not only the protests of the accused by ANY deviation in word or deed of the accusers…"

All of those are from the Salem witch trials 1692-1693, roughly 300 years and not much has changed.

From 1417:

"Should the accused speak in defense he shall be gagged, boxed and weighted for fear he release darkness in words…"

In 1613 one witness refused to testify at a witch trial—for she had no witch marks—three magistrates removed the witness and when they returned the woman testified, "For her witch marks be many."

Yep, the judges dragged her out, beat the crap out of her, then said, "Look what the witch did!" The fabrication has been going on for hundreds of years.

Then I found 1692-1693:

"…albeit the business of witch craft be very much upon the stage of imagination…"

July 21, 2015

"Albeit the business of Actual Inncocence be very much upon the stage of imagination."

1502 and 1714:

"Those who stand for, or by, the accused do but condemn themselves and shall face like consequences and judgments…"

I do believe by the end of this chapter or trial I will more than prove that all of that still holds true today even worse than it did then. There are thousands of good examples from witch trials, in many cases the person was told, "Confess to save your life," then they were hanged—oh, we only meant your spiritual life. Gotta watch them plea deals. If they did not confess, they were also hanged. I could write hundreds of little stories, but I have my own little lynch mob to write about. Before I get too involved here I would like to point out a lying bitch, Carla J. Faletti, she didn't ruin the book but her incompetence made it less—make no mistake—she is in fact a lying bitch!

Between pages 165 to 166 there was a short recess, and it was at this point my so-called lawyer informed me the prosecution had a "secret" recording that would discredit Sally should she testify, and Brandi changed her lie so Sally wasn't needed, but Sally could enter the courtroom. They waited until right after Brandi testified to pull out the secret recording—they removed any mention of it in the Day 1 transcript to the Day 2 transcript.

Sally and I had a long-running argument. In the first break Brandi needed, Sally came in and she was sent to the bank. I tried to explain that in my trial the door was locked and it was guarded. She had entered "when Brandi was OUT!" Then she came in after Brandi testified, SO, Sally why did they fail to mention the recording until after Brandi testified—I WIN!

Hello, Ms. Bailey, are you ready to see ALL the stuff that you as a juror were never allowed to see? There are hundreds of little curiosities in my trial where people change gears that "seems" trivial or like there is no reason for it. In the opening statements the prosecutor made a point that Brandi, "wrote down a little statement." On page 163 he asks Brandi, "Did he or did you write that down?" Answer, "I wrote that down." Over and over he makes a big deal out of the statement Brandi wrote down.

You don't know what's going on, do you Ms. Bailey? I am sorry it took years to pull that rabbit out of the hat. There are two things going on Ms. Bailey as a juror never saw.

Everyone has just seen Brandi hammered about the statement "she wrote." On page 166 we have Officer Caldwell, the main man in this mess. There is a very subtle nuance here few people would even notice, but it was very well done. Caldwell shows up at a possible breaking and entering but then on page 170:

Q. And when you spoke with Brandi did she give you a brief, just verbal statement?

Uh, the prosecutor just asked Brandi did she write that down, why yes, she did, she wrote down a little statement, but tell us Officer Caldwell, about how she gave you a brief JUST VERBAL statement. Uh, Mr. Prosecutor dude, don't you mean what she wrote down? You know, the big deal back on page 163? You still in the dark Ms. Bailey? Don't worry, it comes out later. I can help a little bit though do hate giving away hints. You, Ms. Bailey, now have the police report in your hands. In that police report it clearly states, "Where he removed her shirt and bra." The prosecutor is having fits trying to discredit that should it ever come out. You are not even aware Ms. Bailey, that the judge blocked the police report so it could not enter the jury room.

If one looks on page 168 Caldwell says:

"I'd have to reflect with the report to give you the exact address."

Well hell, let's whip that puppy out. It's the police report from July 9, 2012, the actual report on what was said the day of the event, yet somehow, and one does have to wonder, here we have a, uh—fuck—what we have here Ms. Bailey, is a little statement handwritten by Brandi that was a brief just verbal statement which states I tore off her shirt and bra. That sounds bad to me. As a female would you say shirt and bra were worse than shirt only?

You tell me Ms. Bailey, if that police report had been entered instead of referred to you, as a juror, would have had that in the jury room. But what if you laid that report beside the Jim Shortt video transcript:

Jim: Okay. Alright. Did he ever remove any of your clothing
Brandi: No.
He removed my shirt and bra.
He never removed any of my clothes.

You tell me Ms. Bailey, at any point in my trial were those two points ever pointed out to the jury?

On page 171 Caldwell almost tells the truth. At first Brandi said the sexual assault happened in my house so they did search my house looking for proof, but then they changed the location to Ray Road. It took about five hours but they worked it out.

The best laid plans of mice and men are easily fucked up when all the lies don't match. No matter how well a series of events is practiced it can still go very wrong. A few years ago a Formula One driver was one lap up and 20 car lengths ahead so the race was all but done until a rabbit came out. He hit, went airborne, and shredded his car. No one ever sees the rabbit.

He said he'd pay them 30 bucks apiece.

They was finished cleaning.

Mommy said he'd pay them 30 bucks apiece.

They was finished cleaning.

Q. The house that he resided in would you describe that.

A. ...the inside of the residence was pretty disheveled IT WAS NASTY.

Why Mr. Officer, surely you jest. Three people had cleaned, and cleaned, and cleaned like slaves, morning to evening, been at it all day. According to me, or mommy, or someone, 60 whole dollars were—not paid—to clean—all day. You could not have said it was nasty. You really meant it was double extra eat off the floor eat off the dirt clean. I am appalled, outraged. Don't you realize a sweet little barely 14-year-old angel just said they were finished cleaning? So how could you, officer, attack this little angel with such slander as the house was nasty? How dare you sir to besmirch that little angel's testimony. Uh, excuse me, hey, Ms. Bailey, as a professional juror can you tell me who said the kids would be paid 30 bucks apiece and is the house clean or nasty?

And just maybe you can explain to me, a young girl is assaulted on in a secluded location 20 miles away on a dirt road where her shirt and bra—none of her clothes—were/were not removed. There is a house 20 miles away that may or may not be clean. Do you Ms. Bailey, see any relevance at all between those two points?

Your son is accused of sexual assault on a dirt road 20 miles from your house. You have not washed your breakfast dishes—he is GUILTY AS HELL! Your house is clean, he is GUILTY AS HELL! But hey, Brandi testified, house is clean so that's the truth, the officer testified it was nasty and that is the truth.

Wow, so my super clean house that is nasty somehow proves I sexually assaulted a girl 20 miles away where I ripped off her shirt and bra by not ever removing any of her clothes. Are we all up to speed? You have all that Ms. Bailey? It's all perfectly clear, is it?

Who is lying? The house is clean, the house is nasty. By the way I resent that. The dirt under my missing floor is as clean as anyone else's dirt under their house.

Wait. What the bloody hell ya mean the house was nasty? I just paid (not) two goddamn urchins hard earned cash to clean all damn day and they didn't do shit. Shoulda hired Mexicans. Damn lazy-ass Americans be cleaning all damn day, don't do shit, be leaving the house all nasty and stuff.

Now I don't really give a rat's ass if anyone believes me or not, it's game over for me, but I would hope people who read this think, "What if?" Those who have read my past, a person who was arrested and got his mom shook down for walking too straight, I've had a few run-ins with the police. I can tell anyone, on a lie detector, that I did not stand in my living room and say, "No, I never left the house," then say, "Oh and here is two receipts to prove I'm lying," but that is what was testified to. In fact, that is the prosecutor's entire case.

On July 9, 2012, when the cops got there Brandi said in my house I attempted to lift her shirt. The cops forced me to sit on the couch and I could not move. Hours later I was detained and moved outside. My keys were in my bowl—my wallet was gone. I told the cops Brandi stole my wallet, but I was detained so I could not counter press charges. Caldwell collected cigarettes, energy drink, sunglasses and two receipts from Brandi that had been in my wallet. Anyone who wants the proof put Brandi or her sister on a lie detector and ask her did she steal my wallet to see the truth. Those receipts were never in my pocket.

This is where it gets very convoluted because the entire case is not about the events on Ray Road. If one watches closely, they build a case on one person saying I never left the house, so they set out over and over to prove I left the house. But we will get to that.

Wanna see a prosecutor shit a brick? By page 173 the prosecutor suddenly realized his boy Caldwell fucked up:

Lee: Your Honor the defendant—the evidence so far has been the defendant paid two twelve year olds 60 dollars. I believe that was the testimony!

Hmmm....

"He said he'd pay them 30 dollars apiece."

"They was finished cleaning."

"Mommy said he would pay them 30..."

"They was finished cleaning."

"The house was nasty."

So now Mr. Prosecutor dude, exactly which testimony do you refer to and I bet poor Ms. Bailey hasn't seen the flaw, flaws, in the master plan yet. I can't tell which is lying. They cleaned all day, the house is clean, or the house was nasty.

"He also requested that the complaining witness's younger sister be present and I understand from Mr. Lee that she is present in the hall also." (page 8-9)

Why looky here Ms. Bailey, we have Shania Lyn Shortt, aka House Cleaner Number One. She is right out in the hall. A person who may or may not have cleaned all day. The one I am accused of grooming. Now why are we arguing who paid who or who said what and so on? Call the cleaner to the stand. Oh why not make a big deal out of cleaning but not call actual cleaner who is just out in the hall? Now Mr. Lee, did you know that a Miss Sarah Hale made phone videos of the people in the hall? The younger sister was never present, and the videos were online, and we both know Shania would not lie for you or Brandi. Did you ever find it curious Ms. Bailey, that we had not one but TWO cleaners, a huge deal of hearsay was used about cleaning, but no one ever testified to that other than Dennis Lee prosecutor? Why were those cleaners not called?

There is something very silly about to happen which ends up being one more punch line. On page 174 cop Caldwell calls the investigator then he somehow goes to the scene. Again, should be simple. I can't help with this because I am going by the events at trial from the transcripts. In other words, this is not my fucking mess.

On page 175, and I really do wish my lawyer would have pulled it out, but he wasn't allowed to, Ms. Bailey, would you please refer to the police report where no one ever noticed a stretched shirt? The second page five was amended on March 5, 2015, still no stretched shirt. But if Mike Dennis would release the third page five there is an addendum July 21,

2015 where they just the very day of my trial noticed a stretched shirt. How very convenient we recalled that around six to 10 minutes before we testified. Damn near forgot to remember that, huh! As so, well past three years later her shirt appeared to be stretched.

"Appears, seemed to be."

Also on page 175:

Q. Did you put her in the car with you?

A. She went with another officer and we all rode together.

I am not going to do the idiot dance with these morons. Two cop cars went to Ray Road for a total of nine minutes. I do not know who rode with who, check your call sheets.

Now, if I had to pick my favorite Monty Python moment in my trial, I don't know if I could. I really don't think I can write this with the pure impact it needs to feel real. All I can say is, please keep in mind that for three years I had not seen the police report. I had the criminal complaint, I did not have the supplement. And I do hate to be nitpicky but twice we have established that on Ray Road there will be two red-white-blue beer cans, so here we go, gonna whip out them cans…DNA, fingerprints, fry this perv—game over!

Page 178:

Q. Did you find those cans?

A. yes sir, we did.

Q. And were they beer cans?

A. yes sir, they were.

Q. Did you collect those cans?

A. NO SIR, I DID NOT!

Q. Any reason why you didn't collect those cans?

A. That is just an error that I'm going to have to own up to.

How the! What the! Fucking huh!

I do love the K.E.T.2 channel on TV. Every Saturday and Sunday morning there is a very bendy yoga chick Wai Lana on and she is very calming—she is not on all the time!

Now you tell me Ms. Bailey, your child, your grandchild, your mother is falsely accused of a crime. Your loved one is on trial facing life plus 22 years in prison. There are exactly two pieces of real, relevant evidence—DNA and fingerprint evidence right thereon the ground. It will not match your loved one—collect that evidence. It don't match, your loved one comes home—innocent. Do not collect those cans and your loved one goes to prison for LIFE!

Did you collect those cans?

No sir, I did not.

Then you tell me Ms. Bailey, when you watch your child leave that courtroom to die in prison would you consider the severe criminal negligence of that cop's actions "a little error?" Do you feel the loss of your child for life an error, a little boo-boo?

No one can imagine, and it was my fault, sitting in a cell for three years with bad food and no room to stand up, twice a month or more being dragged out to hear they have the VHS tape, they have two Walmart videos, and they found those cans. Ah, see, my fault, they found those cans. No one ever said they had those cans, but I never caught it.

Can I just say here Ms. Bailey, I am charged with abduction for going to Ray Road. I have attempted rape, Actual Inncocence, contributing, and assault that all stem from Ray Road. The ONLY evidence that would put me on Ray Road was two beer cans, making those cans the absolute be-all-end-all complete and total evidence. My DNA has been on file since 1997, it is collected once a year and it's logged. Cans don't match I am innocent, but:

Did you collect those cans!

Nope, sure didn't.

"Man who is innocent gets life in prison due to uncollected DNA evidence—officer feels life of peon is a little error."

Or how about this Ms. Bailey. Your daughter is brutally raped then gutted like a fish. The only evidence is two beer cans but the killer walks because a cop made a little error by not collecting the cans. If that happened the criminal negligence would be a public uproar but since that only convicted a witch it was perfectly okay.

Ms. Bailey, since you asked about evidence what is your view on imaginary beer cans? Are those okay for evidence? Enough to convince you to fry the pervert? The good thing about "specter" imaginary evidence—it's ALWAYS right where it's needed.

And did you collect those cans?

Nope, sure didn't.

"Mad dog killer rapist goes free because officer fails to collect DNA evidence, how many thousands are at risk due to what he considers a little error—is your child the next to die?" News at 11.

Okay—I'm back.

I don't know about the average person, but I do not consider the loss of my life a minor error. Maybe others who go to prison due to criminal negligence would feel it's perfectly okay. The DNA-fingerprint evidence that would prove me innocent was left lying on the ground.

Then it's just an insult or it's a little worse than an insult. This officer is at a crime where he observes what may or may not be actual DNA evidence and on the one hand—page 176—he has enough for what needs to do, meaning he saw those beer cans which prompted him to make the arrest, and yet the two items he based that decision on, he leaves on the ground. He then tries to justify this criminal negligence by saying that, "an upset female so rattled him he shut it down." So, an upset female at a sexual assault caused a trained officer to miss DNA evidence. Let's all do a sing-along:

"If ya been raped
Put on a happy face
Don't be upset or
He may miss evidence
Or if you've had things
Shoved up your butt
Ya best grin and bear it
Or old Caldwell just might
Forget to pick DNA evidence up."

There's a little ditty I call Ode to Incompetence. Everyone look at the evidence sheet—no beer cans. But that turns out to be the downfall.

"The conceit of specter evidence allowed many to be arrested."

Did you collect the imaginary beer cans!

Nope, sure didn't.

What's wrong with a little "specter" evidence or imaginary evidence at a witch trial? It worked in 1693 and still going in 2015.

Got any beer cans! What a damn shame. Ms. Bailey was looking to see some evidence but nope, no beer cans from Ray Road where there was an alleged sexual assault. Then, and I have yet to figure this out, I do believe I seriously annoyed the hell out of the cops by repeatedly saying, "I want a lawyer," over and over and over for five or six hours. Any question was met with, "I want a lawyer." So, being annoyed, in the police report they invented an imaginary lawyer to go with the imaginary beer cans. On page 179 of the transcript:

"He advised that his lawyer said…"

Exactly where is this imaginary lawyer to match the imaginary beer cans? We use him as an imaginary witness for more specter evidence. I bet the imaginary lawyer would say exactly what is needed to convict me just like the imaginary beer cans mean exactly what's needed. But I don't understand if they are just annoyed or if they mean or imply I lawyered up. Hell, look at my bank statement, I damn sure didn't have one on retainer. So, we have imaginary beer cans, and we have an imaginary lawyer.

Way, way back in the bad old plea deal days I introduced the concept of charge stacking to force a plea deal. I hope I convinced some if not all it is very real. Now let me introduce a new concept known as evidence stacking.

"When a prosecutor lacks evidence in criminal proceedings more often than not he will present a long list of irrelevant unrelated items so it appears he has real overwhelming evidence."

"As codified to be admissible evidence MUST be relevant not just cumulative."

When I wrote about how P.T. Barnum put up an elaborate façade with a sign which read, "This Way to the Great Egress!" I also think of the man who "invented" a solar powered clothes dryer. He made millions. For 50 bucks people would receive a clothesline with instructions on how to put it up. What he said in his ads was true. What was not said cost people 50 bucks for a piece of twine. A good con or show should be viewed for what it is, not what they want to show—always. I am charged with abduction, attempted rape, Actual Inncocence, contributing and assault. Those charges are "the fact at issue!" That or those are what must be proven with evidence. Well, what is evidence?

Rule 2:40 Definition of relevant evidence: Relevant evidence means evidence having ANY tendency to make the existence of any FACT AT ISSUE more probable or less probable than it would be without the evidence.

Rule 2:402 Relevant evidence is generally admissible: irrelevant evidence is inadmissible.

As codified evidence MUST be relevant not just cumulative.

Do you have all that Ms. Bailey? Do you as a juror understand what the fact at issue is, that is, what am I on trial for? I am on trial for sexually assaulting a young girl on a dirt road on Ray Road meaning the only relevant evidence in my trial would be:

Did you collect those cans?

Nope, sure didn't.

How about this one. Evidence must be material not just relevant: Burgh v. Jones 256 Va 136,139 (2003) must be probative of a fact at issue.

Must be probative: Probative: provide proof. Do you see Ms. Bailey, first you look at my charges then you look at a piece of evidence and you decide does this evidence prove or disprove any of the charges. If not, that evidence is irrelevant.

Do you want to know a secret Ms. Bailey? Like you, I am a United States citizen. If you want to leave your house and go to the mall, the store, the movies you are free to do so. I am not charged for "leaving my house" nor is leaving my house a fact at issue. I, like you Ms. Bailey, am under no obligation to report that I did or did not leave my house to anyone including a lying cop. But the bottom line—I am not charged for leaving my house, it's not illegal. If you put Brandi on lie detector, you'd find out we went to Walmart to use bill pay and buy her a poster and her mother was on my couch which gave her permission to go. So now, what do we do when a brain-dead fucking moron leaves DNA evidence on the ground that would prove me innocent:

"If one concedes that specter-imaginary evidence would prove one guilty it must be assumed that same imaginary evidence could prove innocence as well: RMB"

What we do is say hey, look at these not five, not 10, not 15—20! 20 fucking irrelevant pictures! 20 pieces of fabricated evidence. Yep, a lot of nonevidence. Wait till you see this OVERWHELMING nonevidence.

"Are those accurate depictions of scenes and 'evidence' from this crime?"

Well hell, let's look under the hood of this evidence, can't wait to see it. But first there is a small matter here to Ms. Bailey. I was arrested July 9, 2012, and I do believe Brandi just testified we were wearing shorts and t-shirts, yet all these "evidence" photos have snow on the ground. Sally was a weather bug, so arrested in July, trial in July, who and when were these photos made? We have Exhibits 2-12 which are photos of snow in July, I guess.

A photo of MY HOUSE.

I put this photo in the book because it's the only one I was provided. So, exactly which charge "fact at issue" does that picture make more or less probable? Uh, Ms. Bailey, did you hear any argument that a house did not sit in that spot? Do you require proof that at some point in the '20s or '30s someone built a house? Am I charged for any house-related crimes? Do you Ms. Bailey, look at that house picture and say yep, total proof of a sexual assault 20 miles away up a dirt road?

Your child Ms. Bailey, is facing life in prison and you hear:

Did you collect those cans?

Nope, but here is a random house 20 miles away.

Let's see, objection, violation of motion for discovery, violation of rules 2:401, 2:402 and 2:403, irrelevant, misleading, confusing and is inadmissible. But let's ask the expert, Ms. Bailey. Do you see how a picture of a random house, where no crimes were committed, somehow proves any crime on a dirt road 20 miles away where actual DNA evidence was somehow not collected? Just checking.

Did you collect those cans?

Nope, but here's a picture of a house 20 miles away, yep, total evidence to be sure.

"Odd Squad: What's Next!"

On page 182, a photograph of a random road.

"That I believe goes over there somewhere—uh—maybe."

Wow! Oh, that seals it! Anyone who lives in a house near any random road must be a child molester. Yep, random road that goes over there somewhere—uh—maybe is all the goddamn evidence we need! And not only that, but if you take a picture of a random road facing the other way—IT FUCKING GOES IN THE OTHER DIRECTION! GUILTY AS HELL!

Uh, so Ms. Bailey, we have the picture of a random road that goes off somewhere maybe. Do you as a jury member think well hell, a random road—could be 20, 30 or 100 miles from oh, say DNA beer cans—proves, well, anything. A random road proves someone at some point built a road, but I must have missed the argument of who raised the "point of fact" of whether a road existed wherever the photo was taken. Which one of my charges does a picture of a random road make more or less probable? And why is my lawyer so quiet—no objections?

Did you collect those cans?

Nope, but we got a picture of a random road 20 miles away that goes over there somewhere maybe—clearly evidence.

Do you Ms. Bailey, think I sexually assaulted a road? Is that random road what you would call "representation and evidence of this crime?" A random road 20 miles away somehow alone proves abduction? Attempted rape? Actual Inncocence? Contributing? Or assault? I would call the picture of a random road "universal evidence" because it could literally be used as evidence of any crime.

Objection—irrelevant.

Oh, this is a tricky one except for one minor detail. A picture of a store does not prove any crime was ever committed at any other location. Guess what Ms. Bailey? No crime was committed at that store. Buying cigarettes at the age of 48 is not illegal and "there is a total secret you don't know yet, Ms. Bailey."

But here again, that picture of Corner Mart proves WHAT?

That at some point, someone built a store at the place that picture, with snow on the ground, was taken. Do you realize Ms. Bailey, there are thousands of stores in every town, city and country? When you, Ms. Bailey, look at the picture of a store exactly what "proof" did you derive from a picture? First objection—irrelevant. Objection—needlessly cumulative. Objection—violation of motion for discovery. Objection—violation of 2:401 and 2:403. A random picture of a store is not in any way evidence of any crime when no crime was committed at that store.

Did you collect those cans?

Nope, got a picture of a store 40 miles away. Total evidence, we proved it's a store.

Picture of a house 20 miles away.

Picture of a random road 20 miles away.

Picture of a store 40 miles away.

Uh Ms. Bailey, your child faces life in prison for false accusations. The cop just testified he failed to collect DNA evidence that would prove your child innocent. But then he pulls out the picture of a house 20 miles away, a random road 20 miles away, a random store 30 miles away, then says look at all this evidence. Would you see the evidence or bullshit? Only if it was your child—huh.

Did you collet those cans!

Nope, but I done finded a store 30 miles away, so he done did it—didded it? See purty store.

Oh I get it, anyone who lives in a house, near any random road within 100 miles of a town with a store is a child molester—is that the claim here?

"Odd Squad: What's next!"

Oh crap. Ms. Bailey, do you live in the area? If so, take this book to the TruPoint Bank 13250 Gov. Perry Hwy. As of 2022, ask to speak to a Mr. Andrew Baker so he can verify my bank statement. Mr. Baker, you play nice and confirm it's real. Once you confirm to your 100 percent satisfaction that yes, it is my bank statement, then Ms. Bailey, look at page two and you will see:

7/10 200 ATM W/D 15:47 7/9/12

1325 Gov. Perry Hwy

Pounding Mill VA

Yet, OH JOY! We have Exhibit number 5, a picture of the TruPoint bank in Richlands. Now Ms. Bailey, WHO is lying? You hold my actual bank statement, you are free to confirm it beyond any doubt. I nor Brandi was ever at the bank in Richlands. So here we have perjury, we have purely fabricated false evidence to propagate the perjury. Did you happen to catch my attorney trying to correct Brandi to the bank at Claypool Hill? My lawyer was aware of both the perjury and the fabrication—use of false evidence—yet somehow, he just sits there. What do you think Ms. Bailey? Your son is on trial for his life, they use lies and fabricated evidence your child's lawyer is aware of, but the lawyer is taking a nap.

Pardon me a second.

Goddamn it, Sally, would you please tell those damn women why yes, a bank statement at trial would have been a great fucking idea? We haven't got there yet. The bank statement was present at trial but Ms. Bailey, a juror never even knew a bank statement was in contention. They write me and they ask well why didn't I use it at trial if it was all that. Fucking wait for it! After this book I am going to write a book on writing called annoyed shitless by females. Proofread—don't talk!

Okay, I'm back. Well Ms. Bailey, here are some fun facts. When evidence that is known to be false is fabricated it constitutes:

Misconduct: An attorney's dishonesty or attempt to persuade a court or JURY by using deceptive methods.

Fraudulent misrepresentation: A false statement that is known to be false or is made recklessly without knowing or caring whether true or false.

Misconduct: An attorney's dishonesty or attempt to mislead a jury.

Actual malice: Defamation: Knowledge by a person who utters or publishes a defamatory statement—that statement is false.

Gross negligence – breech of duty.

Fabricated evidence: False or deceitful evidence that is unlawfully created usually after the fact in an attempt to achieve a conviction.

Libel: False statements to injure reputation.

And what is the opinion of the jury Ms. Bailey? Here we have not just irrelevant evidence but also completely fabricated false evidence. What "evidence or accurate representation and evidence of this crime" does a bank no one ever went to prove?

Did you collect those cans!

Nope, but I done finded a random bank, no one went there, but tis evidence—he didded it.

"The conceit of specter evidence allows many to be arrested."

Got any objections there, so-called defense dude? No, oh well, back to sleep then.

Now Ms. Bailey, did you happen to hear any argument raised that there was no TruPoint Bank in the spot where the person took that picture since that picture would definitely prove that yep, there's a bank? A random bank 40 miles from the crime scene where actual DNA evidence was left on the ground, not collected, but somehow a bank 40 miles away is evidence.

Breech of duty: Failure to act as the law obligates one to act.

Objection, irrelevant, fabricated evidence, violation of the motion for discovery and Constitutional rights violation—ineffective counsel.

Let's see, anyone who lives in a house near any random road within 100 miles of any town where there is a random store and a random bank is guilty of sexual assault. That sound alright with you Ms. Bailey, because that's the EVIDENCE SO FAR!

"Odd Squad: What's Next!"

Oh sorry, it was at this point that Body Electric came on TV and she is doing pelvic lifts. Brutal to a man in prison—almost as bad as a cooking show, but I lost my train of thought.

Ah, a picture of a random gas station where, yep, no crime was committed. Did you know Ms. Bailey, that for three years a blue million times I had to hear all about (and watch) a stupid VHS tape from Valero and yet here is Exhibit number 6, a picture of a gas station. Curious, why would someone take a picture of a place where they have a VHS tape? So, it's needlessly cumulative and it's not evidence. What's the charge here—buying gas? Do you Ms. Bailey, remember anyone contesting whether or not there was a gas station right at the place where the person took that picture was? But I do wish someone would explain:

Did you collect those cans!

Nope, but here's a picture of a gas station 40 miles away—wow, look at ALL this evidence.

Relevant evidence: Evidence having any tendency to make the existence of any fact at issue more probable or less probable.

Actual Inncocence
Abduction
Attempted rape
Contributing
Assault
Picture of a gas station 40 miles away.
A picture of a random gas station proves abduction?
A picture of a random gas station proves attempted rape?
A picture of a random gas station proves Actual Inncocence?
Did you collect those cans?
Nope, here's a picture of a house.
Did you collect those cans?
Nope, here's a picture of a road.
Did you collect those cans?
Nope, here's a picture of a store.
Did you collect those cans?
Nope, here's a picture of a gas station.
Page 183:

Q. Are you sure that is Daw Road and not Ray Road?

A. That could be Ray Road and that could be the driveway, I'm NOT sure!

A. It appears to be so!

So, ladies and gentlemen of the jury, here we have—hell, I don't know a road somewhere—I'm not sure it appears to be, never mind all the snow, it's July, where we can't collect DNA evidence but three years later, we have a random photo—uh—maybe—he's not sure.

Uh oh! Here comes that damn word again on page 186, "CIGARETTES!" Hey Ms. Bailey, as a professional juror would it be safe to reiterate that cigarettes would in fact pertain to my case? I mean, if someone had oh, some hidden little facts that involve cigarettes, those should come out, should they not? Am I being cryptic? Well here on page 188 we have a Corner Mart receipt. If I was counting the number of times cigarettes came up in the transcript should I count cig pack? CIGARETTE comes up twice on page 189 and on page 190 we have cigarette yet again. I do believe cigarettes would be both relevant and pertain to my case.

Uh, Ms. Bailey, if you were told by ANYONE that cigarettes were not relevant or did not pertain to my case, would it be safe to say that person or persons would be a lying son of a bitch? I won't say it, it's just a random thought.

This was rather, I am not sure if the word I want is sad or amusing when we get to cross examination, but first to Ms. Bailey, your child stops at a store to buy a soda then he is falsely accused of sexual assault. The cop says well, I observed a can on the ground, I did not collect it, but hey, here's a few random pictures from three years later. We have a mall in Peoria, a bank in New Jersey, a gas station in Texas, wow, look at all this evidence! There is no damn difference between a random bank 40, 400 or 4,000 miles away. Fabricated evidence is exactly that. Well, he bought a soda, here's the receipt "we collected," but somehow the actual DNA fingerprint evidence that would have proven your son innocent becomes imaginary—specter—evidence so HE'S GUILTY AS HELL. And due to that cop's criminal negligence, your child rots in prison.

"The conceit of specter evidence allowed many to be arrested..."

I do not expect anyone to be as involved as I am in all this. Maybe one day when it's their ass on trial on false charges they will be a bit more into the boring stuff.

On page 188 there is a minor curiosity that I have to once more blame on Carla J. Faletti:

"We just presented that in order to..."

I bet Ms. Bailey missed it. Everyone has heard numerous times that at my house they did what? Collected not one but two receipts but no one ever mentions what is that second receipt. They collected two, they collect two, they collected two. Uh, they only ever show one. Gee Ms. Bailey, what in the world could that second receipt be? It damn sure don't match the case or it would have been up on the big screen. The second receipt was from the Tennessee animal shelter from my wallet and from the 6th of July that would not have been in my pocket on the 9th, so they replaced it then said on page 188:

"We just presented that to maintain semblance."

Below that it says:

Lee: It is the same. It is the same.

There are a lot of glitches like that in my transcript. That happens when the transcript is reworked or intentionally altered numerous times.

Now Ms. Bailey, I don't really or even expect you to believe me but yep, we stopped at Corner Mart, and I did buy Brandi an energy drink and as much as the prosecutor would love to make true "he forced her to drive," she did not drive to the bank in Richlands and nothing insidious or evil went on. As for cigarettes, I would suggest you Ms. Bailey, read to the end. You, the jury, were lied to seven ways to hell and you were played. Hell, you only saw about a third of the trial. But here I would have to argue. The claim is:

I walked in a store.

Completely at random without ever being asked at all.

I buy someone cigarettes.

Once again on page 191 the prosecutor made the claim, he said he hadn't left the house all day, except I am not on trial for leaving my house. As much as he'd like it to be, "leaving the house" is NOT illegal. People do it every day in the United States of America where we have (supposed to have) freedom to leave our house without being put on trial for it. And you know what Ms. Bailey? Leaving my house is not an issue at fact here because it's not illegal. I was not arrested for leaving my house, so even though the prosecutor fabricated a fictitious fact at issue then he presented irrelevant evidence to prove the fictitious fact at issue, that evidence violated rule 2:403. In other words, he said he didn't leave the house, receipt proves he left the house, so he committed sexual assault 40 miles away. Would that overwhelming evidence be okay if it was your child Ms. Bailey? "He stopped at a store 40 miles away and here we have an imaginary soda can, so he done did it!" Well, she had a stretched shirt NO one added to the police report until three years later, July 21, 2015 around 2:17 p.m. A most convenient recall to be sure.

But I still stand on this from the opening statements—no stretched shirt. Mr. Lee's direct examination of Brandi Lee Shortt—no stretched shirt. Do you Ms. Bailey, find it curious that up until Brandi said it in CROSS examination it was never mentioned? Brandi, like house cleaning, made up a detail so hey, look what your son did Ms. Bailey, three years later.

Well, we got lots of pictures with snow on the ground, a house, a road, a store, a gas station, a dirt road, but we seem to be missing any actual evidence. We got a receipt that is not evidence. You want to see a real crime Ms. Bailey? When your child goes to prison for life on a lie, you walk up and ask the cop, how is it you collected a receipt which proves nothing, but you somehow left DNA fingerprint evidence, the only evidence that mattered, the evidence that would have proven your child innocent, on the ground? Yep, thanks to the criminal negligence of Mr. Fucking Moron, innocent people spend life in prison—good job.

This next part defies all reasonable explanation. It's damn near pathetic or it's more of a "why the fuck bother." Ladies and gentlemen, children over 18, let me introduce Mr. Mike Dennis, so-called defense attorney, in this little stage show. Watch him work. Prepare to be in awe from his astute powers of observation. But first!

I don't think I have actually explained this little tidbit. Why Ms. Bailey, you, your child, your loved ones have Constitutional rights that protest you as U.S. citizens. And under Amendment Six you have the right to counsel, and that assistance of counsel must be effective.

I hate to be legal and boring, but when someone faces life in prison they want to know this. There is a standard in Strickland v. Washington 466 U.S. 668(1984) that says the defendant must show that an attorney was not functioning as counsel and some of those claims can be:

Failure to conduct pretrial investigation

Failure to call a witness

Failure to object

Failure to impeach a witness

Failure to obtain an objection to hearsay

Do you Ms. Bailey, understand what "hearsay" evidence is? "Something one has heard but does not know to be true." "He said he never left the house." "He said (or mommy said) 30 bucks." He said, he said, he said, she said. My entire trial was hearsay. Did you Ms. Bailey, ever once consider that you did not hear me say I did not leave the house, so then the receipt could be used to prove a new fact at issue but instead it was used to resolve a point of hearsay? Your attorney has an obligation to protect you, me, your child, against hearsay—do you know why? It is inadmissible.

From the United States Constitution what it says and what it means:

"Assistance of counsel must be meaningful, adequate and effective."

"If an attorney's performance is not up to a reasonable standard of his profession or if an attorney's ability to put on a full defense is hindered by the prosecutor's misconduct it is grounds to overturn a conviction."

So far, Ms. Bailey, we have exactly two tiny pieces of evidence that are actually evidence not proving an irrelevant hearsay speculation. That would be the DNA fingerprint evidence the super-cops somehow left on the ground, which does make a good book—not so much fun in real life. "Man sentenced to 32 years because fucking moron can't bend his fat ass over to collect DNA evidence that would prove innocent: news at 11."

"Man sentenced to 32 years in prison on imaginary beer cans: news at 11."

My lawyer on page 195-196 is a fucking moron. He is propagating some kind of fucked up fairy tale. Oh, I get it:

Q. "…his attorney told him not to answer questions…"

Uh, yeah. Now we have Mr. Imaginary lawyer to go with the imaginary beer cans. Oh yeah, anyone can look at my bank statement with all those hundreds of pennies. Sure, got me 10 or 12 imaginary lawyers on retainer—we all know how cheap they are. Now, can I call the imaginary lawyer who, obviously, was there and have him contest the imaginary beer cans? I'm not really up on the whole imaginary witness-evidence statutes. Oh, they are imaginary—duh. Is my lawyer helping the prosecution by implying "he lawyered up" by lying or using more, yep, hearsay?

Oh, I forgot on page 194 there is yet another reference to the report that no one ever was allowed to see. About halfway down the page:

"I can't recall."

Wouldn't that alone be enough to bring out the report? Gee Ms. Bailey, what do you suppose is in that report they do NOT want the jury to have?

Do you recall
Best recollection without the report
What is reflected in the report
Typed report
I CAN'T recall

Don't worry Ms. Bailey, that's why I put it in the book to avoid all that. Question I would ask:

Now Mr. Caldwell, you testified upon entering said residence you observed it was nasty. So, if someone said two people cleaned all day, that would be a lie, would it not?

Wow is that a good question Ms. Bailey. I mean, that would be a killer defensive-type question. I guess ol' Dennis missed that one, so not exactly up to the standard of his profession. So, instead of defending me against hearsay, he testifies for the prosecution that I hired two people to clean, all day, a nasty house. Is my house clean or nasty—can't be both.

Page 196: This is a good one. On page 175 they put Brandi in a car and they all rode together except:

"I believe he was in my patrol car."

"Did he go to the location?"

"I would assume so."

Uh, I am betting they did not put Brandi in the car with me, except later I am not in the car, but later than that later I am back in the car again. I wish I'd make up my damn mind.

Now I made an oath that I would not use the word "retarded" in a derogatory context or insult, but if I could use it I'd say my lawyer was fucking retarded, but I can't so I won't. Fraggity-fraggity-waggaty-waggaty-your momma is a faggot aardvark! Sorry, I needed an insult out of my system.

For Ms. Bailey, let me interject a little. Your child, grandchild, your mom, is falsely accused. They are on trial facing life in prison. You just heard a cop testify that he somehow left DNA evidence on the ground that would have proven your loved one innocent.

Did you collect those cans!

No sir, I did not.

That DNA fingerprint evidence would not have matched your child or your loved one, they come home. The attorney who is representing your loved one says (should have said):

Now Mr. Caldwell, would you explain to the court how it is that you managed to leave DNA fingerprint evidence on the ground that would prove the defendant completely innocent?

Ladies and gentlemen of the jury, it is very clear that imaginary evidence that could prove guilt could just as well be imaginary evidence that proved innocence. Mr. Blankenship was never on Ray Road.

Now Mr. Caldwell, would you explain to this court how it is you just noticed this very day, three years later, a stretched shirt you added to the secret police report at 2:17 p.m. today?

Now Mr. Caldwell, had you collected those cans, and his DNA has been on file since 1997, verified yearly, if those cans did not match he would be innocent, would he not?

Mr. Caldwell, if we follow your testimony, when you were at the scene you claim Brandi became upset so you "shut it down," implying her hysteria made you miss collecting those cans, is that correct?

So now Mr. Caldwell, how would you further explain that not one hour later you sat at a computer typing a report where you wrote you found those cans, you then filled out an evidence sheet, but NO BEER CANS. How many hysterical females were around the computer?

Mr. Caldwell, you dispatched an investigator to Corner Mart. You dispatched an investigator to Valero. You dispatched an investigator to Walmart. You did NOT dispatch an investigator to the actual crime scene when you wrote your report, nor did you dispatch a sergeant, a supervisor or go yourself to collect those cans. You knew there were no cans, isn't that right, Mr. Caldwell?

Now Mr. Caldwell, would you explain to this jury that if their children were falsely accused and facing life in prison and you leave DNA evidence on the ground that would prove innocence, how would you justify letting their innocent loved one go to prison? Or Mr. Caldwell, as the report writing would indicate, you lied about the beer cans.

Now Mr. Caldwell, you personally collected two receipts. You personally collected an irrelevant energy drink. You personally collected a pack of cigarettes. You then personally collected a pair of irrelevant sunglasses. All of that shows "duty" and diligence, so how is it you did not collect those cans that would prove Mr. Blankenship innocent? Then you dispatch an investigator to every single location except ONE—the only place where there was a crime scene. How is that?

What do you think Ms. Bailey, if your child was on trial wouldn't those be very good questions, kind of impeach a witness? "At no point in any trial in these United States should imaginary—specter—evidence be allowed to stand or even imply beyond reasonable doubt. Imaginary evidence means reasonable doubt, but when we allow the corruption of the use of imaginary evidence, that evidence could be used to convict you, me, your children or anyone."

You see Ms. Bailey, the problem isn't that he didn't collect the cans, it's that not one hour later he wrote a report, calm, at a computer where he wrote, "and we found those cans," but then (four minutes) later he lists all the evidence—NO BEER CANS! He could have told one of four people hey, go get the cans. The actual investigator is right there. Do you require proof? I can prove it, but you gotta wait. But let's face it, we have two situations here. One there were beer cans on Ray Road—not collected—incompetent criminal negligent son of a bitch. Or there were no beer cans—lying son of a bitch. Y'all can decide which. But I am irrelevant. The real question is what DNA evidence which they fail to collect that would exonerate YOU or what DNA imaginary evidence will they lie about to convict YOU!

Now Ms. Bailey, I believe I asked some very damn good questions. Would you agree? I mean if your child was on trial and they had imaginary evidence, wouldn't it be a good idea to at least try to discredit the specter evidence? But somehow your child's lawyer comes in with:

How did Ms. Pickle get to the scene?

Well, that's all I have.

Who! What! Fucking huh! W.T.F.! This is goddamn pathetic and it's worse later, trust me.

Q. Who went to the scene?

Q. Was Brandi's mother with her?

Wow! Can you believe such powers of defense. I mean, fucking wow, hell of a defense--awesome. I bet Ms. Bailey was just so impressed.

How did Ms. Pickle get to the scene?

Well, that's all I have.

I do not believe there could be a more clear case of ineffective counsel in any trial unless we could count the Salem witch trials 1692-1693 where the accused had no attorney at all. Oh wait, no, it's the same.

How you doing Ms. Bailey, still with us? Were you not impressed with that display of nondefense?

"...those who stand for or by the accused do but condemn themselves..."

"The conceit of specter evidence allowed many to be arrested."

"The failure to contest imaginary evidence allowed many to be convicted: RMB."

You tell me Ms. Bailey, if your child was falsely accused and being tried on the evidence of two imaginary beer cans, would you prefer the questions I asked or would you be okay with:

"Well, how did Ms. Pickle get to the scene?"

"Well, that's all I have."

I, Ms. Bailey, don't think you would give a rosy-red rat's ass how Ms. Pickle got to the scene. She rode a camel with a nine-inch dildo up her ass, nobody cares. How about hey, those beer cans would prove my child innocent, how about we get on THE TOPIC. Beer cans—relevant. Ms. Pickle—IRRELEVANT! Yet:

How did Ms. Pickle get there?

Well, that's all I have.

Here is a picture of a house, no objection. Picture of a store, no objection. Picture of a road, no objection. Picture of a gas station, no objection. House clean, house nasty, no impeachment, how did Ms. Pickle get to the scene? I do believe we have severe ineffective counsel with prejudice, but witches do not have Constitutional rights. It only gets amusing when one sees that defense lawyer Jim Shortt created "house cleaning," then Mike Dennis created "stretched shirt." So far, the only evidence is the prosecutor's imaginary beer cans and the defense's evidence to convict.

Okay, ALL of that was bad. Did you collect those cans? No sir, I did not. How did Ms. Pickle get to the scene? Well, that's all I have. Please keep in mind I AM NOT MAKING THIS SHIT UP! If anyone hasn't yet, now would be a damn good time to smoke pot, take a break, burn one or two and relax, then come back. The next parts are beyond any logical description. In a way this becomes intense Monty Python stupid.

I will admit that I hate writing this part, but I did promise Ms. Bailey some shit she would not see on TV. But this is so messed up it seems made up except NO true crime writer would ever make t his up or write it. It did happen, Ms. Bailey was there.

First we have 197-198 about Layne but he is for later, we are going to Kevin Hale on page 199, a cop for around seven years. So, ol' Kevin, he shows up to investigate a sexual assault—way worse than breaking and entering—but he arrived two minutes after Caldwell then left but he returned (check your call sheets).

"At that time they advised me they needed to change location." He followed in his vehicle to SUPERVISE that situation. Keep in mind here Kevin Hale, Patrol Sergeant, went to supervise at the scene. By page 201 he don't interview, he don't do anything else, meaning HE had one job—supervise the scene.

Page 203 is both good and bad. On the one hand we have the, up to this point, imaginary beer cans, but he does say 150 to 200 yards up a dirt road—thank you, Kevin! I still don't know how long it would take a person to walk 200 yards, or 400 yards total. Here we go on page 204:

Q. Okay was there anything unusual that stuck out in your mind about it when you collected them OR when you picked them up AND LOOKED AT THEM?

A. Yes. I did handle one of them and it was cool, very cool and the liquid SMELLED fresh.

One time Sally took a little girl named Bella to Gatlinburg where Bella rode go-karts. On speaker phone Sally said, "Bella rode the go-karts," and Bella said, "I went about a hundred miles an hour." Bella one-upped Sally. I do believe in prison there are storytellers who constantly one-up one another. Now, Officer Caldwell only observed said imaginary beer cans. By God, Sergeant Kevin Hale not only observed said imaginary beer cans, but he also picked one up to sniff it—did not collect it—but he damn sure one-upped Caldwell.

I have a couple of problems here that I must get out in the open: I am damn annoyed at lying bitch Carla J. Faletti. On page 205 what he said was:

"It was still cold, ice cold and very fresh."

At that point the prosecutor—Lee, not Menefee—threw his finger in the air and screamed:

"AND THE CANS WERE STILL COLD!"

Do you remember that little act on the stage Ms. Bailey? That is not what this transcript says, is it—totally altered. No Ms. Bailey, I would never ask you to come forward to tell the truth. No one ever speaks for the witch. When it's your child no one will speak for them either.

Now Officer Hale, you just testified that the beer can was still cold, ice cold and very fresh, would you now explain to this court how did beer, in a can, stay cold and fresh outside open in July for over five hours?

Ladies and gentlemen, we are faced with a dilemma here. Uh, okay, you are very correct—we are faced with a series of dilemmas here. First, there were no beer cans so old Kev was a lying son of a bitch. Second, there were ice cold beer cans which would literally mean they were no way connected to me unless someone believes beer stays cold and fresh over five hours outside, open, in July. And more importantly third, how is the person, a sergeant who had a total of ONE job to pick up BEER CANS, somehow managed to pick up a can, DNA fingerprint evidence, at an alleged crime scene, he sniffs the DNA evidence—yet—he fails to collect it. Not hard to find when it's in YOUR fucking HAND!

Did you collect those cans!

No sir, I did not.

Did you collect those cans!

Nope, but by god, I sniffed it.

I do believe this calls for a backwards WOW! He arrived to supervise an alleged crime scene, he sees real DNA fingerprint evidence on the ground, he picks it up, he s niffs it, he puts it back on the ground.

"Oh lord, won't you buy me a color TV."

Oh sorry, blew a fuse there for a second. Now Ms. Bailey, as a juror, can you tell us was it Caldwell who observed imaginary DNA evidence and did not collect it, or was it Hale who picked up, sniffed imaginary evidence and did not collect it that carried more weight as purely imaginary evidence?

"Man convicted—sentenced to 32 years, sets new precedence that sniffed DNA, though imaginary, now admissible. News at 11."

Oh hey, Ms. Bailey, how many times on Law and Order have you seen, "Your honor, we observed DNA evidence. Stabler sniffed it, but we left it at the scene."

"And THE CANS WERE STILL COLD! Uh, after five hours outside in July."

Lee: Your honor, at this time we move to enter the ax he obviously used to chop her head off before it grew back. Uh, we don't really have the ax, we have a picture of an ax.

Dennis: Oh, I object. He cut her head off at 1 p.m. not 2 p.m.

Lee: Your honor, I hardly think the hour he cut her head off before it grew back holds any bearing in this case.

Court: I'll allow it!

Caldwell: I see'd the ax on the ground.

Hale: I sniffed the ax.

Guilty as HELL!

Sorry, blew another fuse.

Page 205:

"At that time—I mean I was notifying my superiors and we were gathering other information so I don't recall anything else."

Now Mr. Hale, would you explain to this court what other information would be more important than the DNA fingerprint evidence that

YOU currently hold in YOUR hand that would prove Mr. Blankenship innocent?

Oh hell! I must apologize to my readers. This was supposed to be way funnier in the book. I (we) had a list of stores, 800 stores over West Virginia, Virginia, Kentucky, Tennessee and North Carolina that all use "red price stickers." I lost access to that list.

Q. Was there anything on the can to identify where it came from?

A. I do remember a RED price sticker on the can.

Well holy horse shit, anyone going out to buy beer, bread, soda, water, a can of corn, some sex lube, be sure to ask ol' Kev along. By god, he points at that red price sticker in any one of 800-plus stores. How is that for super cop talents? Uh, if you happen to need DNA fingerprint evidence that would prove you innocent, might want to leave old Kev out of it.

One job, drive to an alleged crime scene, pick up two beer cans, and yet he fucked it up: EPIC FAIL! Yep Ms. Bailey, when they walk your child out of a courtroom to go to prison for life you look back at the man who sniffed the evidence that would have proven your child innocent but he did not collect it and then you feel safe knowing that level of criminal negligence is still on the police force. He feels smug that his lies convicted an innocent person. Your child rots in prison, another dead peon no one cares about.

Misconduct: the failure to act when there is a DUTY to do so.

Now Ms. Bailey, have you ever once thought those cans were collected, did not match my DNA, so they tossed them? Better to lie about imaginary evidence than be honest. Just a thought.

Fraudulent misrepresentation: a false statement.

People can say they observed or sniffed beer cans. They cannot say "he drank his beers!" Malpractice, malicious prosecution, gross negligence, ineffective counsel and breech of duty. Did you know Ms. Bailey, that it is the duty of a police officer to collect evidence that would protect a person from false accusation in the interest of public safety? That means YOU TOO Ms. Bailey, or your family.

You do realize Ms. Bailey, that it was officer Caldwell who "observed" two beer cans then he decided he had enough for what he needed to do—arrest me. So based on that, I was arrested on the imaginary evidence.

"The conceit of specter evidence allowed many to be arrested…1692."

"Imaginary beer cans spur arrest July 9, 2012."

Oh god—NOT AGAIN!

Go ahead there Dennis, so-called defense attorney, you ask all about how did Ms. Pickle get to the scene because NOT the DNA beer cans. NO, we are all dying to know how the hell did Ms. Pickle get to the scene! Page 206 cross examination. Page 207.

Was her mom with her?

How did Ms. Pickle get there?

Who walked up the road?

Well, that's all I have.

Did you collect those cans!

Nope, but I done finded a purdy red sticker only used in 800-plus stores, so he didded it.

Now officer Hale, would you concede that had you collected the ice-cold DNA fingerprint evidence that was sniffed somehow did not match Mr. Blankenship it would, in fact, prove him innocent?

Nope, did not ask that. He, defense lawyer, said how did Ms. Pickle get to the scene, the absolute most irrelevant question he could ask.

"Beavis and Butthead do Cops—one sees evidence, the other sniffs it, no one collects it."

Now prosecutor/acting defense, can you tell how you somehow easily impeach the imaginary evidence you intentionally avoided with irrelevant babble? I am not accused of driving Brandi's mother to the scene. Her presence is in no way a fact at issue. What is at issue is—not my cans—innocent. The prosecutor up to my appeal says he drank two beers but that is a misrepresentation of any known facts and in fact the cans were cold and fresh so were in no way related to this case, unlike cigarettes, which do pertain to the case.

Now Mr. Dennis, I have it on best imaginary evidence that Brandi's mother took a train to New York City, hired a cab to drive her to Nashville, Tennessee where after two years as a dyslexic crack whore—she gave drugs not to have sex—she took guitar lessons but had to pawn her guitar to buy a 1978 VW Rabbit or Bug (that is fuzzy) which she drove back to Virginia where she spent a year under a bridge because she thought it was an open-sided bomb shelter until she won the $20 million lottery which she traded for a moped which she rode to Ray Road. And I fail to see the relevance of your need to know all this because there is DNA fingerprint evidence right there on the ground that would have proven me innocent and shouldn't THAT kind of take priority over how ANYONE got to the scene five hours later? Or could it be Mr. Dennis, you're asking irrelevant questions to aid the prosecution in a conviction because you failed to obtain a plea deal?

Hi Ms. Bailey. If your child was on trial due to imaginary beer cans, which one would YOU feel takes priority, the imaginary beer cans or how Ms. Pickle got to the scene five or six hours after the beer cans? You know, it would really suck if mom planted the beer cans but then Mutt and Jeff failed to collect them.

Picture of a random house.
Picture of a random road.
Picture of a random store.
Picture of a random gas station.
Picture of a dirt road.
One receipt.

There is "the evidence" at this point if we discount hearsay, which is not evidence.

I am not picking on Ms. Bailey. She asked about evidence, and she was on my jury. The problem is she was never allowed to actually see the evidence, so now I am presenting everything as it was, not how the prosecution wants to make up.

Next up we have a curious situation. So did you know Ms. Bailey, you were told I just moved to the area except that was a lie. My mom lived just out the road from my house, and I'd lived there well over a year. If anyone has read my book, I lived with Sally in Grey, Tennessee. I made good money, I built a bitchin' gaming computer, I loved the X-Blade case. I had an eight-piece corner desk and an arm-padded executive leather computer chair.

When my mom had an aneurysm, I had to move and, I am not saying insurance fraud, but someone did not fix the floors in that house. The state of the house or the floors were long before I got there, but the walls and the roof were good, so it could be fixed. The end result here is yes, I had a nice computer, yes, the house I moved into was in serious need of work, but when done it would be my house. I don't exactly walk into a half-built house which did installing cabinets or remodeled house that was all to hell and say, "God, look at these people," yet I am judged and convicted on that scale.

On page 208 we have a situation even more pathetic than the one on Ray Road. Hell, at least Mutt and Jeff did make it to the alleged crime scene. Stand back ladies and gentlemen, make room please, make room for J. Ray Smith, a man so into the Proper Criminal Procedure HE investigates a house 20 miles away from any alleged crime scene. BRAVO, a round of applause please people. Oh do stand, take a bow Mr. J. Ray, we are just all goose-bumpy awaiting to hear just exactly what overwhelming, mind-blowing evidence you found in a house 20 miles away. By all means, take the stand—shhh…listen.

Holy—fucking—hell, shift supervisor!
Patrol cop—observes DNA evidence.
Sergeant—sniffs DNA evidence.
Supervisor—investigates house 20 miles away.

Can I just say one thing: YOU'RE AT THE WRONG FUCKING SCENE, MORON! Seems to me Mr. J. Ray, we could use a wee bit of supervising about 20 miles yon-way where a shift supervisor could, oh, supervise the collection of some DNA fingerprint evidence that the supervisees kinda forgot to collect. Maybe if a supervisor had been around he could have said something very profound like, "Yo, pick up them cans." Now that would have been impressive. So, J. Ray, where were you and WHAT were you investigating 20 miles away?

On page 210:

"I was secondary officer, shift supervisor, just OVERSEEING everything that was going on."

Wow, well let me be the first to say great job of overseeing. Yep, you were so right on top of the DNA evidence two cops somehow failed to collect.

Now Mr. J. Ray Smith, you just testified to the court you were present at the scene during the whole thing yet somehow on page five of the police report you don't show up until March 5, 2015 at 10:34 a.m., just one day before the previous trial date where YOU recall everything in that report except for a stretched shirt that was just added today July 21, 2015 2:17 p.m. Can you explain why it took three years for you to recall or doctor the police report? You J. Ray are not mentioned until March 5, 2015, how is that? Kind of convenient the prosecutor has 20 pop-up photos and witnesses three years later.

Now on the one side at least old J. Ray said I was working on the house. I wonder if he was even there. But hey, let's all pretend he didn't just pop up three years later. Page 212:

Q: Okay. Did you notice anything unusual that seemed out of place to you.

A. The computer system was very out of place.

Wow! That's it? You, Mr. J. Ray, are very damn sloppy. I guess you failed to notice a 40-inch TV on a table propped up on a 2x4 so it wouldn't tip over. How about the Harmon Kardon stereo receiver sitting on top of a dual 18-inch powered subwoofer? Did you happen to see a JBL dynamic center speaker? That little puppy was 1,200 bucks. Did you happen to notice a brand new portable dishwasher that had no sink to hook up to? Hey, look behind you, there is a $1,400 split dresser next to B.C. Rich: Warlock limited edition guitar—body art collection—skulled, that little gem was about 5,000 bucks—without the amp. Now if you'll step this way J. Ray, why look here, a massive brand new side-by-side fridge with both cubed and crushed ice and water in the door that cost more than the room. Oh look over there, a brand new washer and dryer that were never used because my laundry room had no hookups, or floor, yet.

And J. Ray, since you COMPLETELY missed all of that, why did you know there was around 15 to 20 thousand dollars worth of tools in my building?

Now to bust old J. Ray's bubble. See, my computer by that point was pushing over three years old, maybe five years old, so in the computer world my rig was a dual core obsolete paperweight in the land of quad core procs. You, J. Ray, in a blast of super cop observation picked out the one item that actually belonged in the house.

Say J. Ray, just between us criminals, when you broke in to steal my computer how the hell was it you unhooked and left all four external drives? I have been damn curious about that for years. Not one, not two, not three, but four external drives. Did not collect the beer cans. Did not collect the drives. Two terabytes that you did not collect. Oh, I know you can't admit you stole it, but I had to mention it.

Holy-fucking-hell, do you see that Ms. Bailey? Can YOU believe in this day and age that anyone in a house would own a goddamn computer? Oh, that's got GUILTY AS HELL written all over it. We must immediately arrest anyone who lives in any house with a computer. WE

SHALL NOT TOLERATE THESE GODDAMN PERVERT COMPUTER OWNERS! And apparently that is more specter evidence.

So, now we have some fabricated pictures, Mutt and Jeff who fail to collect beer cans at an alleged crime scene, and we have J. Ray investigating a house 20 miles away. Then it took J. Ray three years to do the police report.

Has anyone spotted the rather ironic twist yet? At this point from Caldwell I am still at the house. No wait, he put me in his car where he assumed I went to the scene but then J. Ray says he remained at the residence with me. Page 213:

"I remained at the scene with Mr. Blankenship."

Goddamn it! Make up your goddamn mind. You sons of bitches have got to learn to take notes—you're giving me a headache.

Did you collect those cans!

Nope, but I see'd 'em.

Did you collect those cans!

Nope, but I sniffed 'em.

Did you collect those cans!

Nope, found a computer in a house 20 miles away.

Oh, he's guilty as hell!

You do know J. Ray, that not one damn thing I owned fit in that house and you found the cheapest item.

Now Ms. Bailey, I hate to ask but your child is on trial, falsely accused, and now two cops have left the DNA evidence that would have proven your child innocent on the ground. The shift supervisor then says in the most irrelevant statement that HE found a computer in a house 20 miles away. That has absolutely no bearing or relevance in your child's trial. Would you, Ms. Bailey, be okay with unbelievable fabricated bullshit used to convict your innocent child? Would you see a random irrelevant computer in a random irrelevant house 20 miles away as evidence or would you view that as malicious prosecution?

To everyone else, have I made my goddamn point? He observed a computer in a house 20 miles from the alleged crime scene. Wow, look at all this fabricated, imaginary evidence. "HE OBSERVED." Seems to be a lot of observing—very damn little presenting.

I do like page 214, but I gotta tell ya J. Ray, you sons of bitches gotta learn to take notes. At this point we have Caldwell who says "someone else" put Brandi in a car and they all rode together. No, he put me in his car where he assumed I went to the scene, but Kevin Hale followed while J. Ray stayed at the house with me where he observed my computer in his patrol car.

Then on page 214 he tries to make out I did not call 911. What the hell, check your call sheet, fuckhead. Caller name Blankenship Robert: Caller phone 4236312031: How received 911 call. Yes, I have the call sheets, we put them online so cut the bullshit.

Now Mr. Dennis, do you see any relevance in those questions? If I called 911 I damn sure did not have trouble understanding how to call 911. Hey, here's a better one. Why is your stupid ass in a house 20 miles away investing a NOT crime scene while the two dumb fucks YOU are supposed to be supervising are sniffing but not collecting DNA evidence? I'd say one of us is fucking confused and it's not me!

Now Mr. Dennis, in your cross examination you didn't ask how Ms. Pickle got to the scene—inquiring minds are dying to know I am sure.

Well Ms. Bailey, I am not sure how to present this part but since you did convict me to live in prison I think it only fair you fully understand what you did. I do not hold my conviction against you—you made what you felt was an informed decision based on the information you were allowed to see. You were lied to, you were coerced and you were played, but there was no way they would have allowed me to walk.

I do not know if you know the area but it's important to understand this part. First take this book and go to the TruPoint Bank at 13250 Gov. Perry Hwy, go in and ask for Mr. Andrew Baker, he was there as of 2022. You show him my bank statement and Mr. Baker you confirm said statement, you have my permission.

Once you are convinced that is my bank statement and it is legit, from that bank pull over to Walmart and park around the side on the grocery side, go in on the grocery side, walk back to posters, leave out the grocery side, get back in your car. You, Ms. Bailey, now fully understand the exact route, steps, taken. You now get to be me, congratulations, but then read the next part. The cops were hard to write about, this part is brutal.

On page 216 we have a very, very convenient pop-up surprise witness. For three years we had Brandi's aunt Janet Lester, but she refused to lie for Brandi (can't blame her for that) but hey look we, by a sheer goddamn, almost unbelievable stroke of luck, have a spare aunt. Wow, how very goddamn lucky to lose a witness but no wait, we got an extra. Yep, stretched shirt pops up at 2:17 p.m. the day of my trial and here we have a surprise witness, another aunt the police somehow missed three years ago. Now, I should be upset over a fill-in witness but she was like cream filling in a donut for this book. First we have 20 irrelevant photos as surprise evidence, then we have a whole aunt as a surprise witness.

Ladies and gentlemen, at this time please let me expand on, "stupid witness race." We have Brandi, he told me, mommy told me, he removed shirt and bra, no, he never removed any clothes ever. Need I say bank! We have Caldwell-observed DNA evidence—failed to collect. We have Hale-sniffed DNA evidence—failed to collect. We have J. Ray—finds computer in house 20 miles away. And now entering the stupid witness race please allow me to introduce Crystal Owens. Can Crystal take the lead to be stupidest witness? Let's watch.

Crystal Owens comes in on page 216. Oh, EVERYONE please note on page 217 where Menefee says:

"I'm going to draw your attention back to July 9, 2012." And it is July 21, 2015, so July should be easy.

This turns into one hell of a mess, but we can start here. Janet had taken Crystal to Walmart—Janet is driving. On page 218 she is putting groceries in the truck, good so far.

And how far away from you was she?

I was coming out the grocery side, she was probably halfway between the grocery side and the clothing section. Uh okay, that would be inside Walmart, would it not Ms. Bailey? You, Ms. Bailey, just heard Brandi testify we parked around the side, not out in the parking lot. We entered and we left the grocery side just as you just did Ms. Bailey. You were now seen halfway across the store at the clothing section.

Now Ms. Bailey, you just heard Brandi testify she was held the entire time but Crystal said at first she thought Brandi was alone—there was a man coming up right beside her.

He grabbed her hand and got in the vehicle.

Did you know Ms. Bailey, that two of my wife's friends cannot stand me. They hate me but they proofread the book. Both women who don't like me agree that no matter what ya have to stop holding hands to enter a (cop speak) vehicle. So, according to Brandi she was held until she got to the car, but Crystal says not held until they got to the vehicle. But she saw Brandi get into the driver's side. Then we have a very scary part for Brandi later. Crystal on page 220 then says she did confirm that it was in fact Brandi. Oh my. Well, that was short and simple. She see'd us alright, right there in or near the clothing section.

On page 221 we have cross examination by Mr. Dennis. Keep in mind, no recess, not even five minutes ago Menefee said July 9, 2012. Get it, July.

Here again I do have to mention the lying bitch Carla J. Faletti because she ruined this part.

Q. How do you recall the specific date?

A. I can't say a specific date, but I know it was June.

It was here that she did not say she had her step kids in the summer, she said she had her step kids for two weeks in June, so she knew it was June.

Q. So sometime in June?

A. Yeah.

Q. You saw her in the parking lot getting in the driver's side?

A. Yes.

Now Ms. Bailey, who just entered and exited to walk right out of the grocery side to go around the side where you are parked, how the hell did you then get out in the parking lot? Who is lying here, Brandi or Crystal?

So now Crystal, who was coming out the grocery side putting groceries in the ruck then says by the time she got the truck shut down, but Janet drove her—in June—on page 222—we are now near the clothing section outside halfway across the store.

Again Ms. Bailey, you parked around the side on the grocery side, entered and you exited the grocery side where you back around the side where your car is parked BUT you are seen outside halfway across the store near the optometry door. How the bloody hell did you get way over there in the opposite direction of your car which you were then seen entering in the parking lot on the opposite side of where you parked? Someone is not telling the truth here.

GodDAMN! Page 223, Brandi just testified in and out the grocery side. Crystal just said she saw us halfway across the entire store in between the doors but then she says she just seen her walk out and get in the car.

Q. At first you thought she was by herself.

A. At first I did because I really—you know at first I didn't—

Huh?

"He grabbed her hand and he went to the passenger side she went to the driver's side."

Uh Ms. Bailey, just how goddamn long do you think my arms are?

Ready for the next part Ms. Bailey? If you're at Walmart if you want to go back to Raven, Richlands or Kent's Ridge Road you can only go right onto the four-lane for 338 feet to make a U-turn to go back to the Claypool Hill red light. If you want to go to Raven, you stay right at Claypool Hill and it turns right. If you want to go to Wardell or Kent's Ridge Road, you stay left and go straight at Claypool Hill.

So, Ms. Bailey, you have heard Brandi testify she went straight at Claypool Hill. Brandi was very adamant that she went over Kent's Ridge Road. I put a crude hand-drawn map in Documents that shows to go over Kent's Ridge Road one must go straight at Claypool Hill towards Wardell. So, with Brandi we went straight at Claypool Hill—definitely.

"It gives me a migraine headache thinking down to your level." Megadeth: Sweating Bullets.

Did you ever notice they never put up signs saying "normal children at play?" Only the slow children get signs—there were two signs in Crystal's yard.

So, by page 224 he grabbed her hand to get in the vehicle, he let go of her hand to get in the vehicle—well, that clears that right up. Page 224:

A. ...I lived at Wardell at the time so we were going straight through the lights they were turning off going down towards town.

Q. ...and it turned down at the red light?

A. Yes.

Q. It did not go straight through the red light?

A. No.

Now in case Ms. Bailey don't know, at Claypool Hill there is a huge motel and once a person goes straight they cannot see those who turn right going to Richlands-Raven and that is exactly what Crystal said on page 225:

A. ...I lived at Wardell so I went straight after you pass the motel you can't see nothing.

(Yes Sally, double negative—leave it.)

Q. Was the car in the right lane turning down towards Richlands?

A. Yes.

So, Ms. Bailey, professional juror, who is lying? Brandi said straight at Claypool Hill, Crystal said right at Claypool Hill, so one of those is a lie.

To me it's bad enough that somehow Crystal saw us halfway across Walmart where we never were, then Brandi said not out in the parking lot, but Crystal said out in the parking lot, Brandi said straight at Claypool Hill. So far Crystal had every single detail wrong. Of course, the reader don't know but Ms. Bailey does. On a huge white screen in the jury's face there was a picture—it's in Documents—Walmart picture which is supposed to be Brandi exiting Walmart which would prove it was the grocery side but the photo is a fake, no the photo is real but it's not me.

Would everyone please read 224, 225 and 226 very damn carefully. At this point Crystal went straight and Brandi went right.

Poor Menefee should have took a page from the Mike Dennis handbook. You simply cannot fix or correct the testimony of stupid—but we just have to try don't we, Menefee. Page 226 Menefee:

Q. You said you saw her, they at McDonald's?
A. Uh-huh. (yes)
Q. But you also said you saw her making a U-turn?
A. Uh-huh.

Wow! Now Ms. Bailey, I hope you know the area but when you leave Walmart you turn right onto 19-460 east towards Tazewell for 338 feet then you make a U-turn going back towards Claypool Hill. In between Walmart and Claypool Hill there is a red light at McDonald's, a U-turn there would have to be LEFT, then you'd be going east on 19-460 again back to Walmart. There is no motel at that light and there is right that goes to Richlands and if there was a U-turn now Brandi can't go straight or right at Claypool Hill, she is going to Tazewell. No one going east on 19-460 from Walmart can go over Kent's Ridge Road.

A. No, like I said at the red lights at Claypool Hill I lived at Wardell, so I had to be in the lefthand to—I mean—yeah, lefthand to go straight through and she was in the right lane going to town.

A. It was in between those two lights?

Huh? Are you following all this Ms. Bailey? First at Walmart she did not call out to Brandi because by the time she got the truck Janet was driving shut down Brandi was gone, yet somehow there is a U-turn to the left in 338 then a red light at McDonald's and it's quite a stretch up to the next light. But, and Menefee—in writing this book I have read 224, 225 and 226 (and the whole damn transcript) a hundred times yet I don't seem to have the page where Crystal said she saw a U-turn at McDonald's. If you have that page, could you forward that to me? Ya simply can't do a "turn right U-turn" at the McDonald's light, but Crystal passed us in between lights, so no U-turn.

Now wait. Crystal on page 227 where you say, "lefthand lane to—I mean—yeah, lefthand lane," on the Beverly Hillbillies Jethro always kept his lucky rabbit's foot in his left-side pocket to avoid those left-right confusions—ya might want to get one. Just trying to help.

Q. Okay. In between the red lights. Okay, all right...

Ahhh, poor Menefee, sucks don't it. There was just no way to correct it so Crystal's lies would match Brandi's, but you gave it the old college try. Just like Mike Dennis and his bank-Brandi fiasco you had an epic fail! Uh here, let me give it a go:

"Crystal, you maladjusted, braindead, fucking moron—Brandi said straight at the light, now you get your goddamn lies in line with her fucking lies. Jesus Fucking Christ, back away from the psych-med-stupid pills for five goddamn minutes and get with the fucking program, SHE WENT STRAIGHT! SHE WENT STRAIGHT, fucking twit!"

There you go, Menefee, I fixed it for you, but how about you work on it.

"In response to Mr. Dennis' questions you indicted it was June?"

Q. So, if the date you called her mother was in July 9th that would be the date this occurred?

A. Right.

And the crowd goes wild! In your face, Mike Dennis. NOW that is how you correct the testimony of a stupid witness, it's Menefee for the WIN! Have you ever seen such leading, testifying for, and correcting all without objection in one smooth move—ALL HAIL MENEFEE! MENEFEE! MENEFEE!

Sorry, went off the deep end there for a second. Your honor, I move, in the interest of time, we just let the prosecution testify and all the fucking morons just sit there and nod. Oh, that's what we are doing—good to know.

Now I do hate to ask Ms. Bailey, but from the ATM over to Walmart, park around the side on the grocery side, walk to posters, leave on the grocery side back to your car around that side—how the hell were you seen halfway across the store in the parking lot? So, if someone said that they saw you WAY over there in a court of law, that would be perjury, would it not? And Ms. Bailey, just which way did Brandi go at Claypool Hill—who is lying? Stay tuned to find out.

Had Menefee ended on that high note it would have been perfect. Some people just can't quit when they are ahead. Now I do hope someone gives Brandi this book because even I have to apologize for what happened next, I mean damn, it's bad. Hilarious, yes, but bad. Still on page 228:

Q. Can you remember what he looked like?

A. He was—he wasn't—he was probably medium build, grey hair, I think he may have had a—hehe—BALL—hehehe—CAP-HAHA—ON! (HaHaHa—HaHa—Ha! Ha! Ha!)

Brandi: The sunglasses were on MY HAT!

Yep, poor Brandi, your aunt just confused you—a 14-year-old girl—for a 48-year-old man! Wow, a brutal kick in the self-image. Maybe moisturize, a little feminine care products, might want to lose the hat, dude. Yep, I'm so sorry your aunt thought you were a 48-year-old dude—not a day over 45 I'd swear it.

Well now Ms. Bailey, we have one hell of a problem here, don't we. If Crystal saw me in a hat get in the passenger side but Brandi wore the hat then she did NOT positively identify Brandi.

I am not even going to bring up the flaw in Menefee's one win, but she did mess up. You people really need to read the goddamn police report. Crystal did not call Brandi's mother, sorry. If my brother Don calls, I do not say my brother James called. In the police report it was Janet who called so somehow Crystal called but she said Janet called. It's a minor thing but so far the only person who had any single detail correct was the prosecutor Menefee—I do not own a hat, sorry Crystal.

Are you still with us Ms. Bailey? I do hope you are having a great day, real coffee, good (actual) food all snuggy at home. You get comfy now because this next part is a bit intense. You may want to have a good drink or two to get in a relaxed mood. I hope, Ms. Bailey, you don't mind our little hypotheticals, I just wonder if it was your child on the chopping block in a nest of a lynch mob if you would have paid more attention. Do not think I blame you, I do not, you were only allowed to see what they allowed you to see. Now you will see all the concealed crap. You should know you were monitored, if you chose not guilty it would have been called a mistrial, I was not allowed to win.

If you can Ms. Bailey, for one second I want you to SERIOUSLY consider a 14-year-old girl steals a pack of your son's cigarettes and then she says oh, he sexually assaulted me. Your son is charged with abduction, attempted rape, Actual Inncocence, contributing and assault. The same girl who just stole and lied then says oh yeah, he stole the sunglasses, which she removes from her hat. The police pull what they believe is evidence at Walmart, so on top of all the charges your son, Ms. Bailey, is given a summons for shoplifting. In July 9, 2012 your child has a summons for shoplifting, he is appointed a lawyer and December 2012 he goes to trial for shoplifting. In a grand slam the lawyer finds that hey, this video shows the girl walking into Walmart with sunglasses on her hat, your child pleads NOT GUILTY and he is found NOT GUILTY. Your child has never in his entire life been charged or convicted of shoplifting.

July 21, 2015 your child, Ms. Bailey, goes to trial on his other charges and what do you hear?

"74 – he steals sunglasses"

"75 – he steals sunglasses"

From goddamn start to finish, Ms. Bailey, you hear over and over and over how your worthless piece of trash kid stole sunglasses, he's grooming stealing trinkets, he fucking shoplifted sunglasses, he drove all the way to Walmart to enter where your piece of shit kid did ONE thing—HE STOLE SUNGLASSES!

Now Ms. Bailey, that is not the real kick in the nuts, over and over and over—all over the transcript, "he stole sunglasses!" No, the real kick in the nuts is when YOU, Ms. Bailey, know that the lawyer who defended your son, the lawyer who saw the video of the girl entering Walmart with the sunglasses on her hat, is now the son of a bitch who is your child's co-counsel, and he sits there for the whole fucking trial and NOT ONCE does he ever open his goddamn mouth to correct or offer any defense against the libel and slander being propagated as so-called evidence.

NOW! Ms. Bailey if you, as a juror, would be so kind to peruse back to the book's Documents. There you find two things, page five of the police report—any page five will do.

"I then issued a summons to Mr. Blankenship for shoplifting…"

That report was written by none other than "Did you collect those cans? No sir, I did not," Mr. Caldwell. Then Ms. Bailey, you will find 10-104130 Virginia Uniform Summons. Robert Mckinley Blankenship which Brandi did point out—twice. You will note VA 092 7/9/12 Walmart. And yep, it's signed by our very own Dep. J. M. Caldwell. Over on the right you, Ms. Bailey, will see 9/9/12 10:00 a.m., 10/17/12 10:00 a.m.

and 12/19/12, that Ms. Bailey, would be December 19th, 2012, would it not? Those, Ms. Bailey, are hearing date and time.

Just to be very goddamn clear here Ms. Bailey, if you will now direct your attention to the top left. I see Defendant's Attorney Name M. Letson, is that what you see, Ms. Bailey? If you will peruse down ye old lefthand side, I was present, I plead NOT GUILTY, I was found NOT GUILTY and at the bottom 12/19/12 it is signed by a judge.

Just to be sure Ms. Bailey, would you now please direct your attention to the page Transcript July 21, 2015 page 1(9) Counsel for the Defendant Michael Letson.

Still not convinced, well if we go back to Documents there are two pages from a presentence report and the second page of that is Criminal History Attachment that was created by the probation office, or anyone could just run me online—God knows Sally sure as hell did. But—NO SHOPLIFTING.

So, you see Ms. Bailey, my hypothetical is NOT so goddamn hypothetical. I went to trial in December 2012, and I was found not guilty and the very person who defended me never once said a word.

Ms. Bailey are you familiar with the concept of malicious prosecution: the institution of proceedings without probable cause. Abuse of process: the improper use of legitimate court process to obtain a result that is either unlawful or beyond the processes scope. Actual malice: defamation or knowledge by a person who utters or publishes a defamatory statement when that statement is false or with reckless disregard of whether that statement is true or false. How about fraudulent misrepresentation: a false statement that is known to be false or without caring whether that statement is true or false and is INTENDED TO INDUCE A PARTY TO DETERMENTLY RELY ON IT. How about good old First Amendment libel: false statements to injure reputation.

Now you tell me Ms. Bailey, your child who in December 2012 was found innocent of shoplifting but is now in a courtroom, the SUPPOSED TO BE above reproach land of honesty, a prosecutor repeatedly says your piece of shit son shoplifted. Would you call that fraudulent misrepresentation since it is a false statement, and a jury relies on it to make a determination? Would you say it's libel, a false statement that makes your child a shoplifter? I'd call that damage to one's reputation. And finally, Ms. Bailey, were you as a juror or jury member ever told oh wait, he was found innocent of that? Would you call that meaningful or effective counsel? Would you Ms. Bailey, call it effective counsel if it was your child on trial?

No Ms. Bailey, I am a witch, so I do not expect you to take my word for a goddamn thing, so you take this book, and you go to the bank, you confirm my bank statement, you go to the courthouse, you confirm the shoplifting summons, and when you believe beyond any doubt that I was tried and found innocent of shoplifting, then you move forward in the book. But I do hate to put one more little knife in your back, Ms. Bailey, but in Documents you can see the sentencing order—YOUR handywork. Now I see abduction-20 years, Actual Inncocence-10 years. I see attempted rape-two years, I see contributing and assault, but curiously, I do not see shoplifting. Do you see shoplifting Ms. Bailey? Am I, Ms. Bailey, on trial for shoplifting, you know, the one I am not guilty of? Let's see, shall we.

Starting on page 229 we have Greg Layne. Oh wait, gotta be thorough here just to make sure Ms. Bailey don't get confused—do you know what perjury is, Ms. Bailey?

"Perjury: the willful telling of a lie while under oath." (My other dictionary says "lawful oath.")

So, are we agreed Ms. Bailey, that if your child was found not guilty of shoplifting those sunglasses, ANYONE who then testified that your son, under lawful oath, stole sunglasses that would, in fact, be perjury. Would you agree with that, Ms. Bailey?

So, Mr. Greg Layne on page 229 whatcha got for us today. First we have a very long running setup—all the work but they screw up. Caldwell showed up for a possible breaking and entering but Hale showed up to check out a sexual assault—that's worse. Now on page 230 old Layne pops by to check out an abduction—oh, that's way worse, good buildup though, very nice touch, wouldn't you agree, Ms. Bailey?

No Mr. Layne, would you explain how you somehow investigated an abduction, and you collected all the facts on July 9, 2012, but then Mr. Blankenship was not charged with that abduction until oh, nine months later after he was indicted without an abduction—after he had an actual jury trial lineup—I'd call that a line of bullshit.

In my whole trial this may be one of my absolute favorite lines. But we need a new hypothetical.

Now Ms. Bailey, your daughter, your little girl, is driven to a secluded location, she's beaten, raped and gutted (maybe eaten a little) and the investigator is immediately dispatched to Walmart to prove shoplifting. Well, we didn't quite collect DNA, can't get him on the murder rape, but by god we got him on misdemeanor shoplifting—oh wait, no we didn't. Wow! What an exceptional bit of police work. We just so don't get to see anything like that on that there Law and Order. The victim was raped on 10th Street, quick Stabler, go to Walmart on shoplifting.

Now we have a small problem which I really wish I could fix but I can't and it's not my mess. I can tell the reader what happened, but it won't match all the other versions. But this does get stupid.

Let's go back to what Brandi said. First she said I drove to Corner Mart where I ran in, then she drove to the bank in Richlands, she drove to Valero, she drove to Walmart. In the second version I drove to the Corner Mart, she also went in the store, I drove to Valero (meaning I drove to the bank before Valero), she then drove from Valero to Walmart. Now for Ms. Bailey—I don't give a flying fuck if you believe me or not but I saw it DOZENS of times, you did not.

For three years I was jammed in a cell with two people, can't stand up, no room at all to move, eating garbage I would not feed my dogs. At least twice a month, could be five times in one month, I would be pulled out, taken to a room where a lawyer—including Mike Dennis—would show me a VHS tape from Valero that did show me getting out of the driver's side, pumping gas, then I get in the driver's side and drive away. There is a person in the car but it's not clear who—that person did not get out. At Walmart video one shows us entering, Brandi is not held, and she has sunglasses on her hat. The second video shows Brandi two aisles away alone then she bounds over towards posters. Those were all used over and over and over to hammer away at me, they have you on video so better take a plea deal.

On page 230 we have Layne not going to an alleged crime scene, but he is off to Walmart or Corner Mart, Valero then Walmart.

Well hell, I am so sorry Ms. Bailey, the video at Corner Mart had been down for several months, now we will never know who went into the store, oh darn. Now don't any of you damn criminal types go rob Corner Mart, I am sure it's fixed by now, but hell they'd blame it on me, and they would "observe" evidence to prove it. But hey, we still have Valero. Do you, Ms. Bailey, see on the evidence sheet Valero VHS tape and two Walmart videos? I can't wait to see this.

Q. And after reviewing the tape were you able to make out anything on the tape?

A. No, sir.

Now wait a goddamn minute. I, on July 9, 2012 was arrested on two beer cans:

Did you collect those cans!

No sir, I did not.

I was arrested on a VHS tape—as evidence.

Was there anything on the tape?

Nope, not a thing.

Wow, and exactly how did a blank tape (that's got me on it) suddenly become NOT evidence or when you stop and think we have two cops who fail to collect actual evidence but the investigator does collect a blank tape. He collected NOT evidence—good job. I know, you should take a picture of the tape then just explain what you "observed" on the tape—that's what everyone else is doing.

Now how the bloody hell is poor Ms. Bailey ever going to know who drove to or from Valero? Ya can't ask Brandi, she has three versions already. So, now we have DNA evidence on the ground 30 miles away and it's not being collected, but a blank VHS tape again 30 miles away is being collected.

Page 232:

Q. Did you catch or were you able to find shots of the defendant entering the store.

A. Coming out into the store—no.

Let me help out Ms. Bailey here so she don't get lost. You don't know what's going on, do you Ms. Bailey? You see Ms. Bailey, at Valero you heard Brandi testify that A: either she drove there, or B: she got out and drove from. The VHS tape don't match the prosecutor's case—now—so we toss that evidence out. Now do you recall Ms. Bailey, when you said, "Doesn't HE have to present any evidence?" Well, if you look at the evidence sheet VHS tape at Valero—why I'd love to show you that. But if you Ms. Bailey, would look at page 3(396), why that evidence is not on the exhibits. Where did that evidence go? You will not find two Walmart videos on there either.

Now let me explain, Brandi just said when she entered Walmart she was grabbed but in the video she is not held and she has sunglasses on her hat. So, coming into Walmart, nope can't find a thing, so out goes video one, it don't match the prosecutor's case. So again Ms. Bailey, I'd love to show you that video, but it went missing.

Well now Ms. Bailey, what do you say, your child who was found NOT GUILTY of shoplifting is on trial and they whip out exhibit number 23, a pair of sunglasses to show the sunglasses your lowlife shoplifting son stole—would you be okay with that? So now we have sunglasses as evidence that I stole sunglasses—can you say double jeopardy? Your child, Ms. Bailey, is now on trial for those sunglasses and every single word spoken is perjury. You, Ms. Bailey, are seeing libel, wanton misconduct, fraudulent misrepresentation. You are the front row witness to ineffective counsel, breach of duty and the fabrication of irrelevant evidence, so when you saw all of that did you see it or did you just see a piece of shit who stole sunglasses because the way you saw me—that's exactly how a jury will see your child.

Most people would miss this little point but it all goes together. But first Ms. Bailey, look at the police report evidence sheet:

Cigarettes

Energy drink

Two receipts

Sunglasses

Two Walmart disks

One VHS tape

For those two Walmart disks to be in that report that meant that Layne went to Walmart, then he returned, and he turned over to Caldwell one VHS tape and two Walmart videos. And yet, on page 234 of the transcript we have:

Q. Did you make any stills.

A. We made stills and then we also made recorded video to disk.

Hmmm…and what did he do with those stills he supposedly made? They did not go into evidence nor did they exist up to March 2015 nor were they ever turned over in a motion for discovery, so I guess he somehow turned over the two disks but he walked around for three years with those still in his pocket.

"We want the truth, nothing but the truth—objection overruled."
"Accept."

I kind of have in mind here, in the movie Pink Floyd: The Wall, "Poems, we have poems everybody."

"Photos, we have photos everybody."

Now Ms. Bailey, I really hate peeing on your little parade of overwhelming evidence, but a promise is a promise. But first Ms. Bailey, look at the Walmart picture in Documents. What is bad wrong? You are running out of time!

Now your honor: We fully understand that HE in fact did not steal sunglasses, however, it works better for our case if we just go ahead and say he stole sunglasses and at this time, well, we can't actually show video because it don't match our claims, so what we want to do is a re-enactment but instead of a real re-enactment we will use some fabricated photos to then have someone describe what the re-enactment would look like, if we actually had a re-enactment of a crime he did not commit…"

"I'll allow it!"

You got all that Ms. Bailey? I hope so, you damn sure got it in the real trial. Now I am not going through the bullshit photos they fabricated except for one. But I will ask Ms. Bailey this, the prosecutor by his claims has not photos but actual video that shows Brandi dragged all over the store by the hand, he has video of theft, no stills existed until 2015, why make stills but NEVER enter that video?

Okay, let's play a game. You drive to Walmart, you park on the grocery side, you enter Walmart on the grocery side, you see that black blob on the ceiling that's the camera. You walk back to posters then you exit on the grocery side. You have a window of three to four minutes tops. An investigator then says well, we got her going out but not a sign of her entering. He makes two video disks but then he says he made one video disk and some stills, so he is lying. But then he claims Brandi is held the whole time in the video, so we are not going to SHOW the evidence, we are just going to have someone describe what the evidence would look like if we actually had any evidence. The so-called video was never entered, never shown and they blew it.

ARE YOU READY, MS. BAILEY? We are here, the moment of truth, oh, can you feel the suspense of this moment:

Q. And this last one does it appear that Brandi is being held by the wrist.

You know, don't you Ms. Bailey, that he means the Walmart photo he left up the entire time. It would take a pretty convincing argument to discredit that photo. Did you Ms. Bailey, look at the photo in Documents?

Entrance – Groc Vestibule 7-9-12 4:05:19 p.m.

So, Ms. Bailey, how are you at military time because it's very simple really. If you would please look at my bank statement on page 2 I have marked:

7/10 4.92 DBT CRD 16:09 7-9-12
Doran Grocery
Raven VA

Did you know, Ms. Bailey, that 16:09 is 4:09 p.m.? Now Ms. Bailey, you walk your butt into the vestibule, you stand there, then, and by all means run, you have four minutes to get to your car, get out of Walmart, drive 8.8 miles (13 minutes) to the car wash across the bridge in Raven. If you, Ms. Bailey, cannot do that, that photo is not me, it is a fabrication of what it would look like if it was me. I can assure you Ms. Bailey, and everyone else, my Toyota Corolla did not have hyperdrive or warp drive nor did it come with a teleporter. 8.8 miles, one U-turn, five red lights in four minutes, now I say it cannot be done.

So, you see Ms. Bailey, the goddamn picture you stared at for the whole goddamn trial was not me. But then Ms. Bailey, you have a dilemma because first I was found not guilty of shoplifting sunglasses but then the so-called investigator finds someone putting on sunglasses, then he finds that someone exiting Walmart, but that four minutes proves it's not me so whoever he followed was, BA-BA-BA—NOT ME! So now Ms. Bailey, where do we really stand?

Picture of a random house.
Picture of a random road.
Picture of a store.
Picture of a gas station.
13-18 photos of NOT ME.
Picture of snow on a dirt road.
Sunglasses no one ever shoplifted.
Cigarettes.

That Ms. Bailey, is your actual evidence that is not imaginary or "the conceit of specter evidence allowed many to be arrested." Does it occur to YOU now Ms. Bailey, where was all this, all this fabricated shoplifting evidence back in December 19, 2012 when a judge found me (your child) not guilty? Funny how it didn't exist back then.

Oh you, Ms. Bailey, will love this next part. Here again we have a dilemma, but first—hey lying bitch Carla J. Faletti, NO, I have not forgotten you, I have half a fucking page OR MORE. When the prosecutor claims they went to get to my clothes they were lost—it's missing in my transcript all thanks to Carla J. Faletti.

Okay, I'm back. Maybe Ms. Bailey remembers they said my clothes were lost but hey, wow, just like the surprise aunt popped up how very goddamn convenient for the prosecution to have photos of the lost clothes. Yep, here is a photo of what evidence would look like if we had any evidence whatsoever. But here again we have some random clothes that we can't tie to anyone in any way that we have NOT the clothes, but a picture of some random clothes.

Rule 2:401 Relevant Evidence: relevant evidence means evidence having any tendency to make the existence of any fact in issue more probable or less probable than it would be without the evidence.

On the one hand the man who just committed perjury, who presented purely fabricated evidence in photos, suddenly has more photos of some random clothes with absolutely no way to tie those clothes to me, or to anyone. That is not evidence: that is a fabricated photo of what evidence might look like if they had any real evidence. Or:

Did you collect those cans!

Nope, but here's some clothes—no—pictures of clothes we found at Goodwill. GUILTY AS HELL!

Hey, can you describe those cans?

Can you describe those cans?

Can you describe that house?

Can you describe a computer?

Can you describe that video?

Can you describe those clothes? (p. 240)

Seems to me we have a huge abundance of shit being described. Goddamn Law and Order got it all wrong—don't present any evidence, just make up a bunch of shit.

Now Mr. Layne, would you explain to this court how in a VERY convenient maneuver you somehow managed—three years later—to just happen to have handy photos that you somehow took but also somehow did NOT take into evidence clothes you now want to claim may in some way connect to this case. And you went to the jail where you claim you checked the evidence or property sheet and yet you failed to collect it.

Can you describe what the random clothes you found at Goodwill looked like?

Can you describe that property sheet?

And well hell, looky here, we can present pictures of random clothes without any objection whatsoever.

Your honor, at this time we would like to enter, well, we don't have an ax or a picture of an ax, but we have a picture of my foot that could be a picture of an ax that would be the ax he used to cut her head off before it grew back!

I'll allow it!

Now Ms. Bailey, by this time you are our resident professional juror, you are not looking at my clothes. Your son is facing life plus 22 years and this investigator goes to the jail to "look" at a property sheet, he goes to "look" at clothes, but he does not collect those items as evidence nor did he take photos, no "photos" on the evidence sheet. Three years later he goes to Goodwill and takes pictures of random clothes he then says makes your son guilty as hell. Then your son's lawyer is fine with fabricated imaginary evidence—you, Ms. Bailey, can kiss your son's ass goodbye. Thirty-two years on imaginary beer cans and imaginary clothes.

Then to add insult to injury the investigator says there may have been other items in the bag.

Q. Were there shoes or anything in there.

A. There may have been I can't recall.

You do realize Ms. Bailey, the son of a bitch just said he only removed what matched the prosecutor's claims not everything in the bag.

I do apologize Ms. Bailey, but I can let you off the hook. You were not allowed to hear this but, you see, my lawyer made a motion to enter said property sheet, but the judge blocked it. Do you know why, Ms. Bailey? Because it only had R. Blankenship 7-9-12. You see, they can enter a photo of random clothes taken at Goodwill somewhere on the planet, but I can't enter a real property sheet because it had R. Blankenship—well hell, that could be any one of a hundred R. Blankenships that were arrested 7-9-12. The property sheet listed shorts, t-shirt, underwear, socks, shoes, belt and a watch. Now you know why you, as a juror, never saw that sheet. I'd love to show you some evidence, but it was not allowed. But it didn't end there, the day after my trial all of those clothes were mailed to Sally and Sally reported this to, yep, lying bitch Carla J. Faletti. You can see that Sally Letter in Documents. But we ain't got there yet.

Well, well, well, now upon inspection Ms. Bailey, just exactly what evidence have you seen? The actual, real, tangible evidence is—a pack of CIGARETTES! That is the extent of all evidence presented at my trial.

You did see sunglasses, but I never shoplifted. You have not seen photos of me, of Brandi, or any video at all. I am tired Ms. Bailey. Do you understand what it's like to hear lie after lie?

But what you don't know was at this point there was a brutal argument after you left out on recess. I wanted Mike Letson to step up and admit first the son of a bitch Layne lied there was video of us entering, so he did find us entering—hell—it was four minutes, so he had to. Brandi was not held inside Walmart on any video. I did not shoplift. Mike Letson was made my co-counsel so I could not call him as a witness. To be a witness, like Jim Shortt, he would have to recuse himself then be subpoenaed. Well, isn't that very goddamn convenient for the prosecution. Then I can testify—hey, I never stole sunglasses. Oh yeah, I am sure the jury would be all convinced the child molester wouldn't say anything true and there are things you don't know yet Ms. Bailey.

In my list of crazy I honestly thought I had seen the extreme corruption. He stole sunglasses, that blew me away, but it definitely proved that I was in the land of five prosecutors as a fucking lynch mob out to convict me. And don't forget, we have cop lady on the jury for the inside track. But even I was shocked at the next—DOUBLE—TRIPLE—fuck over on me and worse on the jury.

Now you tell me Ms. Bailey, do you know what a "motion" is in a trial? Well, an example would be on page 67, Mr. Lee has 20 photos, so he makes a motion to use those. The defense then raises, or not, an objection, then the judge rules. Now in my trial it's simple, anything the prosecution wants is allowed and anything for the defense is NOT allowed. But if you Ms. Bailey, would look at page 240 you will see Lee move to introduce pictures 19-20. That is a motion, it's just something that may or may not be entered. Y'all can review the Motions July 20, 2015 transcript to see what motions are. I do not want any confusion here.

There is something Ms. Bailey may not know. Out the back door of the courtroom there is a rather large holding cell for when you, the jury, go into recess, I, the criminal, go to the holding cell. Mr. Dennis, my so-called lawyer, came back and he told me we were done for the day, but the court had some unrelated motions on another case they had to go over. Between page 243 and 246 I was in a holding cell, then at 4:05 p.m. I was brought in when the jury was.

Pay attention here Ms. Bailey, if you have Law-and-Order-itis it's about to be tested. A judge is considered too honest above any reproach—a judge is the shining beacon of honor and honesty—the backbone of our American justice system.

Ms. Bailey please read 246 very carefully.

"Ladies and gentlemen of the jury, we are at a point now where it is 4 o'clock and we are also at a point where the court can take up some issues—SOME MOTIONS—that are not going to require the jury's input…"

Did you Ms. Bailey, clearly read the court had some motions, and do you have a good concept of what a motion is?

I am not sure what he meant by, "does not require the jury's input." Uh…I thought a jury was supposed to watch the input, not input itself. I mean all day the jury did not input but now we reached a point where we don't require what we haven't required all day—in fact, if the jury had input that would be a mistrial unless:

Your honor we move to allow the jury to testify—I'LL ALLOW IT! Hell's bells, it's about the only thing they didn't do. You want to testify Ms. Bailey? Don't worry, just make shit up like everyone else.

Sorry, went off again. Do you see Ms. Bailey, the court, the sitting judge just told the jury they had some motions. Now, in your world Ms. Bailey, at 4:06 p.m. you are released, you are on your way home, you had a good supper, trusting that you had a good handle on the day's events. You believe you had all the facts, saw all the evidence, feeling good, couldn't wait to put your torch in the ol' bonfire under that witch the next day.

Well, before we get by all that how about we finish the trial then light the bonfire. If you would Ms. Bailey, take a gander at subpoena proof in Documents. Every damn time from March 2013 to 2015 that we had a jury trial scheduled I put a subpoena on two people—Robbie Davis and Brad Goff, those are Brandi's probation officers. Now you Ms. Bailey, were told Brandi had what, oh, a minor trespassing which was changed to, oh, a disorderly conduct—awww, ain't she cute. (Hold that thought.)

Now this is a fucking snow job. At the start of my trial the judge asks did I tell my lawyer all the people I wanted subpoenaed and I said yes. What I did not know was they removed my subpoena, tossed out Brad Goff and the prosecution called my witness but neither I nor the jury were in the room.

I may as well get this out of the way now, this damn little tidbit caused one hell of an argument with two of Sally's friends—my adverse proofreaders. Actually, I had several problems out of those two. One argument we had was that they wanted to know, maybe Ms. Bailey wonders too, if my bank statement was all that why didn't we use it—WE haven't got there yet. One of Sally's friends said numerous times, "They can't do that!" Then she ordered her very own transcript from the court which shut her up. The other problem was that at the time of my trial I did not have a transcript of events. I had no idea about the stupid police report evidence sheet, hell, I thought they had beer cans. I had no fucking clue they were going to come out saying, "He stole sunglasses." How the fuck do you defend against something you had no fucking idea was coming and something you were already tried for? I had no goddamn idea what was said on pages 244. Hell, between 3:58 and 4:05 p.m. I was out, then at 4:06 I was back in jail. All of that I did not see until February 2016, so you can't fight corruption after the fact.

This is very simple, Brandi had breaking and entering and some other shit so the prosecutor could not allow her probation officer on the stand in front of a jury, so in super-secret proceedings WHERE A SITTING JUDGE LIED TO A JURY IN A JURY TRIAL to allow the prosecution to call a witness to discredit a defense witness without the actual witness being called.

Yes, at my so-called jury trial the prosecution calls a witness in a super-secret proceeding without a defendant or a jury in the room.

Wait! Hey Ms. Bailey, you were told at 4:05 the court had "SOME MOTIONS" and yet you were sent home at 4:06 p.m. The trial was over, or so you thought, and or so I thought.

Court reconvened 4:34 p.m. July 21, 2015 (page 248).

The court: You may call your next witness.

Menefee (prosecution) calls Robbie Davis witness for the defense.

Uh Ms. Bailey, that is NOT a FUCKING MOTION. The judge did not say they were calling a witness to testify, he said some motions. Now in my neck of the woods we'd call him a lying son of a bitch. The judge lied to the jury and the judge lied to the defendant. I only heard what you heard, "SOME MOTIONS." Then at my jury trial the prosecution somehow calls my witness in a super-secret proceeding, without me or a jury in the room.

Hello Ms. Bailey, you were just lied to by a judge. You as a juror were then put out by that judge and a witness called to testify without you, a jury, in the room.

Tell me Ms. Bailey, do you know much about witch trials? Up until around 1550 there was a process called "boxing." When a person was accused of being a witch before the witness testified they would put the accused in a box. Some were buried and died if the witness took too long. Some they put in an outbuilding or they would be left outside even covered in snow. Now me they just shoved in a tiny cell with two other dudes. Hell, at least the ones who were boxed had a single cell, lucky bastards.

Now Ms. Bailey, please do not think I would in any way disparage your intelligence. You may be way smarter than me. God knows Sally is and she never shuts up about it. But Ms. Bailey, not everyone is up on the United States Constitution—I sure as hell wasn't. But there are some good books. You, your children, your parents, your extended family, supposedly every United States citizen has the Sixth Amendment right to a fast and speedy PUBLIC trial. Then from what it says and what it means the PUBLIC part of that means that you, your child is protected from secret proceedings which means they cannot hold a jury trial without a defendant or a jury behind locked doors.

Then Ms. Bailey, have you ever heard of VA CODE Ann § 19.2-259 a person tried for felony shall be "PERSONALLY PRESENT" during the trial. IT IS an essential process of law: during the trial has been defined as EVERY stage of that trial from the arraignment to the sentencing: the Sixth Amendment protects the right of the accused to be present!

Wow! You see Ms. Bailey, were your son in my shoes his First, Fourth and Sixth Constitutional rights have now been violated.

Did you read that on the VA CODE, it does not state that a person's presence is based upon the content or the context of the proceeding. It states as does the Constitution that a person shall be personally present. Now what is your opinion here Ms. Bailey, is it okay for a judge to lie to a jury, to hold a jury trial without a jury or a defendant, to allow the prosecutor to call a witness in secret proceedings to convict your son? Well, from 4:06 to 4:40 we done went and had a jury trial—NOT a motion—a trial without a jury or the accused present. Yep, witches do not have any Constitutional rights which is okay as long as they are only burning witches, right Ms. Bailey. But I will say I am not even going to write about whatever the prosecutor's witness said because the damage is done—the jury was right there at 4:06 p.m., the judge, the prosecutor and the defense all knew they were going to call a witness. The judge lied to the jury to instigate a secret proceeding and the defense aided the deception. My Fourth and Sixth Amendment rights were violated, case closed.

Now Ms. Bailey, let's run down the old overwhelming evidence we have actually seen.

Picture of a random house.
Picture of a random road.
Picture of a store.
Picture of a gas station.
Picture of snowy dirt road.
Pictures of random people at Walmart.
Picture of clothes from Goodwill.
Sunglasses no one ever shoplifted.
A pack of cigarettes.

Then we have specter evidence. Can you describe those cans, can you describe the can you sniffed, can you describe a stretched shirt no one noticed until three years later, can you describe some video no one saw, can you describe the clothes you found at Goodwill. We had beer cans described that stayed cold for five hours outside in July, we heard an officer describe a computer in a house 20 miles away, we heard an inspector describe what he did not find at all, we heard a witness testify wrong month, wrong person in a hat, wrong location, and contradicted the witness about direction of travel, we heard Brandi testify she had no damn idea about anything the same way twice.

The only cool thing is if one studies witch trials—I had one. All the witnesses were asked to describe the ills the specters caused. And like it or lump it Ms. Bailey, yes beer cans and random clothes are in fact specter evidence—did you SEE IT IN THE COURTROOM!

Did you collect those cans?
Nope, sure didn't.
Did you collect those cans?
Nope, but I sniffed one.
Did you collect those clothes?
Nope, got a picture of some from Goodwill.

1692 the conceit of specter evidence allowed many to be arrested. 2015 the conceit of imaginary evidence allowed many to be convicted.

Yep, we don't need any evidence we can just fabricate any bullshit we need to pretend is evidence. Ya gotta love imaginary evidence, it's always right where it's needed and it means exactly what the prosecutor needs it to mean.

"1397: The accused who stands on any defense only proves stronger guilt that must be ignored."

"1401: A hanged witch will not die until silenced by fire…"

"1745: A witness is held pure above all complaints of the accused."

And having concluded the secret proceedings the lynch mob hung their robes and extinguished the torches. There would be no bonfire this day, but there is always tomorrow!

Chapter 6

Climax

Some people may wonder, God knows I was asked, "What the hell was all that life's story crap when the purpose of this book was the trial?" I had several good reasons but the main one was that no matter how hard anyone digs, what's written is all they will ever find in my past.

On the other side, way back in the book I wrote that, "Anything a person owns can be used as evidence no matter if it's a hundred miles away from any crime scene." It's very easy for the police or a prosecutor to pick out pieces of irrelevant crap or one window of a person's life and claim why look at all this irrelevant evidence. When I lived in Grey, Tennessee happily married, 13 dogs, working in granite, I built a nice computer for Sally and for myself. No huge ulterior motive, no sinister plans, just two married people who needed computer upgrades. And it's okay for a prosecutor to lie his ass off in trial as long as those lies match his case. I had not "just moved" to the area, I lived with my mom almost a year just out the road. When my mom had an aneurysm, I made a deal to move into a house that was run down. It was a mess yes, but the walls and the roof were good. Floors can be fixed. Hell, I've seen, I've lived in way worse. One place I rented had road signs for a bathroom floor. That house was run down long before I got there, so yes, I lived in an older house that needed work and yes, I did have a nice computer. So, Ms. Bailey, was it the house or computer that convinced you someone was ever on a road 20 MILES AWAY? Was that some overwhelming evidence? Or Ms. Bailey, was it the imaginary beer cans that are now one-size-fits-all, universal, can be used against ANYONE, say, like, your children, Ms. Bailey, evidence? Or was it the picture of random Goodwill clothes that tipped your mind to guilty?

You tell me, Ms. Bailey, had a woman been raped or any crime actually committed on that road and the rapist walked because not one, but two cops looked at or sniffed DNA fingerprint evidence but somehow did not collect it, there would be a public outcry and those officers would be fired. But their criminal negligence was perfectly okay because it only put an innocent witch on the bonfire. Tell me, Ms. Bailey, what do you or your children own that will be used as completely fabricated evidence when it's your children on trial? Tell me, Ms. Bailey, do you own a nice car, a nice TV, a nice stereo, a stash of jewelry? Does every item you own "fit" your house? How will you feel when a prosecutor says, "OH! Look what a nice TV. Fifty miles away…GOD! What EVIDENCE! GUILTY AS HELL!" and your child goes to prison. You can't say no. You did it to me, so who's next? Do you, Ms. Bailey, realize that during witch trials no "evidence" was presented? Now, did YOU, Ms. Bailey, see any beer cans? Did you see any clothes? Did you see a computer? NO. You convicted a man on "specter" evidence that can now be used on ANYONE.

Do you, Ms. Bailey, honestly believe that two cops who collected every speck of evidence except two beer cans at the crime scene, or that Caldwell filled out his report before 1 a.m. just an hour later where he wrote, "We found those cans." But he did not notice "NO beer cans" on the evidence sheet. I call bullshit!

What I would like, Ms. Bailey, is to know your opinion on, you see in front of you a Virginia Uniform Summons where almost three years before my trial I was tried for shoplifting sunglasses, and I was not guilty. By all means, run my record on any background check. Yet, at my trial, Ms. Bailey, you were told over and over, look at these sunglasses he stole, he stole sunglasses. Yep, totally stole sunglasses. Every single person who said that committed perjury—NO ONE CARES!

Well, having seen all the perjury the day before and now you, Ms. Bailey, know you were lied to by a judge to conceal a witness to aid the prosecution, I can't wait for the events of day two, though it's not quite as bad.

I do find it curious that somehow Day 1 transcript starts 1(394) but Day 2 transcript starts 1(12) even when Day 2 was made four months after Day 1. Don't try to figure it out. How the hell could it start 1(12)? Where did one to 11 go to get to 12? Day 2 July 22, 2015. We have prosecutors, Judge (lying) Patterson, Lee, Menefee, Dennis, and Letson and for the defense a piece of bellybutton lint. (I'll allow it!)

The year is 2022, the month is June, damn near July (again). The day is irrelevant. "Xena" is on TV, got my coffee, I had slimy, what may have been, egg whites or boiled elephant semen, and a substance some refer to as oatmeal. July 9th, 2022 it will be 10 years in prison and NOW I can finally answer Ms. Bailey's question on "defense evidence." If you would be so kind, Ms. Bailey, you may have the honors of looking/reading out loud page 3(14) Exhibits. You may notice VHS tape from police report as missing. So are two Wal-Mart videos. We have 20 irrelevant photos—fabrications. We do have sunglasses no one stole and we have A PACK OF CIGARETTES!

Do you see EVERY single piece of Exhibit for Defendant was blocked, NOT ALLOWED, NOT ADMITTED! There are some problems here but once again, that is Carla J. Faletti's fault. One hundred percent she conceals the truth. So, you see Ms. Bailey, it wasn't that I didn't have to present evidence. It wasn't that I didn't try. It was that I was not allowed to present ANY evidence. On the upside, there was less blah, blah, blah on the second day.

Now Ms. Bailey, back then you didn't even catch this but I sure as hell did. But first would you, Ms. Bailey, if you reflect back to when Brandi testified, she had a little trespassing charge. Yep, just a little angel. But then on page four, Day 2, why, she never had a trespassing, it was a little disorderly conduct. Why, hardly worth a mention at all, right Ms. Bailey? Yep, just a little innocent angel. Boy, I hope nothing changes that perception.

Disorderly conduct or something like that.

My shock came on page five. Did you recall a Robbie Davis there, Ms. Bailey? Nope because a trial judge said we have motions to go over and sends the jury home to call a witness for the prosecution in a secret proceeding that NO ONE except the five prosecutors know what was said.

Now when you really stop and think here, Ms. Bailey, we are not going to present the clothes, we are going to present a picture of clothes from Goodwill. Oh hey, can you describe those cans you sniffed, then? NOW, your lying honor sir, we ain't gonna present this witness, we are gonna call a witness (with only the lynch mob present) in a secret proceeding in violation of the V, VI, and VII Amendments. Then WE are just going to SAY what that witness said. I'll ALLOW IT!

Now, your lying honor, when he cut her head off with an ax, before it grew back, we have a witness we called in secret who said he saw the whole thing. I'll ALLOW IT! Yeah, what wouldn't you allow, you lying piece of crap? A witness testifying is not a motion, liar. Oh, you won't allow evidence for the defense. I see, good to know.

Still like to know how my witness was called in a secret proceeding but it does not surprise me. Hey Ms. Bailey, do you ever see on "Law and Order" where they hold a jury trial without a jury or a defendant? Hell, why have a trial at all? How about you, cop girl Kalya, you okay with being lied to by a judge, kicked out to have a jury trial without a jury? Yeah, as a cop you don't mind, do you? After all, we are only burning a witch, it's not like it's your family. What's a violated Constitutional right or four? Did you bring your torch for the old bonfire there, Kayla? Nothing like a good old witch burning, hey!

So, I'd call a member of a police force on a jury jury tampering. I'd call swapping witnesses witness tampering. I have no damn idea what a lying judge who is a proven liar in front of a jury. Then, Letson lets the stolen sunglasses slide as does Mike Dennis. That alone is an ineffective counsel claim among 500 others.

Can I ask you Ms. Bailey, would it upset you if you were charged with shoplifting, tried, and found innocent, but then you have to hear over and over and over how you shoplifted, you can't speak and the lawyer who defended you won't speak? Do you Ms. Bailey, think you'd be okay with that? Tell me, Ms. Bailey, if you knew, 100 percent that due to being played in a stage show that you put an innocent man in prison for life—would it bother you? That's okay, it won't bother the jury who falsely convicts your child either. Just another witch on the fire.

Now Ms. Bailey, if you want to see what a real lying son of a bitch, besides the judge, looks at the bottom of page six into seven.

Let me give you the refresher course. Brandi was in detention, Jim Shortt goes with the prosecutor, the cop Caldwell and the witness coach to the detention center to make a video which is supposed to cause me to take a plea deal, but Brandi in true Brandi style lies her ass off. We never went to ANY bank. I only bought cigarettes, no beer, I stole sunglasses

I had been tried for and found NOT GUILTY, but the real kicker here and you can read it, in the police report she said, "her shirt and bra" were removed. You do understand Ms. Bailey, this is a young GIRL on a dirt road who has her shirt and bra removed outside in front of a man. If you read the police report she says I removed her shirt and bra, I grabbed her around the neck, then I just stopped. That was July 9, 2012. Yet somehow May 21, 2014:

"I don't even think he went to the bank. I don't think so. No."

Drove to school, she drove to Wal-Mart, he stole sunglasses, which we now know was a lie.

Now here Ms. Bailey, if you read my story, we lived on Jewel Ridge. We rented houses, we were poor, we rented on Reynolds Ridge, Merry Hallow, Richlands, Shell Street, and when I was 16 we bought a rundown trailer on Kent's Ridge Road about 40 feet past town limits. My family did not have a chimney on Ray Road as Brandi claims is a chimney or a rock, I've yet to find out.

But she screws up every detail until the worst.

On Ray Road I don't drink beer, I get naked, I kick her feet out, throw her on the ground, jump on top of her, and only then try to remove her clothes.

The problem is that you Ms. Bailey, did not see the video. Brandi is deadpan. I mean, she is literally bored. She describes the attack like she would dusting a shelf. The entire video she never has any emotion at all, she is bland. Even though you Ms. Bailey, have no fucking clue what is going on let me explain very damn clearly. They NEVER enter the actual VHS tape, Wal-Mart videos, police report, or the transcript in this book. I mean the Jim Shortt video transcript or the video. There is no way in hell the judge or the four prosecutors are going to allow you, the jury, to have the police report—shirt and bra removed—and the J.S. transcript page seven:

"Okay, did he ever remove any of your clothing?"

"No."

So, you tell me honestly Ms. Bailey, if a man tore off your shirt and bra you would then completely forget and say, "Why no, none of my clothes were ever removed?"

Then you tell me Ms. Bailey, female, a naked man throws you to the ground, jumps on top of you, the naked man is trying to rip your clothes off—you think you would confuse that with, oh, he only took my shirt off?

Did you know Ms. Bailey, that not one but two of my wife's friends, one that hates me, were actually sexually assaulted and both of them say Brandi Lee Short is full of shit? But hey, it's only a jury trial, right, where the lynch mob burns witches. Why let you, the jury, see ALL the facts when we can fabricate imaginary beer cans, show some pictures of a random road, and take a photo of clothes at Goodwill—GUILTY AS HELL—don't forget computer in a house 20 miles away—oh yes, GUILTY, GUILTY, GUILTY. Wait, well he didn't REALLY steal sunglasses, but it works better for the prosecution if we say he did, so here is those NOT stolen sunglasses. Not stolen sunglasses—guilty.

Well now, our witness said he tore off her shirt and bra. No wait, he didn't remove any clothes at all. Oh, uh, let's go with he took her shirt off. Hey, three years later I saw an imaginary stretched shirt to go with the imaginary beer cans and imaginary clothes.

Sorry, I get sidetracked in a rant once in a while.

Hey Ms. Bailey, how would you like to know another secret? The Jim Shortt video is 100 percent video. Not one second is audio. And yet somehow look what Mr. (supposed to be defense) Dennis says:

"It is video and audio but there are just a few seconds of video."

You sir are a lying son of a bitch. If you think it's libel, bring the video and remember, I am not the only one who watched it. My lawyer blatantly lied to help the prosecution convict me. Do you know what that's called Ms. Bailey? Ineffective assistance of counsel that proves he acted with prejudice. He did not enter the police report, the video or the transcript. Then to make goddamn sure no one ever saw it look what they did. Do you Ms. Bailey, know the difference between a CD and a DVD? One is audio, the other video. You can't put video on a CD, so where did the DVD go? It's not on page three Exhibits. They tossed in a CD—did not admit it.

But where we are the prosecutor is desperate to remove two things: the police report and the video. Then, and no one else ever notices these little nuances, in trial we have a Jim Shortt video. Get it? The prosecutor makes a motion to block said video. See Ms. Bailey, THAT is a motion, a motion is not calling a witness. But then the judge rules, well, since the video would show Brandi saying a totally different story in a deadpan bored manner, well hell, we can't have anything like that. I know y'all can just use these transcripts we VERY conveniently already have prepared but, well, since the transcript don't match her testimony we can use it, but not enter it so we don't have to put it in the jury room. We only allow the prosecution's exhibits in the jury room.

Now Ms. Bailey, do not take my word for it. First of all, Mr. Lee, it's all video not a few seconds, so you are a lying son of a bitch too.

From page six up to page 17 let me explain what's going on. The motion to block video was made. The judge then rules that only the defense is limited to the transcript. Only the prosecutor has an open door to allow Jim Shortt, the sixth prosecutor, to lie his ass off, which he does. Jim Shortt makes out like Brandi is all to hell emotionally. She is on a bench seat bored kicking her legs back and forth, her voice never cracks. If anyone wants the truth, Jim Shortt, Mike Dennis, Mike Letson, Joey Stiltner, and Carla J. Faletti have the video.

Then on page 17 there is a motion to strike where I wonder can I use dosecutor for third or fourth prosecutor who is acting defense, so Dennis is defense-prosecutor: D-cutor. Either way, he now testifies there is evidence I removed Brandi's shirt. Huh, there is evidence. Brandi has no goddamn clue what was removed. I mean the only evidence we have is a pack of cigarettes and that don't exactly prove any of her clothes were ever removed. No wait, her shirt and bra. No, oh, only her shirt in this version, but you go ahead and testify for the prosecution, Mr. D-cutor number four.

All right! HELL YEAH!

"The evidence before the court, it's incontrovertible—there's NO NEED for the jury to retire." Pink Floyd "The Wall"

Then on page 18 Lee says:

"While there the uncontroverted evidence."

He used the word and, come to think about it, we have examined the evidence before the court. I see imaginary, I see hypothetical, I see, "The conceit of specter evidence allow many to be arrested." I don't see uncontrovertible. Ice cold beer cans that are fresh after five hours outside, open, in July, that were sniffed—uncontrovertible?

"Controvert: to argue or reason against."

Well, it is hard to argue against imaginary beer cans or pictures of clothes from Goodwill. Now I am sure there are those of you who feel that hey, a fucking pig took them there photos and he wouldn't lie. Excuse you, would that be the same "lying fucking pig" who said he stole sunglasses? Yep, here's the sunglasses he didn't steal, but we are pretending he did. Here is a picture of clothes we found at Goodwill.

Now Ms. Bailey, we get into a bit of a sticky situation here. You see, Brandi did have her mom's permission to go to Wal-Mart with me. Now you, like the prosecutor, could pretend well, he was only going to the bank, not Wal-Mart, except if I was at Corner Mart in Richlands where a bank is just up the road, why would I drive all the way to the bank at Claypool Hill beside Wal-Mart? I was going to Wal-Mart. So, this is fun, the abduction was "with the deception of going to Ray Road," and the sexual assault would be the "attempt to defile." But Ms. Bailey, if I did not go to Ray Road then you are now left with one charge, contributing. Now me, I think 32 years in prison would be "cruel and unusual" punishment on a misdemeanor contributing. If I was never on Ray Road that is. Wouldn't that be a kick in the ass. (See bank statement: innocent.)

I have always found this a curiosity. Lee argues on page 27:

"There is clearly evidence to…"

Uh, which clear evidence does he keep referring to? We have imaginary ice-cold beer cans, a witness with three stories, a picture of Goodwill clothes, and we have multiple lies about sunglasses. We have a computer in a house 20 miles away. Where is this clear evidence there, Mr. Lee? Of course, it does help when the defendant don't have a lawyer. Oh, we do have hearsay evidence if we count the house cleaning Brandi made up.

You know Ms. Bailey, I spent years, literally from around 2004-05 up to around 2010-12 trying to explain how fucked up the legal system is when it's put under a light. Now I could spend days, weeks, years telling people even one item, but they have law-and-order-itis so they are not going to believe it. Sally didn't until I put proof in her face for over five years. My point being here that if I needed an example that covered every point in a corrupt out of control system, my trial would have answered that wish. The problem is, there were so many little fucked up twists and manipulations I have a hard time picking my favorite.

You don't know me, Ms. Bailey. You have read my story, but you don't know me. I love to read and write, I have thousands of friends from our dog rescue, I do love Monty Python, I am male so I like Xena on TV, and I love a good ironic twist. I was not joking about the solar-powered clothes dryer. One man ran ads in hundreds of papers, and I read the ads. Every word he wrote was true, but it was just a clothesline.

So, Ms. Bailey, my trial was a snow job from hell. While I am not real happy about the 32 years in prison, I still have to admire the P.T. Barnum level of bullshit they pulled off. Here is a damn good example.

We have to go back to July 20, 2015 in the motions. There was a probation psychological report done on Brandi Lee Shortt where she threatened to lie about sexual assault. The judge ruled that anything exculpatory would be able to come out for the defense. On July 21, 2015 the same judge said what he pulled out was the only relevant information and my lawyer then said yep, nothing else pertains to him. We have two redacted statements which are in Documents. Those are what the judge ruled that we, the defense, were allowed to use.

In a seemingly unrelated topic, let us reflect on Crystal Owens. Here we have an aunt who saw two random people, in June, in the wrong place going the wrong way and yet everyone grills the hell out of her about what she obviously didn't see. Do you remember all the questions Ms. Bailey, that they hit Crystal with?

Now Ms. Bailey, I have not one but two hypotheticals for you. A girl lies about sexual assault on your son. Would you really want your son's lawyer to call none other than the girl's mother as a witness? Do you think the mother of the girl your son allegedly sexually assaulted is going to be, in any way, all warm and fuzzy towards your child, innocent or not? I believe the absolute last person you or your son would want on the stand IS THE GIRL'S GODDAMN MOTHER!

I don't give a bully-bull's dick who called that bitch, SHE WAS NOT my witness, she was a witness the defense conspired against me to put on the stand. When Mike Dennis called her, I was like, what the fuck, dude!

Now here again Ms. Bailey, your child is on trial and right now his only defense are two redacted statements. That is all he has, period. Those two statements are the only infinitesimal slightest shred of hope. You could say your child is hanging by one thread and your child's lawyer somehow thinks, hey, let's put a person on the stand who will then discredit the only tiny piece of your son's hope. Would you, Ms. Bailey, be okay watching your son's attorney call the prosecutor's witness to cut the only thread your child has?

Oh, you want proof, is that it? Just imagine, Ms. Bailey, one day, a normal day, sun is out, it's warm but not too hot, you are talking to your sister on the phone. You are thinking about cooking supper, maybe a pizza or throw a meat entrée in the oven with potatoes and rolls. Your sister is rattling on about a brand new, eight-speed vibrator she just bought after the dog chewed up her last one. It cost $85, but so worth it. And you're thinking, "Damn, that woman wears out more vibrators than a gaggle of nuns."

All of a sudden—BAM—your little girl, your angel, rushes in, hair all fucked up, stretched shirt, she is a goddamn hysterical mess. She has been sexually assaulted. You are right there on the scene, a witness to her condition. You may or may not have gone to the scene, but damn, you were right there. They have grilled your sister seven ways to hell about what she may have seen in a 4 minute window but when you take the stand they do not ask you one question about, "your daughter's" state.

Then hey Ms. Bailey, did you know that you cannot perjure your own witness? So, if the prosecutor called you, you would have to be honest, but if the defense, you know, if for some ungodly fucked up reason the man who assaulted your little girl was to call you as a witness, well hell, you have an open book, you can say anything you want and no one can perjure you. You, Ms. Bailey, have a license to lie your ass off in a court of law and no one can touch you.

But then Ms. Bailey, there you are on the stand, and no one ever mentions, not one question at all about the day of the events. No one asks you hey, what was Brandi's state when she came home? What happened? Hey, tell us again about $30 each for cleaning, and MR. DENNIS, don't you think it a bit odd you ask Caldwell how did Brandi's mom get to the scene? Well fuck, now we will never know. You know Mr. Dennis, Ms. Bailey wanted to know all about how Brandi's mom got to the scene. Hell, could have been a game changer but you never asked, "Brandi's mother."

Do you now have a very goddamned clear image of what is going on on page 30? The defense conspired to call the prosecutor's witness to discredit the two redacted statements.

Now everyone, even you Ms. Bailey, can read from page 30 up to page 37 and there is not one question about July 9, 2012. The entire process or the entire bullshit, which was practiced out in the hallway, is on page 35. But again, let me help out Ms. Bailey here. The prosecutor, if you follow these events, see he wants to impose the lie that the little sweetheart, Brandi, was being beaten by an evil stepdad with a belt and "JUST ONCE" the little angel said if he didn't stop, she would holler rape. That was the sole purpose of putting Brandi's mother on the stand, so she could perjure that line on page 35, and no one could bust her for lying under oath except—she was not my witness.

Hey, I got two statements as evidence. I know, let's call a witness to discredit my only evidence. WOW, what a great fucking idea!

Now me, I would call this little scenario ineffective counsel. He literally discredited my ONLY evidence on purpose. The ONLY questions asked were about the probation report so that was in fact the only goal. Would you agree with that assessment, Ms. Bailey? Your son's lawyer just discredited the only evidence your son had, that okay with you? Do you, Ms. Bailey, find it just a little odd that your daughter, your little girl came in all fucked up on July 9, 2012 and yet no one asks, at all?

Okay, I do believe I proved my point on that score. The prosecutor's witness committed perjury but it's okay, it's only a witch trial put on by a lynch mob. Then the next so-called witness comes up and this is even more hilarious. Keep in mind here folks we had Greg Layne who had a completely open door to lie about sunglasses, lie about some random Goodwill clothes, yep, he had an open door to lie away.

Then they call Darlene Bradley and say here, you can only speak what we highlighted. Hell, here, let's write down your testimony and/or hey, we will testify, and you just nod. She is only allowed to speak about the two redacted statements. I here have to say again, first Brandi's mom then my—gagged—witness. I may not like the result, but I do love watching the pure manipulations. I love it when every single witness for the prosecution can blatantly lie but a witness for the defense, here is ALL you are allowed to say.

"This Way to the Great Egress!"

HOWEVER! (he used as an exclamation)

Ladies and gentlemen, children over 18, please lend me your ears. At this point in our little tale of woe once more it's time to pull another little rabbit out of the hat. Uh, it's a big damn rabbit so it will take a few years, but let's say on page 45 we can see the tips of the rabbit's ears.

Q. "And Brandi denied that anyone had EVER sexually molested her?"

A. "She denied it, right."

That was actually done in June 2012, so yes, it was before me but MS. BAILEY, would you mark this page for future reference?

There is one rather funny thing about Darlene Bradley but only if it's put into proper perspective. It must be remembered that this is not a random report, this report was created to be turned over to probation that the Commonwealth would use to roast Brandi like a pig if needed to be used against her. But when the report don't work in another trial the Commonwealth, who would not hesitate to lock Brandi in detention, then claims on page 44 well, she's an angel, the mother is just difficult. Now excuse me there Mr. Lee, no one lands on double probation or gets thrown in juvenile detention for having a difficult mom.

Q: "And when you talked to Brandi she denied that anyone had ever sexually assaulted her?"
A. "Correct!"
Q. "And Brandi denied that anyone had ever sexually assaulted her."
A. "She denied it."

Keep in mind here on page 45 that that is prosecutor Lee who's asking the questions. "Oh, what a tangled web we compile when we attempt a jury trial." I know, Ms. Bailey, you don't have a damn clue what I'm doing, huh? That is the point—YOU DON'T KNOW.

Well hello Jim Terry Shortt. Man, it's been a while. Why, I haven't seen you since that time you, the defense attorney, went to create some brand new evidence to help convict me, the defendant. Good times, huh? Page 48 we have Jim Shortt, creator of the house cleaning propaganda that is still hearsay which last I heard was not even evidence but hell who cares, it's only a witch on trial eh, Ms. Bailey?

Oh God!

When Jim Shortt visited in 2014, he had a video of Brandi Lee Shortt that he was there to show me how consistent she was, so I better take a plea deal. When that video started, I was laughing, and he did not know why. HE, my defense attorney, had not read the criminal complaint. He had no fucking clue that Brandi said shirt and bra removed. For the first time in two years he read the police report—in 2014. But on page 53, oh, he spent time reviewing those.

I would first like to direct everyone's attention to a couple of little facts here. First, no accident, Jim Shortt bypasses both Corner Mart and the bank.

See, shit like this drives me crazy. Jim Shortt sits there saying Brandi told him that I drove her from the high school to the Wal-Mart. NO. Brandi said I drove (in this goddamn version) to the high school then forced her to drive to Wal-Mart. I don't mind a fucking lie, but goddamn it, people, can we all get on the same goddamn page—FUCKING PLEASE! At least try to get all the lies in one ballpark.

How about this Ms. Bailey, we are obviously having a multidimensional overlap. Me one, me, and me three. Y'all put the wrong me in prison.

A piece of rock, a chimney? Fuck, would someone please go see what the bloody hell they keep talking about? I mean, I've heard it a hundred times, no fucking clue what it is, what it means or where it fits into this story. I do not even have pictures of the rock so this must be some more of that specter evidence—irrelevant, but it's a rock.

Wow! "Buck-a-roo blows it," (Ready Player One)

Uh, Jim Shortt, YOU fucked up. On page 56 you said, "police report." Did you not get the memo? We do not use the words police report in this trial. The police report is hidden from the jury, so we call it a little statement Brandi wrote down or call it a report but do not say police report. We are keeping the "shirt and bra removed" under wraps.

I FUCKING LOVE IT!

On page 60 the prosecutor is now objecting to the police report. The report in his words he would object to "A DEFENSE WITNESS" would refer to when he had not one, not two, but four witnesses refer to! And can anything be more ironic than a prosecutor objecting to a report—A POLICE REPORT—the report that was the basis for every criminal charge I am charged with, a report that lists ALL of his so-called evidence that he put me on trial for. I propose if we threw out that report HE had NO grounds for arrest, no evidence, and the charges were brought without probable cause. Word up you son of a bitch, I am on trial. That report was entered the minute I walked in.

And this is just wrong on so many levels, the prosecutor is now saying that the police report he turned over to Jim Shortt to defend me against what was in that report he now objects to. Wow!

Now Ms. Bailey, I am sorry, if you read from page 60 up to page 63 there is a huge argument that I am sure most of which made no sense. I would have solved the whole damn mess by just giving the jury 12 copies of the police report and 12 copies of the Jim Shortt transcript and said here, read it. At least now it's in the book. From 2015 to 2022 you, a juror, never read those so I printed them.

If you read through those pages Ms. Bailey, you will see a hell of a lot of "-" or "--" marks. Half of what was said was removed so it's chopped all to hell.

Now, everyone please help me out on this one. When you have a jury trial you subpoena a witness which is a paper that compels a person to appear in court. WHY? What is the one job, what is the reason to have a witness in court at a trial?

Mr. Lee: And I will object to his testifying without being requested.

Uh-huh! Your honor I'd like to subpoena this witness, not to testify or anything, he is going to hang around for no reason at all. If anyone subpoenas a witness would that not constitute a request to testify, or did I miss the point of the whole subpoena thing?

I will object to A WITNESS testifying without being requested to do so. Uh, Ms. Bailey, do you understand that one up there on the jury and all? How does one object to a witness testifying without being requested? Damn, at least with Darlene, they let her testify, told her what to say, but allowed her to say it.

On page 63 the court says:

"Not give the—well—"

"And I agree obviously Mr. Dennis, we've got the situation where we are now, not give the—well—"

You don't have a clue what's going on, do you Ms. Bailey? Again, need some help?

Mr. Blankenship began to take his clothes off.

He kept taking his clothes off.

He was fully nude.

Mr. Blankenship had taken his clothes off.

He took all of his clothes off.

He was fully nude.

He was fully nude.

He was still fully nude.

Ah, yep, that was hammered away at over and over and over. Now correct me if I'm wrong, but Jim Shortt was asked to point out the inconsistencies. So, Ms. Bailey, before you picked this book up could you tell me even one inconsistency? I mean, if you read this, don't you believe the actual inconsistencies should have been stated, you only heard, "appears to contradict," but you never heard, "contradicts what?"

A girl, Ms. Bailey, says your son drove her to a secluded area, he tore off a shirt and bra. But then she says, "No, none of my clothes were ever removed." In trial a jury never hears shirt and bra removed, and no clothes removed was barely mentioned at all, but your son's so-called defense attorney repeats eight times he was nude!

Oh Ms. Bailey, you may like this part. There is an exhibit number 24. Now, do keep in mind "WHAT IS EVIDENCE."

Relevant evidence means evidence having any tendency to make the existence of any fact at issue more probable or less probable than it would be without the evidence.

You do realize the fact at issue here is abduction, attempted rape, Actual Inncocence, contributing and assault. Now, the prosecutor moves to enter a list of names from a detention center from 2014, May of 2014, that absolutely has no ties to any aspect of my trial. Evidence to be relevant must in some way be connected to one of the crimes that are on trial.

Now, if Jim Shortt came out and he was on trial where he said he never visited that detention center, then the prosecutor would have grounds to enter a list which would prove he was there. Jim Shortt is not on trial, I who am on trial was never at that detention center and Jim Shortt not only said he was there he also has a dated transcript, so why are we entering fabricated evidence that violates every rule of evidence there is? It means nothing, it does not prove any fact at issue.

Do you see Ms. Bailey, when you asked didn't the defense have to enter evidence, a better question may be, would you know what evidence is no matter who presents it?

And, Ms. Bailey, do you recall that list? Did you notice that Brandi Lee Shortt is listed four times in a row but it's the visitors they blacked out, not the people in detention? They left Jim Shortt but they blocked out Lee, Caldwell and the witness coach that were all present when the video was made.

Uh! Isn't my lawyer supposed to, oh, enter evidence that would be exculpatory? I mean, here I have a police report in my hand that says shirt and bra removed, but I also have a report in my hand that says no clothes ever, at all, removed. Then the witness completely revamped a story for trial to a third version. But we do not enter those so they would be exhibits in the jury room. Then the same attorney who somehow has no fucking clue what rule 2:401, 2:402 or 2:403 is, he does not object to even one piece of irrelevant evidence. My attorney was ineffective counsel with extreme prejudice.

Now Ms. Bailey, on page 71 you just heard the prosecutor make a motion to enter a list that is irrelevant but then hey, this motion at a jury trial must be done without a jury. You know, like the witness the day before.

This part is so goddamn funny it is posted online, and it had a fan following. It's actually one of the things I was accused of making up because it's so ludicrous. You may not understand just how damn funny this is Ms. Bailey, but you will.

Now Ms. Bailey, I am sure when you were young you never landed in juvenile detention. Well, neither did I, but I did have friends who near lived there. This is not a convent or an orphanage, this is a prison for juvenile criminals. Nor do you get there by having a disorderly conduct. On page 72 the prosecutor tries to play this like oh, we have a pure of heart little angel who is in a traumatizing environment where a scary lawyer dragged her off to a room in a coercive environment with officers with guns, things of that nature.

In other words, the prosecutor who locks people up in the detention where on a daily basis they are visited by lawyers is somehow now a system shock. Bullshit. If Brandi was in detention seeing a lawyer in a room with cops and guns around it's probably any given Tuesday. She was well aware, and bored, by the drill. I doubt if any lawyer visit even upset her lunch because long before one gets to juvenile detention she is well aware of the process—Brandi more than most. The only funny part is, he put Brandi in the so-called coercive environment he is now trying to discredit. He locks people in detention where they see attorneys under the conditions he created, but now says they are coercive. Uh, it's supposed to be scary. It's prison for criminals, not little sweethearts. Hell, she probably had a few hundred lawyer visits by that point.

Does everyone else see the irony here? He locks people up in a jail to talk to a lawyer but talking to a lawyer there is coercive. Well, I was in a coercive situation about a thousand times. In other words, the prosecutor is objecting to a person in prison talking to a lawyer. Uh, yeah!

Okay, y'all can read all the Jim Shortt crap if y'all want to. It came down to yes, we can present a picture of some clothes from Goodwill but we cannot see a real video of a witness lying her ass off.

"How much FUCKING STUPID can you cram in a two-pound sack."

Then Ms. Bailey, here we have a huge glitch that, thanks to lying bitch Carla J. Faletti, I cannot resolve, sorry. If we look on page 99 at the top of the page Mr. Lee and Mr. Dennis go into secret conference, then they call a side bar. What's going on, Ms. Bailey? Then all of a sudden at 10:54 to 10:55 they boot the jury and me out of the room from 10:55 to 11:05. What happened? The court pops up and says, "Alright, we are ready to go forward." Where did Letson go?

Here we go again. Do you remember the probation report, Ms. Bailey? You know, the two redacted statements the court gave your son, his only evidence now, Ms. Bailey. When that jury goes into deliberations, they will have not one but two statements where the girl who lied on your son had threatened to lie about sexual assault, even rape. Do you Ms. Bailey, think boy, if a jury had those, they might consider your innocent child innocent? Shouldn't "evidence" be up to the jury to decide on? Those statements may save your child's life. Nope. When the defense tries to enter the one and only lifeline your child has, on pages 100-01 they are blocked. So, we can enter a completely irrelevant picture of clothes from Goodwill but a statement where the witness threatened to lie about actual rape—we can't have that.

Now Ms. Bailey, you get to see the beauty of a defense acting as a prosecutor. Unless you slow it down you will miss it.

"It wasn't substantive evidence. It only went to the credibility of the witness and THEN IMPEACHED BY THAT TESTIMONY." (Brandi's mother.)

What a good word. Substantive. Now Ms. Bailey, if your child were on trial falsely accused, would you consider a picture of clothes form Goodwill more important than a statement where the girl threatened to lie about rape? Which would YOU want the jury to have? But when you read that it proves my point. The defense conspired to call the prosecutor's witness for the sole purpose of removing those statements from ever reaching the jury room.

That was bad. Just think Ms. Bailey, your son's defense attorney just cut your son's only hope to help convict him. But then another of my absolute favorite things happened. Not my favorite, but this is in the top five for real.

Damn I missed one on page 102. I hate stupid shit. You do realize Ms. Bailey, that you just sat there watching a whole goddamn section where Jim Shortt went through the video transcript. Yet somehow the so-called lawyer does not move to enter the transcript, he moves to enter the DVD which in May 2016 is then altered to CD. Of course, it's not admitted because it was Brandi's second lie.

Then we come to my favorite section. Well, maybe my third favorite. I can tell you Ms. Bailey, what you are about to read set off a bad argument at Sally's house, it was damn near a war. At Sally's there was a 3-2 split because three people said no way in hell did this ever happen in any court of law—ever. It is so improbable that no sane person would believe it, but it happened. It is a damn shame you missed it Ms. Bailey, but as you were on the jury you missed half the trial, and you missed two-thirds of the actual evidence.

I am not going to make any crazy claims here, just a very simple one. Look in Documents at my bank statement. By all means go to TruPoint and confirm that it is "a bank statement" if anyone don't know what a bank statement is. It has "Statement Period" on top of every page, and it has cancelled checks with my name signed by me. When we all—ALL—agree that is in fact a bank statement, then we can move on.

On page 103, can I just say or interject here—NOT ONE GOD-DAMN PERSON AT MY TRIAL SAID "BANK RECORDS!" Did you get that, lying bitch Carla J. Faletti? Hey Carla, got that transcript yet?

My so-called defense attorney moved to enter my bank statement because it proved, proves, Brandi Lee Shortt did not drive to the bank in Richlands. We never went to that bank, so the picture of the bank in Richlands was purely fabricated false evidence, irrelevant and in violation of every rule of evidence. I do believe perjury, the willful telling of a lie while under lawful oath, is illegal. Y'all know, like he stole sunglasses.

Ah-ha! My bank statement terrified the prosecutor and I wish they would have left this part alone in the transcript, it was hilarious. The prosecutor objected. He doubted the AUTHENTICITY—WOW! Just FUCKING WOW! He is a man who just entered a picture of random clothes, NOT CLOTHES, the picture of random clothes from Goodwill. No name, no property sheet, not even a bag, just random clothes and yet here is a bank statement with cancelled checks and the prosecutor posted up on a huge screen the Corner Mart receipt, Name, date, time, debit card use, location and amount area all reflected in the bank statement, the 2 documents were mutually authenticating.

The authentic ploy failed so he then objected by saying, "items were missing."

Now by god that is fucking phenomenal, exceptionally amazing, STU-fucking-PENDOUS! Here is a man, nay, here is a God-like being so in tune with the space-time cosmic universe he can pick up not just a three-year-old bank statement but also a final bank statement, printed over three years later, and at a single glance with powers of observational perception that would give Sherlock Holmes a hard-on he instantly knows every single expenditure three years ago in a minute time frame from June 18, 2012 to July 15, 2012 and declares that items bought are missing. Fucking WOW! A round of applause, no, a standing ovation, please!

Anyone, anyone at all, take any three-, five-, 20-year-old bank statement up to Dennis Lee and in under 10 seconds he will examine the correctness. Did the bank fuck up five years ago? Here is THE MAN-GOD of bank statements on planet Earth. May we bow in awe. Hey Ms. Bailey, you will not see that shit on TV. Damn shame you missed it in real life. STRIKE TWO!

Now I might concede that current purchases may not reflect on a current statement, but statement period June 18, 2012 to July 15, 2012 and final then printed July 21, 2015, I am guessing if it ain't cleared in three years it ain't going to, UNLESS TruPoint Bank hired J. Ray Smith who does take three years on paperwork.

That ploy did not work so then the prosecutor in a last gambit said, "I don't know what a bank statement is," and the judge ruled: page 104.

Court: "Without agreement as to what type of record it is I do not think it would be admissible."

Now we can have a picture of random clothes with no idea what Goodwill they got them from, but we can't use my bank statement because a sitting court judge "does not know what a bank statement is!" If I told someone I am in prison because three grown men, one of which is a judge, did not know what a bank statement is, they would call me a liar. (Believe me, I know.) But it's in the transcript, when the Judge said, "without agreement," he is in fact saying, "I don't know what a bank statement is either."

Can you, for one damn second Ms. Bailey, imagine that your child is on trial falsely accused facing life plus 22 years. Your bank statement proves your son innocent, and the judge tells you that you cannot use a bank statement because HE don't know what a bank statement is. When your son is chained and taken to prison for life you go home with a bank statement. You sit for 10 years, know the girl lied about the bank, she lied about Ray Road. Your child rots in prison because a judge had no idea what a bank statement is. And the jurors who sentenced your child to life had no clue that a bank statement ever existed at your child's trial.

And that ladies and gentlemen you for goddamned sure will not see on ye olde "Law and Order." We will put this topic on hold for a bit, but it comes up again later. Even I, the Majestic Robert Mckinley Blankenship, do make mistakes but some of my mistakes are just damn lucky.

Here again I do hate to be overly persnickety but can someone please put page 104 in front of lying bitch Carla J. Faletti and ask her why was that objection, for the record, not noticed or fixed. By that I mean what the judge said was:

Court: "This is just purely a matter for the appellate court."

Dennis: "Yes, that's fine."

Does everyone see the difference on page 104:

"This is just purely—yes that's fine."

The transcript had been reworked four times at this point, so shit got fucked up as they say. And NO, I am not unjustly picking on Carla J. Faletti. That mess was 100 percent ALL HER FAULT!

I personally feel it's bad to be fucked over. "He stole sunglasses," "I don't know what a bank statement is," "got a photo of Goodwill clothes," "GUILTY AS HELL!" But it's worse when they go ahead and set up future fuck overs also.

On page 105 I am not even going to try to explain the mess with my aunt Mary, but I would ask everyone to note one line at the bottom of 105:

"Mr. Blankenship may be a victim in a later case where SOMEONE has stolen his wallet."

Oh, I'm sorry, Ms. Bailey was out of the room for all this hoop-to-do. Did you know Ms. Bailey, that my wallet was stolen? Everyone knew except the jury in a jury trial. Again, two-thirds of a jury trial had no jury. But it's very important to remember that line for later. Are we still in the dark there Ms. Bailey? Do YOU still want to know about the defendant showing evidence? I got bunches I'd love to show—NOT ALLOWED!

Here we have one of the worse arguments or maybe one of the stupidest arguments that went on at Sally's. Some parts I could explain back then and some were under wraps—some I did not know. Did you Ms. Bailey, wonder why I chose not to testify? Sally and friends were all sided against me. If I had the WHOLE transcript, this would make sense. My lawyer moved to enter the police report, it was blocked. My lawyer moved to enter the Jim Shortt transcript, blocked. The Virginia summons, blocked. The jail property sheet, blocked. Every single thing I could say was blocked. Do you know why Ms. Bailey?

Well Ms. Bailey, let me ask you this. You or your child were charged with the shoplifting of sunglasses. You went to trial almost three years ago and were found innocent. Then you sit there, and a prosecutor and multiple witnesses blatantly lie about the sunglasses you, your child, stole and do you: A) Jump up and proclaim NO, I did not steal any damn sunglasses, or B) Do you maintain ass-clenching composure and never once say a word? Then why not testify and say hey, I did not steal sunglasses? Because if you did Ms. Bailey, you would look like a babbling idiot, and it would be worse for you.

You, Ms. Bailey, may not be aware even now. If you reflect back to the motions the day before and the morning of my trial, when they moved to enter the prior conviction the statute states that the prosecutor can tell you, the jury, the charge (Actual Inncocence), the date (1999), and the place (Hickory, North Carolina). However, we have where the prosecutor claimed he would not use the police report and the judge ruled he would not allow the use of the police report. That was bullshit and you know it Ms. Bailey, don't you? There is a little stipulation that if I testify it's considered "opening a door." That means the prosecutor could move to enter the police report from 16 years ago and you Ms. Bailey, can bet your ass Mr. Judge would allow it. But that is only side A in the equation.

I am not allowed to mention the plea deal from 2013. I am not allowed to mention bank statement, shoplifting, clothing list, Ms. Maynard leaving, the statements from the probation report. Hell, the list of shit I could not say was longer than all the evidence lists combined.

It is true that the Sixth Amendment and the Virginia Code 19.2-256 does protect the right for anyone charged with a felony to be present during all phases of the trial from arraignment to sentencing. But should a defendant's actions be adverse, haranguing or erratic, a person can be ejected from the room—and tried in his absence.

Do you Ms. Bailey, have any goddamn idea what it took to sit there and hear over and over and over that I stole a junk-ass pair of sunglasses when I held the goddamn summons in my hand that proved me innocent, but I could not use that summons without the son of a bitch Letson, who was on lockdown as co-counsel? To see a person put up a random photo and claim, "look what he stole," to hear a prosecutor say, "oh look at the grooming by stealing sunglasses," to be stabbed over and over and over with the same blade? And I never, not once, flinched.

As long as I never spoke, the use of the police report from 1997 would be double jeopardy; and, I would be ejected, tried in my absence.

But this is rather ironic. Should I testify, I cannot mention a plea deal on the current charges from just two years ago, but I can talk about a plea deal from 16 years ago. I am not allowed to mention the police report from July 9, 2012, the day of my arrest on current charges, but I can talk about a police report from 16 years ago. And, if I so much as say one word on any topic including shoplifting, I will be ejected, the old police report entered, and an open floor to say whatever they wanted.

How many prosecutors does it take to screw in a lightbulb? I don't know, but it took five prosecutors to fuck a Robert.

Oh, by the way, the recording that was supposed to discredit Sarah Hale, the secret fabricated phone recording never mentioned in the motion for discovery, was pulled on page six. No objection, of course, and my lawyer is threatening me with it. I do believe we have ineffective counsel again.

Here we have a whole bunch of hoop-to-do bullshit. I would note Menefee on page 128. "She didn't ask him to steal those sunglasses." Well, there you go, she didn't ask, I didn't steal them, so the rest is bullshit.

I do believe one of my favorite lines is on page 161 which is about as messed up as it gets. The prosecutor Lee now says:

"One way you can tell when a person is lying is when they tell the same story again and again..."

Well hell, that would make Brandi Lee Short the most honest person in America. She has never told the same story twice in a row, even when testifying.

Now, I do admit that yes, on some details, what color were Brandi's shoes, I do not know. What did Brandi say going to Corner Mart? I don't know. But there is no way in hell a young girl was driven to a secluded location where her shirt and bra were ripped off in front of a man outside. Then Brandi says why no, none of my clothes were ever removed. Nor would any woman or girl be slammed to the ground with a naked man on top of her that she would confuse that with he only removed my shirt. Brandi is a lying insult to any woman who was ever sexually assaulted.

Now Ms. Bailey, would you please refer to page 174 where the prosecutor says, "The Wal-Mart video matches up." There is NO Wal-Mart video. NO video was ever shown or allowed. In fact, we have a missing Wal-Mart video, where did it go?

Page 174-75 we have beer cans, so that is corroborated. Uh, well, it would seem gee, those are missing too. We have "specter" beer cans that magically stay cold for over five hours outside in July. "The conceit of specter evidence allowed many to be convicted."

Oh my, my, my, my, the best laid plans of mice and prosecutors, gotta watch that ego, it will bite you in the ass.

I did grow up with three younger brothers and I know for a fact there is nothing more fun, or more annoying, than the game of, "I know something you don't know," and we just HAVE to kick in a little hint to show off our superior knowledge. Yep, we just can't help but rub it in a little. On page 176:

"He told me was going to rape me, HE TOLD ME HE WAS GOING TO KILL ME…"

What a most curious choice of words there Mr. Lee. Oh, you are correct, it would be a better lie indeed. Gee, I wonder if maybe she already used that one before and YOU Mr. Lee knew something we don't. Maybe someone forgot to mention—maybe.

Hey Ms. Bailey, you are on point here. Did you know in the jury room you Ms. Bailey, would have access to the exhibits? Well, not ALL the exhibits, you would have access to the prosecutor's exhibits YOU the jury are allowed to see. You will NOT Ms. Bailey, have access to ALL the exhibits. WE ARE NOT having a FAIR trial here. This is a lynching. Did you Ms. Bailey, bring your torch and matches? Burning the witch is awesome when YOU put the torch on the fire.

Okay, I have mentioned this a few times. We are now damn close to my absolute number one favorite moment in my trial, 32 years in prison was worth it for this one little moment in time.

There is extremely good and there is extremely bad. Above every other item in my trial this is where the biggest animosity towards the lying bitch Carla J. Faletti comes from. This part of my transcript is more fucked up than all others.

The jury went into the jury room into deliberations at 2:18 p.m. but even though the transcript does not reflect it, the jury came out at 2:58 p.m. First, they asked for a trial transcript.

Wow, let's see, it took me until May 2016 to get most of it, but I got three more pages in 2017 and in 2022 I have an altered transcript so yeah, good luck with that in 40 minutes. Nope, no transcript for you, until now.

LET THE FUCKING SHIT STORM COMMENCE!

I am not going to ruin the surprise at this point but just so we are all clear, Exhibit One is the prior conviction from North Carolina instead of the Final Order. The page with the charge date and place the prosecutor entered the entire plea deal, but in this instance the prosecutor's own corruption bit him in the ass. Now Ms. Bailey, a plea deal, which you can see Plea Agreement 2-11-2013 (the one I can't mention) in Documents is a series of questions. You will note Ms. Bailey, that the one I provided is very clear and legible. The one provided to the jury is a fucking ink blot. The plea deal is in a series of illegible ink smears. To keep it simple, the prosecutor provided a document no one could read. His intention was to provide a long document that of course everyone would think, wow, look at all these "details" when it does not have any of the details at all. But there is nothing more exciting than a game just missed or more damning a document than one no one can read. Kind of leaves what's there up to the imagination. So, the jury comes out and they say, "Hey, we can't read this damn thing, got a better copy?" which of course he don't because he ink blotted that one just so it can't be read. "Somewhat FUZZY!" Uh, no, it's an ink blot.

"Now Ms. Bailey, what do you see in this ink blot Rorschach Test?"

"I see Robert is fucked!"

"You passed!"

2:58 to 3:00 p.m. then the jury is back in deliberations. Nope, 3:24 p.m. the jury is right back out again. For those who are bad at math that is 40 + 24 = 64 minutes. Hey Ms. Bailey, you ever hear of rule 2:403? That rule states that relevant evidence may be excluded if it has the likelihood of confusing, misleading or is prejudiced. What the fucking hell could be more confusing or misleading than a paper no one can read?

Now Ms. Bailey, you tell me, here is a police report that says your son took a girl to a secluded location where he "only ripped her shirt and bra off." Here you have a report that the same girl says no, none of my clothes were ever removed. You have a report that says the same girl said no, she was thrown down and a naked man was on top of her. No, that didn't happen at all, he only removed her shirt. And here you have a pile of ink blotted, 16-year-old papers that no one can read. Now honestly

Ms. Bailey, which of these would YOU like the jury to spend the whole goddamn first hour of deliberations studying?

At 3:24 the jury is back out and now ladies and gentlemen we are at the very edge of my absolute favorite moment of my trial. Once again, twice in the whole first hour, the jury comes out to say they would like a magnifying glass in an attempt to read the ink blot provided to them. The jury for the whole first hour has now been reading a 16-year-old plea deal THEY CAN'T READ.

All y'all ready for this?

When the jury came out to request a magnifying glass, they literally held 12 copies of the plea deal, but then they said the only part of that report they could read was the police report!

Poor Ms. Bailey. Now if Ms. Bailey reads this book, she will now know you, a juror, was not supposed to have that report. Plea deal, okay. Police report, double jeopardy. The prosecutor thought he would be slick. He can't legally use the police report, so let's make 14 copies, slip them into the jury room, then after conviction destroy copies. No one would know. Had the dumbass provided a clean, legible plea deal it would have worked. But nope, he wanted to give all the ink blotted pages to make all the boring questions seem like a huge report, so his own corruption did bite him in the ass.

Does anyone know a Mr. T.M. Whisnant? He is a cop in Hickory, North Carolina. Well, if so, they may want to pass this book along--he will not be happy. It was Mr. Whisnant who wrote said police report. That would be the goddamn North Carolina police report I mentioned a few times in the "Police Report Blues" chapter. It was Mr. Whisnant who told Sally that an act of God would not unseal that police report, and no one would ever read it. Well, it would seem God has not met Mr. Dennis Lee, prosecutor.

When the jury said all they could read was the police report, on a whim I asked Mike Dennis for a copy, which he took from a juror and he handed it to me.

And the world fucking stopped.

You did read, did you not Ms. Bailey, that the prosecutor said he would not use that? You did read the court would not allow it, and yet Ms. Bailey, there you sit with it in your hands. And even worse Ms. Bailey, you are fucking clueless. Do you even know why that record was sealed? Well, it's to protect the victim. If your little girl is molested that record is sealed to protect your little girl. Did you know Ms. Bailey, that nine serial killers and over 75 child rapists have served multiple times on jury duty and here we have a prosecutor who just handed your little girl's information to 13 random people? A jury is not righteous by divine right. Any one of them could be a hardcore killer and the prosecutor just handed your little girl to him. Now he can leave the courtroom—to hunt. Did you know Ms. Bailey, Jeffrey Dahmer served on four juries. Heard of him, have you? If throwing your child to a serial killer would win the prosecutor's case, he would not, he did not, hesitate to do so.

For three years I was married to Sally. For three goddamn years I got to hear over and over and over, "Well, what does the police report say?" For three years. I had to put with HER little superiority complex beating me with the North Carolina police report whip. Three years I was slammed with, "What does the police report say?" repeatedly. And for three LONG years I tried every humanly way known to man to lay my hands on that report to no avail. I even damn near begged a man just to read Sally what it says—no names—but it was a brick wall.

Yo, Sally, when I get out, bend over, bitch. YOUR ass is getting a tattoo, literally! Sally's ass is not that big and it's a large report so, yep, her ass gonna be sore. I HAD THE NORTH CAROLINA POLICE REPORT! I HAD IT IN MY HAND!

On the inside I was doing the happy dance of sheer joy. Sally was just two seats behind me. Oh, I did so want to put that goddamn report in her face, I did not even look at Sally. I sat there in a Zen of calm that would put Buddha to shame and I very, very casually slid that under my papers. Yep, nothing to see here, I am just taking some notes. NO ONE at this table has any papers. They are the ONE thing on the planet we are not supposed to have.

Use of said police report was double jeopardy. Now, we could ask Ms. Bailey to come forward but she can't. Those who stand for or by the accused do but condemn themselves, and it's okay Ms. Bailey. No one will stand for your child either when they are falsely convicted.

Now, way, way back in time I did say I burned Sally's ass on all points. I do admit, 32 years in prison to win an argument may be a bit over the top, but I WON! IN YOUR FACE, SALLY!

You do now realize Ms. Bailey, that the United States Constitution says you, me, your children cannot be tried for the same crime twice. You had the police report, so it was double jeopardy. Either you stand for the

Constitution, or you stand for nothing. Witches do not have Constitutional rights. Pray your child is not the next witch.

Of course, you do realize Ms. Bailey, that you as a juror at a jury trial do not have the police report from the day the incident happened just three years ago. You know, the police report to go with the charges that the person is on trial for where YOU are the jury. But you do, somehow, have a 16-year-old police report. Now, just exactly what did you read from 16 years ago that absolutely proved to you a crime was committed—16 years later. Or was it the imaginary beer cans or the pictures of clothes from Goodwill or was it the NOT stolen sunglasses? Just curious, feel free to drop me a letter sometime. I assure you I hold no ill feelings, you had no choice.

I do believe it's a goddamn insult that my so-called lawyer does not object to the police report-double jeopardy, but he does object to the magnifying glass used to commit double jeopardy. Well, WHY the hell NOT.

Then we finally wind down to the name of my book. I have said a million times, Sally said a million and seven, what does Actual Inncocence mean?

"Albeit the business of witchcraft be very much upon the stage of imagination."

"Albeit the business of Actual Inncocence be very much upon the stage of imagination."

If evidence that confuses a jury cannot be used, what about a criminal charge?

Page 184 the jury requests a written definition to ONLY one of my charges, Actual Inncocence. So, they had no trouble understanding what the accused was supposed to have done until it came to that charge that NOT one out of 12 people had a damn clue what it meant.

"Indecent exposure with lascivious intent."

Wow! Yeah, that cleared that right up. So, it's exposing something like an ankle that some consider indecent, and they might do something later.

You do realize Carla J. Faletti, that had your lying bitch-ass fixed my transcript, you would have heard the jury had the police report and your lying bitch-ass would have FIXED THE GODDAMN TIME!

Okay I'm back--sorry.

There is a major glitch or "let's do the time warp again" thing coming. Life can be strange.

As those who have read this far may know, I do love Monty Python. In the movie, "The Life of Brian," there is a spot in the movie where an old man is chained to a prison wall and he is yelling, "You lucky bastards, you lucky, lucky bastards," at people going to be crucified. The other day I saw on TV a man was found guilty after the jury deliberated for a whopping two days, and another man was found guilty after four whole days of deliberations. Lucky bastards, indeed. My jury was allowed one hour to get it done. This is hard to explain but from 2:18 to 3:40 with two interruptions the jury has been in deliberations—sort of. And never forget for the whole past hour the jury has been stuck trying to read a 16-year-old ink blot plea deal.

At—you will not read this—at 3:30 the judge sent the prosecutor to poll the jury to see if they convicted me yet.

Then we can look at page 185 where:

"Well actually, basically they've come to a conclusion on three charges they cannot—two charges they agreed on, and three they cannot, and they said they are not in agreement. I guess WE can do one of two things. WE can bring them in and determine—I can do the Allen Charge!"

It's the background you Ms. Bailey, don't see, or what YOU didn't know. The reason the judge sent the prosecutor ("we") to the jury room was because if you tried to say not guilty, the judge was going to call a mistrial before you came out, but since you, the jury, had not decided he chose the "attack the jury" ploy. But that is not a shock. What is a shock is look at WHO came to my defense, the GODDAMN FEMALE PROSECUTOR! Where is my (one of my) lawyers? Why is the only person in the room who is speaking up for me the prosecutor who is trying to put me away?

Or, how fucked up is the corruption when even the one honest prosecutor says whoa, that's messed up, but even she cannot be honest.

Menefee: "Yes. I mean, they've only been at it two hours. That's not…"

Goddamn lying bitch Carla J. Faletti, do you see that? "That's not…," what? All your fault. She said it was not justifiable legally. The jury was not gridlocked they were polled, that's why the court came back with, "Yes, I mean, you know, we'll go on the record…" Then Menefee has to go to the jury room to get Lee. She does not send Brandon to get him. Now this is not easy to spot, but it's funny as hell once it's seen. Do not blink! At this point this is what we have:

Court out   Court in   Minutes

2:18	2:58	40
3:00	3:24	24
3:26	3:40	14

We have a total of 78 minutes. Now in my world 60 minutes is an hour, so I count one hour then 18 minutes. But in Menefee's world 39 minutes is an hour. But Menefee raised an objection. The prosecutor defended me, the accused. I don't know if they did one on "Law and Order" or not.

2:18 court in recess
2:58 court reconvened
3:00 court in recess
3:24 court reconvened
3:26 court in recess
3:40 court reconvened
4:41 jury in (no recess)

Uh, yeah. Look on page 185, the court reconvened at 3:40 p.m. There is maybe two minutes of talk on page 185, but on page 186 we go from Menefee saying, call him please are we ready—BAM it's a one-hour jump from 3:40 to 4:41. That would mean that the court sat there a whole hour with no recess doing nothing, saying nothing.

Carla J. Faletti, I do not hate you, but I'd be happy—or not so rude—if you'd fix the transcript. This little screw-up threw off the whole timeline, bad. It was so bad it confused the court reporter.

Legally I would like to propose the argument that a jury in deliberation is a stand-alone entity. A trial by jury means a trial decided by a jury, period! When a jury is in deliberations and a judge pulls a jury, he in fact changes the location of the deliberations, he does not change the fact that the jury is still in deliberations. He is neither adding nor detracting any evidence of a "fact at issue." He is in fact now joining in those deliberations. It is no longer a trial by jury, it is a trial by a jury and a judge. When one joins a jury in deliberations the words spoken are irrelevant next to the fact that now a judge has joined, and is saying any words to, a jury in deliberations, thus he joined deliberations. When we allow any corruption to invade what is a Constitutional right, we no longer have a Constitution. Trial by jury should mean trial by jury. How long before a jury is allowed five-minute deliberation or no deliberation at all? How long until there is no jury? The Allen Charge is pure jury tampering in every sense of the word.

Tamper: to interfere with

Jury: a group of people who hear evidence in a law case and give a decision

"Substantive (actual) due process: bars certain arbitrary wrongful actions of government regardless of the rules or procedures used to implement them: Zimmerman v. Burch."

The jury had heard all the allowed evidence, they were in deliberation, they were deciding a verdict, a judge removed them from a jury room—he tampered.

The last time I checked, the Judicial Branch that includes all courts is a branch of government.

Arbitrary: not fixed by rules, left to one's judgment or choice.

So, the Allen Charge is an arbitrary action by government, a process to attack a jury, legalized jury tampering.

I am not alone in my thoughts. Twenty-eight states have banned the Allen Charge. Many courts have written:

"The Allen Charge is laden with deception and meant to browbeat a jury..."

"The Allen Charge is coercive..."

"The Allen Charge is imposing an implicit deadline that can and does impede the quality of decision-making and encourages jurors to bow to the pressure of a simple majority..."

"The Allen Charge removes individual choice and the right to choose..."

The Allen Charge has been banned in Alaska, Arizona, California, Colorado, Hawaii, Idaho, Montana, Nebraska, Nevada, New Hampshire, New Mexico, North Dakota, Ohio, Oregon, Pennsylvania, Rhode Island, Tennessee, Wisconsin, Kentucky, Louisiana, Maine, Michigan, Minnesota, and Wyoming, so those are the states that still have real jury trials.

"The Allen Charge allows the attack on choice by unscrupulous judges..."

Well, my judge already lied to the jury so the question of unscrupulous has well-past been answered.

Here we go. How about you Ms. Bailey, your child who was falsely accused has just been through the ordeal of a trial to match mine. You have seen shit no one would believe. The jury now exits to go into deliberations. This, Ms. Bailey, is your absolute last, final and only hope that at least some of the jury will see that something ain't right. You sit and you wait, the fate of your child's life is in that room.

What's the prosecutor doing in there?

Then out of nowhere a judge attacks:

"…get your stupid fucking asses out here, goddamn, a whole fucking hour, ain't you son of a bitches found this fucking worthless peon guilty yet, goddamn, do you stupid fucks NOT SEE THE EXPENSE, THE GODDAMNED INCONVENIENCE! ESTABLISH GUILT! Get the fuck on with it, I am going TO LET you go back, I am in charge, and I will haul your stupid asses back out here in a goddamn very short time, DO NOT piss me off, fucking morons!"

Page 186:

"I am going to send you back."

Page 187:

"ADDITIONALLY, YOU MAY WANT TO CONSIDER THE EXPENSE AND THE INCONVENIENCE!"

Page 187:

"A unanimous verdict."

Page 189:

"It is your DUTY to agree upon a verdict."

Page 190:

"ESTABLISH GUILT…"

Page 190:

"I am going TO LET you go back…"

"I WILL bring you back…"

Now you tell me Ms. Bailey, your child faces life in prison, do you really want his life considered by a jury to be an expense, an inconvenience? Do you see your child's life as just a worthless peon, an expense, just an inconvenience? Do you view your child's Constitutional right to a trial by jury, the backbone of the American judicial system, a right to be judged by a jury as an expense, an inconvenience? Your falsely accused child had just three jurors who felt he was innocent and they were told that, NO, it is their DUTY to put your innocent child in prison.

I would further propose, this is not Fred the barber talking, this is a sitting trial judge. He is viewed as the ultimate authority, so for him to use the words:

"Decide the case!"

"Establish GUILT."

The context of the words is irrelevant. He did not say establish innocence, so which one would you Ms. Bailey, prefer to hear at your child's trial? The judge just told the jury that it is their duty to find your child guilty—you okay with that? Or how about, I, KING IN CHARGE, am going to let you go back, and I, KING, am going to haul you back! Does that sound like imposing an undue time constraint? Take all the time you need, you have one hour. That sound right to you, Ms. Bailey?

So, YOU have the right to a jury trial, as long as it's not expensive, uh, as long as it's not inconvenient, uh, and don't take over an hour. Yep. Oh, you can't show any evidence. Yep, total right to a jury trial, only slightly modified. You don't mind if we, oh, call some witnesses when the jury goes home do you? Oh, we already did. Now you can testify but only about this part, not the other parts, and we will attack the jury if they take too long.

We understand you were found innocent of shoplifting, but well, it works better if we say you did it. Go ahead, we dare you to say one word and you are out of here.

American Justice 101—lie!

The NEW American Justice—We have decided imaginary (sniffed) evidence will be allowed.

Now your honor, we didn't actually collect the weapon but Boo-Boo the dog sniffed it, so GUILTY AS HELL—I'LL ALLOW IT! Now your honor, we ain't going to call any witnesses, we will just tell the jury of two officers, what was said, and we don't have any evidence, so we have some pictures of what evidence might look like if we had any. Well, some photos, store, house, gas station, a cat, a motel in Texas... Uh, I think this is vacation sand or cat litter. GUILTY AS HELL—I'LL ALLOW IT!

Your honor, we have here a document that proves he didn't do it, but we object—I CAN'T READ ENGLISH! Without agreement, well hell, we can't admit that.

Sorry, I went off again but, prosecutor: "I don't know what a bank statement;" Judge: "me either!" I am fucking entitled.

Here once again we must call upon our resident lying bitch Carla J. Faletti for ruining my book in yet another spot. There is a worse glitch here than even the one-hour time warp with no recess. The next glitch is just silly.

There was not one Allen Charge at my trial, there were two, and here the court reporter became very frustrated, for good reason. Did y'all know that Sally was a school teacher so she saw this a few times? Big shout-out to Bella here—see, I said I would. Well Bella was a little girl that Sally would babysit, and she would help Bella with homework. On one math test Bella decided it would be a good idea to just mark "10" for every answer. Yep, a whole page of tens.

So, on my transcript first we have to go back to the 3:40 to 4:41 time jump, then we get to page 190:

"We are getting close to five o'clock."

Should be:

"We are getting close to four o'clock."

At that time, it was 3:46 not 4:46 p.m. Then look at:

3:46 (not 4:46) court recess

6:03 court reconvened

6:03 court recess

6:03 court reconvened

Uh, Bella, "10, 10, 10." Court reporter, "6:03, 6:03, 6:03, 6:03." She got so frustrated trying to adjust the time to correct the alterations she said fuck it, make 'em all 6:03! I got bad news—I was in my cell, Sally was at the motel, and Ms. Bailey was long gone by 6:03 p.m. I do admit here I only have two ways to prove this. One would be if Carla J. Faletti gets my transcript or if Ms. Bailey came forward with the truth. In other words, I'm-ah fucked puppy! By the way, Sally went to get a burger and was at her motel by 6:03.

At 3:46 the jury went back in to deliberations. At 4:30 (not 6:03) the court reconvened, the jury was pulled then read the Allen Charge again, except that time the judge said, "His guilt seems obvious." Do you recall the second Allen Charge, Ms. Bailey? It's not in the transcript, is it? At 4:47 the court was in recess again. At 5:07 I was found guilty, but it was actually funny now. At 4:47 the prosecutor had gone to the jury room, and he told the jury hey, just find him guilty then give him the minimum sentence. Sally paid a lot to get that information, but the prosecutor did not say that the minimum was 32 years in prison would be life for me.

Sally loved my trial notes. July 21, 2015 at the start on Kayla Nelson, cop lady, I wrote, "Yeah, make this bitch foreperson, find me guilty and call it a day." And there we are July 22, 2015 and yep, there's cop lady Kayla, foreperson. Was that Lee's idea? Either way, good move.

Well, I am in prison, so the verdict was not exactly a surprise. We only had guilty and mistrial to choose from. I didn't care, I was kind of anxious to get out of there. Do not forget I have the North Carolina police report buried in my papers. Yep, guilty, get on with it.

But before I get to that, would everyone go to Documents and look at the letter Mr. Lee wrote to Jim Shortt where HE did the three-year guidelines. Does anyone see in that letter anything about mandatory 10 years? Nope!

Well, he damn sure didn't forget on page 198, statute 18.2 – upon a second conviction… yep, so his three-year guidelines made him a lying son of a bitch—proven—I WIN! Virginia does not have parole. There is a geriatric parole, but I will never be eligible, so no parole for me. That comes up way later.

On page 213 there is a line of bullshit. My so-called lawyer pretends he came up with minimum sentencing that had already been done in the jury room.

There is a sentencing transcript anyone can read, but it's kind of ridiculous. The page numbers are 1(357), I, 2(358), and so on.

The day after my trial both Mike Dennis and Mike Letson recused themselves. Mike Dennis took over as Commonwealth Attorney, so the prosecutor my paperwork would go to to keep me in prison was the defense attorney who prosecuted me. Uh, WOW! I did put a page in Documents to show Mike Dennis, Commonwealth Attorney. And of course, due to the "sunglasses" corruption Mike Letson had to bug out, so I had no lawyer, but that's a WHOLE other story.

There is more to write but I would be very remiss if I did not write this part. When I got back to my cell, I put the North Carolina police report into some legal work and I had 15 copies made. Five copies went out to Sally and friends with the instructions to scan then upload the text file under any name they could dream of, plus they made five copies each which were in turn mailed to five people with the same instructions. Then I made 10 more copies, every week. Every Monday for two years I mailed Sally a police report with a note: "Read the God DAMN N.C. Police Report!" or, "What does the police report say!"

I honestly do not give a fuck about anyone else, but I honestly was glad I put that report in Sally's hands. It cost me hard, but I WON! The best part was that Sally was right there in the courtroom. There was no room for any doubt where it came from, she held a bonified copy of the North Carolina police report.

I have no damn idea how many times or under what names that text file was uploaded as. I do know over 5,000 copies are on Facebook. It was uploaded as how to change hinges on Toyota trucks, 5,000 free high school shower webcams, the lottery number secret code, Social Security supplements, marijuana license how-to, all of those are a few examples, but when someone downloads the text file, they get the North Carolina police report.

Back in the real world the real report was put in over 700 file cabinets in random workplaces that will never be found or thrown away. It was a game.

Oh, Christmas, birthday, Valentine's Day, any holiday for two years Sally got a police report. She was most annoyed but hey, it was not an ass tattoo. It is kind of ironic that 18 years after the fact I finally got to read the North Carolina police report. It was only then that I realized what a fucking idiot I was. Talk about going in blind and stupid. The charge of Actual Inncocence was NOT justified, at all. But there is another little matter I must get to first to avoid confusion.

I ran into a hell of a dilemma. Who owned that file? Here is where I can get into a legal bog. Luckily, and I did not work this out until 2017, the Virginia State Bar finally worked it out. If anyone don't see my dilemma it's simple. That file, the entire file, was in North Carolina under seal which we are all aware of when the prosecutor obtained that file he then used under 18.2-67.7:1 or Supreme Court rule 2:413. The prosecutor was supposed to enter the date, the charge and the place, but under that statute:

"The Commonwealth shall provide to the defendant photocopies of the final orders that it intends to introduce…"

So, it may burn old Mr. Whisnant's ass, but the Virginia State Bar said very clearly, whatever the prosecutor used I must be provided a copy of. If that record was sealed and there was no mention to unseal that record the fault lies with the Commonwealth and that record is now MINE! I can do whatever the hell I want with it. MINE! MINE! MINE! ALL MINE!

Okay, one group I will apologize to is the 4,500 people who downloaded "The King James Bible Mistranslations" only to get the North Carolina police report. I heard there was some negative feedback on that one. Totally my bad as that was my idea. It was also uploaded as the Muslim Coded Attack Plan, and I bet the government is still trying to decode it. Yes, I am not normal but ya gotta have some fun.

Two years, 104 copies of the police report. I got Sally a card and I asked, 32 years in prison to obtain police report—are we cool on the kielbasa and rice thing? I was forgiven—YEAH!

Anyway, I was writing 16 to 18 years after the fact I found out I was a moron or a bigger moron. First, I do admit that at that time I had no damn idea what "Actual Inncocence" meant. I did not study the law, I worked in a furniture factory and had never been in serious trouble. I did not know any of the things I write about now which his kind of why I am writing this book. I walked into a nest of corrupt vipers, blind and stupid. On the current charges I walked into a nest of corrupt vipers with no fear of being bit. I had purpose, I will die in prison—this book will not.

"Corruption is like a sewage pail. Sooner or later it overflows for everyone to see just how nasty it is: RMB"

In a very roundabout way, my lawyer in North Carolina did not lie to me but he sure as hell did not tell me everything. I need to revisit Documents in my book. I have added NC-Sample where there is 1-6 circled. Pages one and three are plea deal samples that are ink blots, but page two is actually The Final Order. In other words, it was page two that the prosecutor should have used. It shows the date, the charge and the state, but he got greedy and tossed in an illegal plea deal.

That brings me to the rest. The problem is the mother said I had been picking up Ashley Renee Bradshaw at the house of another woman, Robin Haynes, in Longview IN MY TRUCK. Now me, I believe much like, "he stole these sunglasses," one should at least try to be a little honest, and I do love some good old facts. I more than welcome anyone, hell everyone, feel free to run me on any DMV in all states. In my life I have owned exactly one truck, a 1999 Ford Ranger that I bought and registered in Kingsport, Tennessee when Sally and I had met. Now legally, I propose there was no way in hell I drove a 1999 Ford Ranger bought after 2003 back in 1997—again, no time machine. In North Carolina, hell run my record and read this book, I barely owned a car. But the claim by Brenda Bradshaw Townsend that I picked Ashley up in a truck was pure bullshit and to make it worse, I was never at Robin's house, ever, and I'd take a lie detector on that any day. It would not have been hard for the police to find out I did not own or drive a truck. Brenda lied! And that is called generating a false police report, by the way. I could ask Robin

Haynes to come forward and tell the truth if she is still alive or COVID didn't get her.

Then I come to the good stuff. I put pages four and five which is the police report, yep, hey Whisnant 4557, do YOU see that, view an act of God now. Not only me but the whole damn world can read MY report. I also included two handwritten pages of the report:

Reference Interview with Ashley Renee Bradshaw W/F DOB 8-25-90:

"How many times did he do it?"

"One time."

"What was he wearing?"

"He had his clothes on. IT WAS DARK, I DON'T KNOW IF HE HAD HIS PANTS UNZIPPED OR NOT."

"What kind of CAR were you in?"

"A red car."

"I asked Ashley if he ever touched her privates and she said no."

On this score we have two things. I did drive Ashley in a red car, so she is right, but here is where I found out my lawyer violated my right to counsel. He did not do an investigation and he was unaware of the law, or he ignored it to net a plea deal. If he had have bothered on the school check-in sheet, I put R.B. on Bradshaw, Ashley one Tuesday and one Thursday. Ah, but look above Ashley Bradshaw—I see Brook Haynes and it would seem that a V.A. picked up Ashley and Brook the Tuesday I drove her to school. Now why would I drive all the way to Robin Haynes' house when there was a Brook right there going to school?

But, and you have it right from the judge's mouth, Actual Inncocence is indecent exposure, so we have Ashley who never saw if my pants were unzipped and we have Brandi who never saw if I am circumcised. Thirty-two years in prison and not once has any underaged person seen my dick; but, it makes for a good book.

I do hope everyone sees that the North Carolina plea deal is an ink blot and the police report is perfect. Yep, good play, but it did backfire, and I got the police report which was cleared as ALL mine! Then I found out had I had a lawyer, not a cop in law school, he would have known that Ashley rode with Brook, I did not own a truck and I only drove her twice and I was never exposed—the charge was not justified. So, off the bat we have violation of my right to effective counsel.

Now I do have one little nit to pick. I am not even upset by this, but on my jury when I was convicted there was a big ol' fat bitch just grinning her little heart out. I do hope that wasn't you Ms. Bailey. I haven't got there yet but my bank statement proves beyond any doubt that Brandi lied, we did not go to Ray Road and I am innocent. I was convicted on imaginary specter evidence and perjury.

And do you know what, big ol' fat grinning lady? There are thousands of little Ashleys and Brandis out there. One day one of them will rob and lie on your children or grandchildren and there will be some other big ol' fat bitch grinning just as broadly when your innocent loved one is convicted. And if you, big ol' fat grinning bitch, have any evidence your loved one is innocent, NOT ALLOWED—GUILTY AS HELL. I wonder if your grin will falter when your innocent loved one is put in the bonfire—one good witch burning deserves another. Who is next?

So, fat grinning girl, in your simple little mind when your child sits on trial will you grin when DNA evidence is observed—sniffed—not collected, lies about what your child stole, or they haul out wow, a picture of clothes found at Goodwill. Will you, grinning girl, proudly wear your "WE BURN WITCHES!" t-shirt when your child, your neighbor's child, ANYONE'S CHILD, is cuffed, chained and sent away for life? When we convict an innocent man on hypotheticals and imagination, when we in every sense of the word take that man's life, we are the face of evil every morning in the mirror. We cannot do better in retrospect for our damage is done. You, fat girl, are forgiven for not only putting an innocent man in prison but also for enjoying it. You proudly wear your, "we burn witches," t-shirt." The you pray some little Brandi don't steal your loved one's shit and lie about sexual assault.

A minor correction. Would Robin Haynes, last known address 168 23 st. N.W., Longview, N.C. ph. 328-8239 please stand up and tell me the truth, I was never at your house and who is "VA" that picked up both Ashley and Brook.

And to Ms. Bailey, did you know you were told a doxen times, "he said he didn't have on underwear." Did you ever once wonder, where is the jail property sheet from the day of my arrest that was only referred to by Layne. Why would a prosecutor not parade that list in front of a jury and say here see, no underwear.

See, Ms. Bailey, you missed it again.

I will correct this now to be very plain. If you, Ms. Bailey, look at Day-2 of my transcript there is, 1(12), 2(13), 3(14) an 11 page offset, in all there are 40-138 pages missing. But the consistent 11 page offset is where motions were removed. Only now can Ms. Bailey read they did try to enter my bank statement, they did try to enter my stolen wallet; but, there are motions you can't read.

The first attempt to enter the Jim Shortt video, the prosecutor entered the detention check-in sheet to counter the transcript. The first ruling was, for the defense it was transcript only so we could not enter the DVD. Then the second time after it was used the Judge rule DVD, no transcript. That way in deliberation the Jury had a dvd they could not see but not the transcript. They pulled the transcript but left the check-in sheet which was then irrelevant as it was not evidence of any of my charges. Then, in the 3rd rewrite of the transcript, DVD was changed to CD, if the video objection was raised on appeal the Court would only find a blank CD, no video. (Can you say fraud.)

Now if Ms. Bailey had those 11 pages she'd see a motion to enter the jail property sheet from the day of my arrest, it listed, t-shirt, shorts, underwear, socks, shoes, belt and watch. The list was not allowed because it only had R. Blankenship 7-9-12. That could be anyone. But, you tell me Ms. Bailey, how many R. Blakenships do you think were arrested near midnight 7-9-12.

Then the motion to enter the police report, which beside the video transcript is mutually exculpatory so it was not allowed. No way could allow the Jury to see Brandi's lies in deliberation.

Then we had the motion to enter the Virginia Unifor summons that showed me not guilty of shoplifting, it's a legal Court document that is free from hearsay but did you know, Ms. Bailey, it was blocked because Mike Letson was the Co-Counsel and could not testify. Then it was ordered, if I so much as farted "did not steal sunglasses" I'd be ejected.

In that 11 pages there were 7 separate motions on defense evidence all removed. That would mean, you Ms. Bailey, who asked about me presenting evidence literally missed two-thirds of the evidence, or the motions to enter it so you, a juror, could see it. Look at page 3 exhibits.

All those missing motions are the fault of Carletta J. Faletti, hey Carla, July-3-2017, to, November-2022, got that transcript yet.

Hold on we are off to war on a front as bad as the trial.

Chapter 7

Transcript Wars

My sentencing was November 19, 2015, or 11-19-15. Now I can present what is up with the transcript. Look at the sentencing page "i" transcript which shows:

Document	Date	Date Filed
Sentencing	11-19-15	12-16-15
Motions	07-20-15	12-16-15
Day 1	07-21-15	02-08-16

Uh, yeah. If the sentencing transcript was made December 16, 2015, how the hell does it list Day 1 transcript from February 8, 2016 in the index? That transcript was reworked after February 8, 2016. Excuse me, where is Day 2? There is no Day 2 transcript listed, where did it go? Now let me explain.

Document	Date	Date Filed
Motions	07-20-15	12-16-15
Day 1	07-21-15	12-16-15
Day 2	07-22-15	12-16-15
Sentencing	11-19-15	12-16-15

I do have letters online I, sadly, do not have access to at this time but the letters are from a judge who says that the court orders a transcript be made. The court does not parcel out days or in parts so on 12-16-15 a complete transcript was made. Sally ordered and paid for that transcript, and I fucked up—again. When the officer said the cans were cold, ice cold, and fresh I put that and many other things in a habeas for ineffective counsel. Immediately the entire transcript was pulled, and it's used as a "sealed record" in the Office of the Attorney General. They returned Sally's money, and they used my habeas to alter the hell out of the transcript due to my trial notes I filed before I had the transcript in hand.

Then I was appointed Joey Stiltner in the same office as Mike Dennis and Mike Letson. The second transcript was made making:

Motions	07-20-15	12-16-15
Day 1	07-21-15	02-08-16
Day 2	07-22-15	02-08-16
Sentencing	11-19-15	12-16-15

There was then a huge boo-boo. The second Allen Charge was still in the Day 2 transcript. Hell, we can't have that, so out went Day 2, the entire transcript was pulled, then the only alteration was to remove Day 2 from page "i" in the sentencing transcript, then it was reposted. Sally had already ordered the transcript. Her order was rejected because the transcript was pulled then it posted. She ordered it, but I was missing Day 2. Where the hell did Day 2 go?

When I was found guilty back in July 2015 three days later they mailed Sally my clothes which the prosecutor claimed lost but that is in the missing pages along with the motion to use the clothing list from the jail. What they mailed Sally was my actual clothes, blue jean shorts, t-shirt, underwear, socks, shoes, belt and watch.

Hello Sally's friend Missy. If you're reading this, do you remember when you asked me why didn't I just report my altered transcript? Read on.

I know a lot of people think my trial was a one-off or something, but my trial is par for the course for anyone who refuses a plea deal. I was made an example of, and the entire court could not let me win, I had to be convicted. What happened to me has, and will, happen to thousands more. I know that right now there are thousands being processed into jails thinking they will fight whatever it is. They are about to be slammed hard with reality.

What happened to me, first it was just pure retaliation for refusing a plea deal, but it was also an example. Every lawyer involved is probably at this very minute telling some lost soul, oh, he could have had just three years, but he got 32 years. No matter what they had to do I had to be convicted. That's why the judge concealed facts, lied and used a second Allen Charge. Anyone who feels a judge won't lie is in for a rude awakening. Have I failed yet to prove a point?

So, by February 2016 I hold a transcript missing Day 2 and I have Joey Stiltner for an appellate lawyer.

I am going to reiterate a few items here. In my transcript when they broke for motions there was a motion to enter the jail check-in sheet which the judge ruled since it only had R. Blankenship 7-9-12, it might not be me. Like my bank statement, it was objected to, and the objection and ruling were preserved for appeal. That entire motion was completely removed from my transcript, completely. The officer testified the cans were cold, ice cold and fresh which would have been impossible after five hours outside in July, but my lawyer never once, at all, even mentioned beer cans. That alone is the very definition of ineffective counsel. The prosecutor screamed, "And the cans were still cold." That's when I laughed but the whole section was altered. The gag order on Ms. Maynard was removed. The motion to block any testimony regarding the police report from the date of my arrest was removed from the transcript. When the jury came out to request a magnifying glass, they stated all they could read was the North Carolina police report which proved double jeopardy was removed from the transcript. The second Allen Charge was removed. The second Allen Charge alone was enough to overturn my conviction but even I had no idea how bad my trial was. But my transcript and trial records were altered all to hell which again denies due process. The one thing I wish they had have left alone was in the first transcript it said police report not admitted, VHS tape not admitted and two Wal-Mart videos not admitted. I would love to have the first transcript, but I don't.

Then I go to page numbers:

Motions   :1(378) to 16(393)
Day 1   :1(9), i, 1(394) to 256(649)
Day 2   :1(12), 2(13), 2(10), 3(11), 3(14) to 223(234)
Sentencing :1(335) to 17(373), 18, 19, 20

That comes out to:

Day 2   10 to 234
Sentencing 357 to 373, 18, 19, 20
Motions   378 to 393
Day 1   394 to 649

Uh, yeah, see, simple. I would bet my publisher is damn glad I do not use a court reporter's numbering system. Did I really have to state to ANYONE hey, this thing is fucked up? But remember in February 2016 I don't have a Day 2. By the way, the 18, 19, and 20 on sentencing were added in a year later.

First, I told Joey Stiltner that Day 2 was missing, and he said, "I thought it was a one-day trial." And this is the mo-fo handling my appeal! But then I told him first that they mailed Sally the clothes and Sally saw that the jury had the North Carolina police report, she was there. I still get angry. Joey Stiltner said he'd love to talk to her, to talk to someone who was there.

Well there Joey, let me help you out with that. Whoever you're on your knees in front of (blowing off) look up. Chances are it's one of the trial lawyers since YOU are in the same office as both defense attorneys. YOU wanted to discredit my witness, you stupid son of a bitch. How about as a damn appellate attorney you get or read the transcript? Then, what does this fuck do? He moves to file my appeal with Day 2 missing, then he says well, it couldn't really matter. I filed a Virginia State Bar complaint because he would not get the Day 2 transcript.

I wrote to the court reporter. In Documents there is one letter from January 2016 where the reporter claims she has not received any order for any transcript. So uh, why was two parts already made in December? I wrote to the judge the first time and I said why was transcript not ordered. He said my transcript was ordered back in November. So, in February 2016 she makes a new transcript, but then Day 2 is removed. Then she claims, the court reporter claims, she had just then received the order for Day 2. I wrote the judge, and I told him first the Day 1 transcript was altered intentionally and why did he only order Day 1. The judge told me the transcript is not his responsibility, I should contact the appeals court, and the judge said that he did not order the days separately. So, I contacted the appeals court, and the appeals court told me to contact the appellate attorney which would be the moron who tried to file with Day 2 missing. Finally, in May 2016 I finally get Day 2 of my transcript which is the disaster that is in the book. By 2022 I still do not have a transcript.

Motions	07-20-15	12-16-15
Day 1	07-21-15	02-08-16
Day 2	07-22-15	05-05-16
Sentencing	11-19-15	12-16-15

Keep in mind what set this shit storm off was my habeas, so I wrote an addendum which was a motion to review to the trial recording due to an intentionally altered transcript. My motion, in Documents, was returned because it was unsigned except from the court it was signed. Then when I refiled it, they said it was past the limit for an addendum. Then in the response to the habeas the court wrote that on my transcript alterations that would have to be handled in the trial court on a separate habeas.

I filed a second habeas with the trial court who said it was rejected because it was not included in the first but then in the first habeas the motion to review that had not been allowed was then denied so it was in fact in the first habeas and the rejection of the habeas was based upon what they knew was an intentionally falsified document. And the worst part was in the actual habeas. It was ruled that, "ALL OF THESE POINTS SHOULD BE RAISED IN REGULAR APPEAL!" That was in Habeas 160484 which I had in a neat layout to show my appellate attorney had I ever been given the chance.

On a word here there is a file online at http://surftofind.com/transcripts. "Some tips about court transcripts and protecting yourself." I do highly recommend that file and there are thousands of examples of intentionally altered transcripts online. The only point here is, do not trust any judge, lawyer or court reporter—get the transcript and read it. The harder it is to get a trial transcript the more likely it is to be severely altered.

I contacted the trial court to say, "Hey, you know that transcript you son of a bitches intentionally altered, would you mind fixing it?" So, the trial court said that they were only responsible for providing the transcript to the appeals court and any questions of an altered transcript should be taken up with that court.

The trial court also told me to contact my appellate lawyer. I went to the trial court a second time that my appellate attorney refused to correct the transcript. Then I went to the appeals court, and I told them point blank that my transcript was intentionally and severely altered, and the appellate court said they were not responsible for the accuracy of a transcript. The court operated on a strict basis of "assumed correct." So, in other words the first set of son of a bitches alter a transcript and the second set of son of a bitches say that's perfectly okay. The appellate court then said the sole responsibility of my transcript fell to one person, the appellate attorney.

I wrote to seven separate lawyers, two separate courts, two separate habeas, the attorney general of the United States and the attorney general of Virginia. I wrote to the trial lawyer Mike Dennis who was then the Commonwealth attorney. I am asking the person who is fighting my appeal who was the defense attorney to fix my intentionally altered trial transcript that HE would know was altered, but he cannot get involved as my defense attorney now represented the office that would deny any fair due process on appeal.

Every single person up to this point is a flat-out lying son of a bitch. If they don't like it, bring the recording and I'll bring my transcript and we will do a public review. But not one of the lying son of a bitches will step up, they can't. I WIN!

By this point I have two letters from the Virginia State Bar saying they found no inconsistencies in my transcript. I was told not one thing was omitted and that they did a complete investigation. However, they did say if I felt there was a problem, I needed to do one thing, report to the appellate attorney. Every single person or entity told me the exact same thing. In my second habeas it stated that my claims, including the altered transcript, should "ALL BE HANDLED ON A REGULAR APPEAL."

I did include one State Bar letter in Documents. I love where they write, "Mr. Stiltner said he discussed with me the idea of pursuing a delayed appeal rather than moving forward with an incomplete document." Uh, excuse you, the whole goddamn complaint was that Mr. Stiltner attempted to move forward on not only an incomplete document but the part we had was severely altered so that whole line was bullshit. Make no mistake, lying son of a bitches protect their own (don't they, Carla).

Up until 2017 I still did not have a complete trial transcript. The pages 18, 19 and 20 were not added until March 2017 which was why those pages do not match the other numbers.

It was also in 2017 that something crazy happened. Remember when I said that those reading the transcript had information I did not have? I had not seen my own bank statement, then it was mailed to me.

Holy Hell! One of the reasons for this book is right here. Neither Brandi nor I had even thought about the damn pizza. I honestly completely forgot about the pizza and thank God I did. What with being arrested, the whole jail ride, the threats over the abduction charge, and then the whole life plus 22 years, the pizza slipped my mind. But the best part was that Brandi forgot the pizza too, but then someone who can have their shirt and bra ripped off in public then completely forget that probably couldn't remember a $4.92 pizza. So, in a way the entire book comes down to 22 minutes and a five dollar pizza.

CRIMINALS LIE!

Yep, I suppose one could say oh, he just made up an entire bank statement. Not sure how I'd pull that off when I am in a cell but to those people I would say take a look in Documents. I put TruPoint Proof 1 to 4. Page one is the envelope they scanned at the prison, a letter to me from the bank. "K.M.C.C." is Keen Mountain Prison. I am (was) in C-336 when I received it. That's building C cell 336. Page two is a letter from Mr. Andrew Baker at the TruPoint Bank 13250, Gov. Perry Highway. Pages three and four show what and how Sarah Hale paid to get my statement, my account and dates. Do not try to use Sally's card number, it's long dead. Anyone who still don't believe, take this book, WALK INTO THE FUCKING BANK AND ASK.

In 2017 exactly two people in the whole world knew about the pizza, Sarah Hale and myself and she was sworn to absolute secrecy. She never wrote about nor mentioned it on the phone, period.

Now I can have some fun. No matter what one thinks or believes, Brandi committed perjury all the way around.

In my trial Brandi testified she drove to the bank in Richlands. My bank statement shows 13250 Gov. Perry Highway. Brandi then testified when we left Wal-Mart we went down across Kent's Ridge Road to Ray Road where we stopped. I cannot really estimate how long it would take to walk 195 to 200 yards up a dirt road, drink two beers, walk another 195 yards back to the car then drive to Raven. It don't matter, but let's say 10 minutes. Sally estimated seven to 12 minutes depending on which of Brandi's three lies one went by.

In Documents I have included an actual Google map that goes from 13250 Gov. Perry Hwy. over Kent's Ridge to Raven which is 12.1 miles, 22 minutes if one drives at speed nonstop. I apologize for the map, but they are not easy to get in prison. But the route Brandi testified to my statement proves she committed perjury. Just to make damn sure, Sally came to a hotel for two days and she drove the exact route Brandi claimed five times over two whole days. With the u-turn and four red lights it took her 27 to 34 minutes just to drive from Wal-Mart to Ray

Road. Anyone can check the route on any map program then look at or confirm my bank statement. Brandi lied because we were never on Ray Road. So, in fact if the imaginary beer cans were real, they would prove to be not mine.

Then the stupid part came. My bank statement was objected to and a ruling made in error because no grown man can claim I don't know what a bank statement is. Sally spoke to a "lawyer friend," not sure if it was pussy for legal advice but hell, I'd pimp her out for a honey bun and coffee so why not legal advice. The lawyer told Sally that on appeal I could prove the judge erred and the witness committed perjury. Hell, my bank statement even proved the Wal-Mart photo was not me and of course no one has mentioned I was innocent of the shoplifting anyway.

Oh joy! Joey Stiltner recused himself—in the wrong court! Are y'all sure this dude's a lawyer? So, then he recused himself in the correct court.

I will write this as calmly as I am able, but there may be a few derogatory outbursts that are inappropriate. Fun, yes. Warranted, definitely. But still inappropriate. I was appointed Carletta J. Faletti for my appeal. In June 2017, damn near two years after my trial, that my transcript was severely and intentionally altered and the only thing I wanted was a clean, true transcript. I, AND SALLY, made it very clear. Every single person that I made complaints to told me the exact same thing—the trial transcript accuracy was dependent on one person, the appellate attorney. Carla knew I had exactly one shot at obtaining an honest transcript for my appeal. That meant that me being in or out of prison was solely up to Carletta J. Faletti. All she had to do was fix my transcript so it had the second Allen Charge and the rest of the removed motions and testimony.

Four, FOUR separate times I spoke to Carla on the phone. Four times I made it damn clear—DO NOT file any appeal until I had an honest and true transcript in my hand. Carla told me with everything that Mike Dennis did, and did not do, in my trial that we would file on ineffective counsel, the previous conviction, the jury had the police report, and the second Allen Charge. Carla told Sally she would file on all of those points.

Please see Carla Letter-1 in Documents:

"I do understand your allegation that the trial transcript was not a fair representation of what you recall happening at your trial."

Okay first of all, I do not "recall" a goddamn thing, I have exact fucking notes. Why don't you, Carla, listen to the goddamn recordings? Why don't you listen to the cop say the cans were cold, ice cold and fresh then the prosecutor scream the cans were still cold? Then you read my goddamn habeas that says that was not what was said. Why don't you, Carla, listen to the clothing sheet be denied because it only had R. Blankenship? Why don't you listen to the second Allen Charge where a damn judge says, "His guilt seems obvious!"? Tell me Carla, do you see a gag order on Ms. Maynard's part? Do you see a gag order on the damn police report?

"At this time there is very little to do on your appeal!"

Yeah, like make sure the records are not altered all to hell maybe.

"An appeal must be upon errors within the proceedings…"

I am well aware of that, but tell me this genius, if those proceedings are removed or altered then that denies due process does it not?

(e.g. motions granted or denied.)

And so, you're saying that if a motion in my transcript to enter a bank statement and a sitting judge ruled that it would not be allowed because HE did not know what a bank statement was that may be raised on appeal since it was in fact a motion and there was a clear objection.

So, tell me Carla, are you aware that over 1,400 cases have been overturned on appeal due to the wording of an Allen Charge? And where do you stand on, oh, lying about stolen sunglasses, double jeopardy, and what happened to the ineffective counsel YOU were going to use?

"I will do everything possible to assure that the transcript submitted to the court of appeals is accurate."

"It is my intention to file a motion with the court to ask that the transcript be typed anew."

"I intend to visit you to discuss your appeal once I have been able to review the transcript AND COMPARE IT TO THE AUDIO RECORDING!"

Would the 100 percent lying bitch Carletta J. Faletti now stand up and tell the world just exactly which of any of that did you do.

Every goddamned word a fucking lie. She flat out lied in writing. That letter was from July 3, 2017. I was told repeatedly by Carla that she was waiting on all the records to be in or transmitted to the court. Then Carla told me she wrote a motion to the court that a brand new transcript be made. She said it could take maybe 30 to 60 days. The lying bitch then filed my appeal behind my back. August and September both Sally and I were waiting on a new transcript.

October 4, 2017 – Carla Letter-2

"Enclosed please find the appeal that was filed."

You filed a bullshit appeal on one item but by God, it was not on my behalf. You, Carla, were covering up for the other lying son of a bitches by joining the ranks. Don't get me wrong Carla, you do talk a good game. You fooled Sally but I saw you for the pure lying bitch that you were. In the October 4, 2017 letter:

"I realize you take exception to the transcript itself."

Uh, I also take exception to a lying bitch who files an appeal on what she knows is an intentionally falsified document then only files a half-ass appeal, and I do take exception to being lied to by a lying bitch.

"I only hope you are satisfied with the petition."

Am I satisfied they appointed me a lying bitch who intentionally blew my appeal? Uh, nope. I'd be satisfied with an honest, unaltered transcript to start, but you Carla, are a lawyer so an "honest" anything is beyond your realm of capabilities.

Please see Carla Letter-3 in Documents. I will now attempt to answer some of Carla's questions from that letter.

In the October 29, 2018 letter:

"I have explained to you and to your wife…"

So, Carla did talk to Sally.

In this letter Carla claims she filed a motion for the recordings except when I contacted the court no such motion was ever filed. There was a motion to preserve the recordings but not one for the recordings, so another lie.

"I have a hard time understanding why you insist on being continually threatening towards me in your tone."

Well let's see, how about you are a lying bitch—on paper—who I knew was out to lose the appeal so you wouldn't be blackballed by your fuck buddies at court. You lied from the start and you, Carla, didn't like that I saw you for the lying bitch that you, in fact, are. you were not the only attorney to work on my behalf. Jim Shortt created new evidence to help convict me, Mike Dennis never mentioned oh, he was innocent of shoplifting, objected to the pictures on numerous grounds. How about Mike Dennis trying to correct Brandi to the correct bank not to defend me but to correct her testimony to convict me? How about the jury had the North Carolina Police Report? Mike Dennis just stood there and even handed it to me. Then there was Mike Letson who sat through the whole trial, and he heard repeatedly that I was stealing sunglasses when he was the son of a bitch who defended me. Then Carla, I end up with your lying ass, so I'd say you worked on my behalf the same as the others.

"Working on a misconception the purported inconsistencies in the trial transcript are relevant to this appeal. They are not."

But in your first letter you stated that the appeal depended on motions granted or denied, but there are seven motions that are missing, as was the second Allen Charge that can, and has, overturned cases on appeal. So, I would say I am under no misconceptions at all nor am I under the influence of a lying bitch who I see for exactly what she is.

"I am extremely fortunate!"

You tell me Carla, did you read Brandi's probation report? Exactly. Where was I anywhere near fortunate? You told me, Carla, you would put a true transcript in my hands. You told me you would file an ineffective counsel. You Carla, blatantly lied to my face. I am sorry I do not call that fortunate, I'd say that's as far from fortunate as one can get.

Oh gee, I am so sorry, why that makes absolute perfect sense now that I see it on paper, I totally agree. What's life in prison, years of mental torture? What's the life of a worthless peon when there is only a trifling $900 in it? Shit, that's not worth getting out of bed for huh, Carla? So sorry my entire life only nets a paltry 900 bucks, totally understandable. What better reason to be a lying bitch than when it only taps $900.

But do tell me why, Carla, did you spend "several hundred hours" on what you knew was an intentionally altered document? You should have spent the first hour actually writing the motion for a new transcript because since you did not the rest were just wasted hours.

Now on page two Carla, let's be fair, I was never threatening. I said when you lost the appeal, I would write your lying ass into a book for the world to see. You lied from the start, and I wrote a book. I have never threatened anyone, I was being blunt. You lied Carla, on paper, so you are in fact a lying bitch. I did not do that. You were informed in June, you said in July. You'd have a transcript made so why did you lie? I do not believe in conspiracy, I believe a pack of lying son of a bitches cover for each other and you Carla, are the top of the pyramid.

In Documents I have placed a Sally letter. In the Sally letter there are parts where she talked to Carla even though Sally fell for Carla's line of shit. Carla told Sally that she did file an ineffective counsel, but Carla did not. Sally does say in the letter they mailed the clothes to her which matched the list the judge blocked had Carla bothered to fix the transcript to the see the motion.

Sally wrote:

"10:20 a.m.: OK I just got off the phone with Carla and she and I agree you need to calm down."

Uh, not sure what they mean there. I think considering the shit I've been through I am calm. Carla is a lying bitch, I called her a lying bitch, that's not un-calm, that's just stating the overtly obvious.

On page two of the Sally letter first paragraph, Sally shows Carla filed (said she filed) on ineffective counsel. Also, on page two Sally wrote about her lawyer friend. Sally said Carla was shocked the clothes were mailed to her, but Carla never bothered to fix the transcript to hear the whole argument.

The one lie that pisses me off says:

"She (Carla) asked about them offering you a good deal!"

You stupid bitch, Carla. Are you saying it's justifiable to put a person in prison for life but hey, they were offered a good deal? Fucking plea deal on the goddamned brain. I have been to kangaroo court, how about we think appeal not stupid plea deal.

Next to last paragraph Carla starts talking about ineffective counsel but of course Carla never filed on it. But I did save a part to the last I will now explain. In the Carla letters and in Sally's letter Carla said I had not told her the specifics of what was wrong:

"She's (Carla) trying to find out what you're objecting to about the transcript."

Well Carla, back in time Jim Shortt set up for me to watch the Brandi video, which is 100 percent video not audio. As we watched that video, I pointed out that Brandi lied but she did not show one emotion. Feel free to watch the video, Carla. Look at the transcript. MIKE DENNIS, defense attorney said it's audio—he lied.

If you watch that video Brandi says a naked man walks up, slams her to the ground, jumps on top of her trying to remove her clothes for two whole minutes, but she is 100 percent bored, she is completely deadpan.

The point here being as soon as I told Jim Shortt the lies in that video, he ran to the prosecutor to file a motion to remove the video and most of what I said was in that motion. In my trial he lied.

In my trial, in December of 2012 I went to trial where Mike Letson watched the Wal-Mart video of Brandi walking into Wal-Mart with sunglasses on her hat and I was found innocent. My entire trial Mike Letson never said a word, he was appointed so I could not call him.

Now you tell me Carla, when Brandi said she drove to the bank in Richlands she lied, I told Mike Dennis she committed perjury, I gave him proof she committed perjury, and he busted his balls not to defend me, but to correct her testimony. He even said, "BANK AT CLAYPOOL HILL." Why was my defense attorney trying to correct her to that bank? He led the hell out of her.

Then you, Carla, tell me where the fuck is the logic that I would put the girl's goddamn mother on the stand to discredit my own goddamn evidence? My trial was far outside ineffective counsel, it was malicious prosecution.

Every single time I pointed out anything that would help my defense, the so-called goddamned defense attorney with the prosecutor altered the paperwork.

"I don't know what a bank statement is!"

Bull-fucking-shit!

You may wonder what my point is. I never told you what was wrong in the transcript because you lied. I knew anything I told you you would not have used in my appeal. You, like all the others, would have altered the facts.

Let's say I would have said my bank statement shows I bought a pizza in Raven which proves by the time shown that we did not drive to Ray Road. You would not have defended me. You, Carla, and your fuck buddies would have pulled the transcript again. You would have rewritten it so Mutt and Jeff would have found a pizza box, would not have collected it, but they would have observed it. Except for Jeff, he would sniff it and it would still have been hot. Hell, by then good ol' Smith would have found my guitar in a house 20 miles away and good ol' Layne would have me shoplifting a wide screen TV.

On the other side, Carla, it's actually kind of perfect because you being a lying bitch worked better for the book.

By the way, when the jury came out to request a magnifying glass to read the ink smears, they said all they could read was the police report. The police report from July 9, 2012 was "entered not admitted" only in the first transcript, meaning the only police report used in my trial was from the previous conviction which you, Carla, would have known had you fixed the transcript. But because you, Carla, did not fix that in my appeal I had to read:

"The statute allowed for its admission and the arguably inflammatory and fact-specific aspects of the prior conviction were NEVER considered by the jury. The trial court did not abuse its discretion in admitting the prior conviction."

Wow! So now Carla, you not only fucked up everything else, but you also fucked up the one point you attempted to file on. The jury had the police report from North Carolina, so I'd call that inflammatory and fact-specific, wouldn't you? And yet you, Carla, what was it you said?

"That the purported inconsistencies in the trial transcript are relevant to this appeal—they are not." October 29, 2018

So, according to the above since the jury had the North Carolina police report that would have resulted in the trial court's abuse of discretion which I believe damn sure did concern even the half-ass attempt you made on an appeal but fucked up.

I have included a page nine from my appeal. In the footnote the words "inadvertently omitted," are bullshit. After all I went through, including three separate transcripts, nothing was inadvertently omitted, but it would seem the Commonwealth has no trouble finding intentionally omitted items when needed.

I do love the top of page nine, "The defendant did not present any other evidence."

Well, let's start with the bank statement which proves Brandi never drove to the bank in Richlands. I'd like to present the VHS tape from Valero. Oh, it's missing. I'd like to present the Wal-Mart video-1 that shows Brandi with sunglasses on her hat. Oh, that's missing too. How about a bank statement that proves the so-called Wal-Mart picture only leaves four minutes to go 8.8 miles or that there was no way we went to Ray Road?

Oh, I know. How about I enter one little piece of evidence, Brandi's probtaion report—the whole psych report. Yeah, that would make some people very nervous, would it not? So, what would happen if I said the judge's ruling, the defense attorney's remarks, and Brandi's FULL probation report were posted online?

Hey Corletta J. Faletti, do you know what the deal is with Brandi's psych report? Talk about ineffective counsel. Read on, we will get there.

On one upside while all the so-called appeal crap was going on, I went to Wallen's Ridge Prison. I was 230 pounds. I went to segregation for seven months and I came out of seg at 139 pounds. Wallen's Ridge weight loss plan—don't put any food on the trays or they serve soured beans a goat couldn't eat.

On a presentence report I had not wrote about yet, one lady had an attitude like I was not in daily contact with Sally. As it turned out once Sally had the North Carolina police report and everything else then we wrote each other three to five letters a week. We worked out all the differences. This is the grand tragic love story portion of the book. On September 9, 2018 Sally and I were married at Wallen's Ridge Prison. In 10 years I was only allowed two contact visits and the wedding was the second one. But I was three for three on no sex on the wedding night. I do like the September 9, 2018 wedding day though, easy to remember as long as I don't use Tennessee math.

Then comes the shocking plot twist one loves in these true crime novels. When Sally was in college, she met what's called an acquisitioner, a person who looks for new books he then presents to various publishers that he works for. I wrote an outline with a few small details, and he was extremely into the book. From the start I wrote a very rough first chapter, but Sally didn't get it at first. Then I made a copy of that to send to Sally. I would write around six pages that had lawyer visits, what went on that day, every detail and experience. So, we worked on both, each chapter and day-to-day crap plus backups of every piece of paper I had. Then we had backups of the backups held by other people and we had backups online.

The appeal died in 2019 and yep, Carla took off faster than a cat with its ass on fire and I cannot even get my case file from her.

I would say, "And then something crazy happened," but this may rank as either crazier or craziest.

Y'all ready for this!

From 1963 to 2021 this book has waded in and out of very odd situations, so I am not easily surprised, but then I was truly shocked.

First, to make the proper impact here we need a recap because right when I thought I'd been kicked in the nuts about as hard as a person could be, I had a double or triple kick.

First, on page four of motions: Brandi's probation report:

"We are asking the court to release ANY information that may pertain to her credibility and issues that would undermine her credibility or attack her credibility."

Page 13: Day-1 The Court:

"The court has pulled out relevant documents."

Page 14: Day-1 Defense Lawyer:

"There was no additional information that pertained to Mr. Blankenship's case."

Well, all of that seems perfectly clear to me. On Brandi's probation report they found some adverse statements, I believe the prosecutor called it "two or three" lines. So, the court reviews said report, then the court states that it has pulled out the relevant information that may undermine Brandi's credibility, and my lawyer says yes, that's all there is, there ain't no more. The court said yep, here's the redacted statements, nothing else relevant to see here.

There was a line in my appeal that there was only one incident:

8: B.S. (Brandi Shortt) said she would holler rape if he [her stepfather] didn't stop beating her.

Transcript Day-1 page 32:

He buys a package of cigarettes

He gives the cigarettes to Brandi

Page 78:

He gives her the cigarettes

Page 96:

Cigarettes: cigarettes

Closing argument: he buys her cigarettes.

I could go through the entire transcript, but I do believe I made the point that yes, cigarettes are a huge part of my case. They were hammered away at start to finish.

Oh, the drama, the suspense, the on-the-edge-of-my-seat anticipation. What in the hell could be so built up? Okay, one more, let's not forget the prosecutor's little remark:

"But if she wanted to lie, do you not think she could have made a better lie? He told me he'd rape me, HE SAID HE WAS GOING TO KILL ME."

Gee there, Mr. Prosecutor dude, maybe she already used that one on someone else, like where you got that line from.

Ladies and gentlemen, children over the age of 18, I, Robert Mckinley Blankenship, now present, "The Brandi Lee Shortt Probation Report," to the severe consternation of all involved parties since said report was unsealed, but to see the whole picture, please read the redacted statements in Documents. That read:

"Mom reports being unable to find Brandi on several occasions, has contacted the police, reports Brandi hangs out with older and negative peers, continues to smoke, mom suspects drug use, curses, screams, threatens to say she is sexually and physically abused, kicks and hits things when she doesn't get her way. RECENTLY BRANDI WAS CHARGED WITH BREAKING AND ENTERING AND DESTRUCTION OF PROPERTY, court date is scheduled for July 2012."

Let's see, in my trial I do believe the prosecutor said Brandi had a minor trespassing and maybe a fight, then he claimed it was oh, a disorderly conduct. That's quite a stretch from breaking and entering. But I can help with one thing. When I went to Tazewell or when I went to Sally's, Brandi was playing lick kitty with her girlfriend at my house. That's the times she couldn't be found.

From the psych report:

June 17, 2012 Threatening to say they abuse her and threatening to say her stepdad sexually abuses her.

Brandi is not concerned about the upcoming case of breaking and entering.

May 21, 2012 Brandi leaves without permission, has been unable to find her on many occasions, lies about where she is LIES ABOUT WHERE SHE IS and who she is with, has been with older boys on numerous occasions, continues to smoke, has been involved in numerous conflicts in the neighborhood, has been bullying younger kids."

Uh-oh! Look what it says next!

"BRANDI AND TWO OTHER KIDS IN THE NEIGHBORHOOD BROKE INTO BRANDI'S HOME, TORE UP THE DOOR, BRANDI BROKE INTO HER OWN HOME REPEATEDLY TO STEAL CIGARETTES, BRANDI STOLE MONEY ON TWO OCCASIONS."

THE COURT pulled out all relevant documents or information.

Defense: Nothing else pertains to Mr. Blankenship's case.

So, Mr. Judge—YOU LIED! Brandi broke into homes repeatedly to steal cigarettes and that alone makes the judge, yep, a lying son of a bitch in fact! So, Mr. Judge, which is it, is it the court's claim that the cigarettes in that file are in some way not cigarettes or is it the court's claim that no cigarettes were involved in my trial?

To continue the report or Brandi's probation report:

"During the investigation Brandi was slurring her words, passing out, officers recommended drug testing…"

"On numerous occasions police have been called by neighbors for disturbances at the home, Brandi is out yelling, screaming, cursing, DEMANDING CIGARETTES, beating a mailbox, threatening to say she was raped at one or two o'clock in the mornings."

May 12, 2012 Brandi is STEALING, LYING, THREATENING TO SAY SHE IS SEXUALLY ASSAULTED, is disrespectful and disobedient.

Brandi is belligerent, angry, refused to get out of the car, kicking, screaming, threatening, blowing the horn, kicking doors, cursing, and LYING.

Therapist is concerned about numerous remarks Brandi made about STEPDAD RAPING HER escalating until police were called on numerous occasions.

Mom reports whenever Brandi gets mad or doesn't get her way she threatens to say her stepdad raped her.

The police have been called to the home several times due to Brandi for various disturbances and mom calling the police herself.

May 15, 2012 BRANDI WAS DEMANDING CIGARETTES, calling her stepdad bald and a rapist, cursing, threatening to say her stepdad raped her.

Brandi is not where she is supposed to be. SHE IS LYING, STEALING, police reports have been filed on Brandi, she bullies little kids.

January 19, 2012 Brandi gets mad screaming and yelling out the window wanting the window down on the way home from the bus stop, she got mad when stepdad said not to roll the window down because it was cold, she was yelling, screaming, and threatening to say he sexually abused her.

Mom reports Brandi and her sister fight and they often have bruises.
Brandi has threatened to say DAD sexually abused her.
(Note that is dad, not stepdad)
Brandi gets mad, steals, lies about what she does or says.
August 24, 2011

Brandi recently reported that a person at TDT touched her inappropriately and she said, "HE THREATENED TO KILL HER IF SHE TOLD," but then Brandi DENIES SEXUAL ASSAULT, she blames person at TDT.

August 27, 2011

She has breaking and entering charge, she was threatening to say her stepdad and HER DAD raped her unless she GOT CIGARETTES.

May 21, 2012

Brandi started her period last month for one day, has not had any more periods.

Damn, that file only goes back to August 24, 2011, but Brandi broke into homes repeatedly to steal money and cigarettes. She lied about sexual assault on another person, and she threatened to accuse multiple people multiple times for months, and all of that information would have severely attacked her credibility. But let's all give a round of applause to Ms. Maynard who out of 13 people was the only one who knew the truth and she left. I can see why she said her opinion would be clouded where Brandi was concerned.

"During the trials many witnesses stood silent for fear of retaliations, accusations and strong public opinions, many feared ruined reputations so did not speak for the accused."

That little tidbit was written in the 1400s when seven women and four men were put to death for witchcraft in just two days. Not one witness stood for the accused, including family members. So, no one could blame Ms. Maynard for bugging out. Had she stood for me the others would have hated her even when she knew the truth.

But I would say, first, I don't even know how to present a lying judge, so I put together enough pages to prove a judge lied and I sent it to the A.C.L.U., The Innocence Project, several news agencies, and I filed a motion to vacate on the entire mess, but I do not expect any justice at all, not after reading that file. Malicious prosecution, nonrepresentation, ineffective counsel, judicial misconduct, severe abuse of discretion, misrepresentation.

I never had a trial, I had a lynch mob who forgot to bring a rope.
Now y'all tell me,
The court: Pulled all relevant information
Defense: No other information
Prosecution: Minor trespassing

I do believe there is a difference between a fair trial and a lying judge and a room full of prosecutors.

All the way up to my appeal they tried to play it like poor, sweet little Brandi who only had minor trespassing and would yell rape if her stepdad did not stop beating her, but I believe the psych report discredits that whole line.

Of course, it is now damn funny when the prosecutor tried to paint Brandi as a barely 14-year-old choir girl when at 13 she had already racked up breaking and entering, destruction of property, multiple police reports of theft of cigarettes and money. Then she actually falsely accused another person of sexual assault using the same words the prosecutor used in closing. I guess he did, obviously, know something we did not know.

I have only included three pages of the psych report. Thank God it was unsealed and sent to me. I hope everyone sees the first page. I was arrested July 9, 2012, and they had the file on July 17, 2012, just eight days later, but they buried it for three years then lied about it.

One does have to admire, "This Way to the Great Egress!" My trial was one of the best cases of misrepresentation. Hell, that was a stage show worthy of a movie or at lest one hell of a play. And here we are, that probation report is like a baby's diaper—sooner or later shit comes out.

But hey, let's pay a visit back to Ms. Bailey on the jury, except it's your child on trial. Brandi or one like her could tag your child any second. In the trial the judge says he pulled out all relevant information from a file, then he conceals said file. Then years later while your child rots in prison, your child is innocent and nobody cares, then you receive that file that says the accuser broke into multiple homes multiple times to rob money and cigarettes, the accuser had threatened to lie about sexual assault on multiple people multiple times for months, and the accuser lies about where she goes, what she does, but not a speck of that ever came out at trial.

I still do not know how the record was unsealed. I expect I know who did it—guilty conscience would be my best guess. I did find it funny when Sally's friend Missy got mad at me because it popped her fuse that a sitting trial judge blatantly lied flat out, so she wanted to accuse me of creating the file, but it is the court copy, it's on record. Then Missy started to be an advocate for me.

We did decide, just in case, to put the whole probation report online in differently named .txt files. As of 2022, one of my better ideas, Brandi's probation report has been downloaded over 700,000 times. One has to love the internet because there are fetish sites for damn near anything anyone could think of, so I had Brandi's probation report named "Brandi's First Period Log," and it was uploaded to over 500 menstruation fetish websites. The file counter shows just on one site it is downloaded around 60 times a day.

The probation report was uploaded as "Crazy Cake Recipe" to cooking sites. There is a file, "Who Really Wrote Star Wars," then my favorite, "B. Clinton Diary Pages," "Proof Brandi Lee Shortt: The Pope's Love Child," "Long John Silver's Bathroom Webcams," "SS Number Scam." All of those text files are the Brandi probation report. One of the best ones was done by Connie in Florida. She uploaded the file as an internet trace test. It instructs anyone to rename the file then upload it to see how good the tracker works. The funny part is it was the "B. Clinton Diary Pages" that had the most downloads.

Back in the real world I did send transcript pages and the psych report to over 20 groups who are victims of sex offender laws to prove how corrupt the system really is.

Damn.

I don't guess anyone saw how damn ironic all of this is. In North Carolina I was told by my lawyer ALL the police report was that Ashley said it was one time and she did not see if my pants were unzipped. I did not know about all the other lies and bullshit. But I never read the report because it was written then a judge sealed it. I was a moron who knew absolutely nothing about the real system. At Tazewell I fought tooth and nail that if it was involved in my trial, I read it or I saw it, all except for exactly one file—the damn Brandi probation report. Look at how fast the judge said, here are a few lines, that's all the relevant information and this record is sealed! How many innocent people are in prison due to blatant, outright lies by a judge, or sealed records?

Keep in mind the exact same judge who blatantly lied about the police report, the probation report and questioned the witness then blocked the two statements HE said we were entitled to. Then he attacked my jury twice in under two hours.

Then we have a couple of cool items in Brandi's probation report. Numerous times it said Brandi LIES!

1697:

"Lying wenches who accuse innocent neighbors by pretending… blood thirsty ministers and judges encourage these lies with bigoted zeal stirring up blind and mostly bloody rage—till they themselves are accused."

1750:

"…and concluded that innocent people had died, imprisoned, because of lying, self-indulgent girls, cowardly adults afraid of accusation and credulous judges—fraud from start to finish."

1867:

"He thought from the start the girls lied from the beginning egged on by judges who had manipulated the terror to gain power…"

Then I had one of Sally's friends who had been so against me, she slammed the hell out of me because she had been sexually assaulted. She accused me of altering the transcript until she literally ordered one from the court. She had the worst case of law-and-order-itis possible. She then found out that they did pull a fast one. They gave the CD to the records, but it's blank so the upper court never saw the police report or the Jim Shortt transcript and the CD was not a CD, it was a DVD in the first transcript. Sally's friend now knows I am innocent, so I have cured two cases of law-and-order-itis. The lady was sexually assaulted when she was 11 on a school bus and she said Brandi is full of shit. On the other side, one of Sally's friends don't like me but she believes me innocent.

In a lot of witch trials girls between the ages of seven to 12 would say the specter of a person was torturing them. They would bind, gag, and in several cases they blinded, the accused. People were tied "neck and ankle" in outbuildings where some died. The judges changed from "what vexes" to "who vexes" the accuser.

In some much earlier witch trials they would put the accused in one of several boxes for the witness to point to. If she pointed to the wrong box, they would switch the boxes around so she pointed correctly. In some trials the accused was gagged and eye movement was used to plea, but left was guilty, look right was guilty, look up, down, or close eyes were all pleading guilty.

The court: "The court pulled out all relevant information."

I do find it funny that I sit here writing and on the news I see stories. One man was just arrested for sex crimes that were supposed to have happened between 1964 and 1984, wow. "He touched my ass back in

1964" and off to prison he goes. Anyone can put anyone away at anytime and they do not need evidence, or if they do hey, just observe some beer cans, soda cans or any item on the ground.

But it does bother me when I see a man who had seven counts of anal insertion with pictures so there is no room for doubt and he plead out to four years. He fucked a 10-year-old girl in the ass, and he took pictures seven times, and he walked with four years. They just showed that between 2020 and 2021 a man made over 40 videos fucking a 12-year-old and he plead out to 15 years.

I get my wallet stolen and I get 32 years for refusing a plea deal. My bank statement proves I was never on that road.

Then I have a part I wanted to save until after the psych report came out in the book because I guess one could say the probation report was the icing on the cake, but this part is like the little sugar flowers on the icing. After I was convicted, I had to go for a presentencing report, kind of a sexual evaluation. I only put two pages in Documents because there is a little shock on the cover page. It says:

"Incident Report regarding theft of Mr. Blankenship's wallet, 2012 – Tazewell County Sheriff's Dept."

That is under sources of information. I think in the Queen of England's voice "WE ARE CONFUSED!" For all of 10 seconds I thought damn, someone did a police report where Brandi stole my wallet but nope, it was just more fucking bullshit and a very goddamn poor level of bullshit at that.

I will go over the presentence report to nitpick a few items.

On page three, for three years I had been crammed in a cell for 23 hours a day with two other people with no room to even stand up. There were no hair clippers and, not every week, but on a good week we could shave once out of seven days. On a really good week the showers actually worked, both of them. But in this report the observer said I looked unkept or unkempt. Uh yeah, put that bitch under the same conditions for a year. That "unkempt" would change to "looks damn good considering the deplorable conditions."

Then my favorite:

"He has tattoos (first ones ever) on the top of each hand which were self-done during his current incarceration (not a lot to do in jail). A marijuana leaf on his left hand and a skull with a middle finger on his right.

Mr. Blankenship reports the middle finger represents his thoughts about the Tazewell County legal system…"

As of 2022 the middle finger still represents Mr. Blankenship's thoughts about the Tazewell County legal system except I should have made it bigger with "TZ-CO" on the nail.

On page 4:

"He is writing a book about the corruption in the legal system and the injustice of his case."

This report was done August 12, 2015 when I said I was doing a book. Here is said book after many, many revisions.

Oh, on page four they omitted Brandi Lee Shortt's name, but should anyone wonder what Brandi Lee Short's name is, it's Brandi Lee Short. For the record, I do feel "B.S." is way more appropriate in this instance. Maybe Brandi should consider a name change to B.S.

Then I came to a damn curious point in the whole file on my wallet being stolen:

"This statement does not align with a police report Mr. Blankenship made regarding another female stealing his wallet."

Ho-ho! This plot thickens. Another female, a witness to the pizza, we have another witness, oh joy! Uh, I recall the bank at Claypool Hill, I recall the sold-out poster, I recalled the pizza, then Brandi's sister came, and they left. Damn it, God knows I have a string of bitches (don't I Sally, uh, wife?), but then to find out not only was one of the bitches there: she stole my wallet. Oh, I know, let's get the police report, I gotta find this witness so I can't wait to see what I said.

GODDAMN IT!

"It gives me a migraine headache thinking down to your level." "Sweating Bullets" by Megadeth.

Simple, I wrote a letter to the Sheriff's Department to request a copy of the police report I filed concerning the theft of my wallet in 2012, it's listed on my sentencing report.

Everyone please look in Documents, I have included what was returned to me from the Sheriff's office.

"Mr. Blankenship

Enclosed you will find a copy of an incident report from 2011 involving another female named Ms. Bourne. The incident report you are asking about can't be located in our jurisdiction with any information in which you provided."

Holy Hell! Or, Goddamn Almighty, June 21, 2011. For fuck's sake, who the bloody hell is Ms. Bourne? I wonder if someone was watching, oh, Jason Bourne when they made that up. Wrong goddamn month, wrong goddamn day, and wrong goddamn year, no name in the report, and ARE YOU FUCKING KIDDING ME!

Sally was most amused by, "brown wallet." Oh, so close, a good guess, but let me clue you in. When Sally and I were married in Gatlinburg, TN the first time at one shop Sally bought me a pair of real moccasins, a wolf shirt, and she bought me a black and white cloth tri-fold wallet. It had a tribal symbol for wolf with black swirls around the edges.

But evaluator Cheryl A. Clayton would you please, for God's sake, explain to me how the hell did I report my wallet stolen on July 9, 2012, way the fuck back in June 21, 2011? I, and the readers, would love the answer. Why is 2012 on the front of that report and 2011 on the police report? The report is at my house. I was having sex with three women, two of which were involved (and wife Sally) but none were anyone named Bourne, no first name.

How did Cheryl A. Clayton read 2011 and bump it to 2012? Hey, let's just all play make-shit-up-as-we-go-along. Although to be fair, the whole June thing did match Brandi's witness. There has to be three or four of me and one of the mes is banging Ms. Bourne back in 2011.

I am mentally worn the hell out. I do remember when we lived on Jewel Ridge. When I was in second grade mom had a wringer washer and cloth diapers she had to wash. Drop in some diapers and the shit is stirred loose. That is every damn facet of the Tazewell County justice system—when it's washed the shit continues to roll out.

Then I had an even bigger shock. When I told the snitch bitch on the wire all about Brandi offering sex for money, the lying son of a bitches put every word in the report. I have never made any statement to anyone anywhere. Sally knew, this book is my statement. Pages two of five to five of five are all pure fabrication, a false report to go with the false police report. Can y'all Cheryl A. Clayton please fix the goddamn date on the falsified police report? I know it's bullshit but come on, at least try to get it in the same year.

Also, when you wrote about Tennessee I was never incarcerated. I sat at the desk talking to the cop, I made bail, then I was home before the ice in my drink melted, but I was supposedly "released from incarceration." Sounds better for lying son of a bitches.

And would you fix the whole bullshit about "2 or 3" times in the North Carolina police report? I have the report and so do thousands of others. She said it was one time and she never saw if my pants were unzipped.

On page five-family I did say Sally and I were in constant contact because we were, and Sally knows the police report is fake. As of May 3, 2022 Sally had 27 days of visitation left but it won't be renewed.

On page six I would ask the lying bitch Cheryl A. Clayton to review the trial transcript. I tell people I took electronics for two years which I did, I never say I graduated, not in the book, not on trial, so stop making me out to be a liar after your ass pops in a fake police report. Whether I graduated or not was irrelevant in my world, not a lot of call for electronics in woodworking. College was a waste of two years.

I did attend church with Sally at Buffalo Ridge Baptist Church. The after-church corruption hour (or four) was so worth it. Sally was very good at after-church corruption hours.

And finally, it was in this report that my complete sexual history was speculated on and here it is from Grave Sex Girl to Sarah Hale (call me Sally). That's all there is, there ain't no more.

On page nine:

Defendant reports that he plans to write a book, publish a book titled, "little tin gods: a modern day witch hunt," (no caps). The title changed but here is the book in its completed state. At this that time I did have a publisher that Sally dealt with through the acquisitioner.

There are so many mistakes in the report I wonder if the creator is related to the court reporter. Or, like a court reporter, makes up whatever because they are little tin gods. Who would dare question our shit no matter how bad it stinks.

"2. Mr. Blankenship is in need of comprehensive sex offense treatment to address his sexual offending, HIS PROBLEMATIC personality traits, his history of noncompliance with previous treatment obligations, his level of hostility and his lack of community social supports he is unlikely to be responsive to community-based treatment until substantial gains are made on issues interfering with treatment amenability."

Oh my!

"Amenability: open to persuasion: syn: obedient."

"In the event he is referred to community-based sex offender treatment upon his release from incarceration his participation in treatment should be on a probationary basis and contingent upon his willingness to acknowledge his offending and some degree of motivation in the change process."

Wow! Where to start on that one.

Failure to participate in the past. I told the son of a bitch shrink I did not do a goddamn thing other than accept a plea deal to avoid life in prison. If he don't want the truth he can still go outside and play hide and go fuck himself.

As to "amenable" if one means since I was court ordered to attend a S.O.A.P. program y'all think if I sit in prison long enough I will break. I am told in that program one must write down what one did or be considered in denial. Let me help with that. Ten years in prison and I was not guilty when the lying son of a bitches locked me up, I am not guilty after 10 years in prison, and I will be not guilty when I die in prison. You want the truth Cheryl A. Clayton, you put Brandi on a lie detector, and you ask her if she stole my wallet. She steals money, cigarettes and she lies. Until you get the truth instead of fabricating false police reports you are just another turd washing out of the diaper.

Then Cheryl A. Clayton, where the hell do you come off calling me a pathological liar? Like Hoggle said in the movie "Labyrinth," "I wonder what your basis for comparison is." You, Cheryl A. Clayton, who includes a false police report with the wrong day, month and year call me a liar. Such audacity.

Hey, here's some good ones:

"He tore off my shirt and bra."

"No, he never removed ANY of my clothes."

"He removed my shirt."

Gonna be damn hard to admit what I did when the bitch can't make up her mind. As to my hostility, can anyone reading this book honestly say if this happened to them, or their child they would say, "Oh, what a wonderful experience."

Tell ya' what there Cheryl A. Clayton, are you still at the probation office at Claypool Hill. Why don't you pick up Ms. Bailey, juror, then go to TruPoint Bank,13250 Gov. Perry Hwy. it's only one minute from the office. You go in and you personally confirm my bank statement and when you know it's legit. You pull around the bank to the ATM and set a watch for 22 minutes mintues.

You pull over to Wal-Mart, you park around the side on the grocery side, enter the grocery side, walk back to posters, exit the grocery side.

Then you drive the route Brandi testified to, the Google Map, with a 12 minute stop on Ray Road. Then you drive the River Road. If that 22 minutes runs out before you can get to the car wash, Doran Grocery, Brandi lied, I am innocent.

In the immortal words of Blackie Lawless, W.A.S.P. "Harder Faster," "you can suck me, suck me, eat me raw." Or tag up with the shring ass-hole in N.C. and you can both go outside and play hide and go fuck yourself. I AM INNOCENT.

Pathological liars, huh:
The court has pulled all relevant information.
Defense, nothing pertains to Mr. Blankenship.
He bought her cigarettes.
She repeatedly broke into houses to steal cigarettes.
Prosecutor: She had minor trespassing.
Brandi goes to trial for breaking and entering.
Mr. Blankenship is innocent of shoplifting
HE STOLE SUNGLASSES

There was only one incident where Brandi would yell rape--if stepdad did not stop hitting her with a belt.

Brandi falsely accuses a person at TDT.

Brandi makes multiple threats of lying about sexual assault on multiple people spanning months.

Do you, Cheryl A. Fucking Clayton, see the goddamn summons for shoplifting in the book's Documents? Do you know how many goddamn times it was blasted to a jury HE STOLE SUNGLASSES and the son of a bitch who defended me just sat there—not a fucking peep? That summons was written July 9, 2012 for sunglasses in which I went to trial in December. Do you see a goddamn shoplifting on my record anywhere, ever?!

And Cheryl A. Clayton, do you realize the prosecutor put the Wal-Mart picture on a huge screen for my entire trial? Now you, Cheryl A. Clayton, go to Wal-Mart and stand in that spot, look at my bank statement, then drive to Raven in four minutes. If you can't then that photo is not me, it is fabricated "SPECTER" evidence.

Here's a good one Cheryl A. Clayton. You read Brandi's probation psych report then you walk up to Judge Patterson and you ask him to his face why HE lied. I say CIGARETTES were involved or more than damn well pertained to my case, and I would say Brandi breaking into houses just to steal cigarettes REPEATEDLY could have oh, undermined her credibility, attacked her credibility.

Here's a new play there, super honest Cheryl A. Clayton. Why don't you question hey, where did that VHS tape go, where are the two Wal-Mart videos? You, Ms. Cheryl A. Clayton, watch the Jim Shortt video then you come and tell me is it video or audio, then you Cheryl A. Clayton, point out who is lying. Then on top of all that, I pick up a report that says in 2012 some other woman stole my wallet or that somehow the only person who has not spoken is a pathological liar.

So yeah, maybe I am a wee bit hostile, can't imagine why. Luckily, from working in appliances I learned a neat trick about anger—take it out on the bill. Well, this book is my bill.

As to the others, think on this Cheryl A. Clayton, had I ever been going to say I did it it would have been on the plea deal, one charge for three years, long before any abduction bullshit and I would be home now. Sally posted all of the paperwork online so the people can decide, and thousands know I am innocent. I will never take any program no matter if I sit in prison until I die.

But I will make a deal. You put Brandi and her sister on a lie detector, and you ask them both if they stole my wallet, then I will take a lie detector every single day for a year. While you're at it, put Judge Patterson, Jim Shortt, Mike Dennis and Mike Letson on a lie detector, in public, to see just who the pathological liars are or if you have the ability to know the difference.

Until Brandi is on a lie detector, all any of you will ever get is NOT GUILTY—FUCK YOU!

I did, however, add in Documents the criminal history that the pre-sentence report provided. Keep in mind December 2012 I went to trial for shoplifting. Does anyone see shoplifting on said criminal history?

I would love to actually ask Ms. Cheryl A. Clayton exactly where am I a pathological liar? You sit in your little tin god world and you operate on the premise of those now proven to be pathological liars. Have you ever once questioned any situation no matter how ludicrous it is? And then Cheryl A. Clayton, you read:

The court: The court pulled all relevant documents

Defense: Nothing else pertains to Mr. Blankenship's case

He bought her cigarettes.

She repeatedly broke into homes to steal cigarettes.

Now who lied!

Damn it, fix the damn date in the false police report then call me a liar, please. See, I said please, not hostile at all until annoyed.

Damn it! I do hate it when one of Sally's friends corrects me, annoying nude female proofreaders. Yes, in the movie, "Labyrinth," it was the Goblin King (Bowie), not Hoggle, who said, "I wonder what your basis for comparison?"

See Cheryl A. Clayton, that is what a correction looks like you should try it sometime instead of putting out falsified Court documents "2012 police report." I bet had my stolen wallet been raised on appeal your little falsified document would have been argued by the Commonwealth, not to worry, lying bitch Carletta J. Faletti never raised the point. You do know the falsification of Court documents is fraud don't you.

Come to think of it, Cheryl A. Clayton, at the probation office, did you happen to review a little file, Juvenile and Domestic Relations Court Progress Report on Brandi?

You should compare Redacted Statement-1 with the reports page 2. How very goddamn convenient that statement was cut out just below, "Brandi lies, Brandi steals," and cut out just above, "Brandi has breaking and entering, destruction of private property Court date sch. For July." The Redacted Statement-2 was cut out below it was the police that had been called on Brandi, by neighbors, numerous times. That exculpatory evidence was intentionally concealed in violation of Due Process.

Then, You, Cheryl A. Clayton, go review the trial recording against the posted transcript the YOU tell this so called "community" who the liars are. You personally review all the evidence against the testimony.

But, for fuck's sake, fix the goddamn date in your falsified police report. Then call me a liar.

Chapter 8

Actual Innocence

"When Sarah Good was accused of being a witch, she did not believe it. When she was arrested, tried and convicted, she did not believe it. When they put the rope around her neck, and she dropped, in that eternity of seconds between her last attempt to gasp for air and her final thought before death, then she believed. If, at that moment, we could look through the eyes of Sarah at the spectators, some with grins, watching her die, I wonder if even one of them ever thought...'What If I, or my child, are the next to be falsely accused?' If Sarah had tried to warn them would they have listened." Sarah Good, Hanged as a witch July 19, 1692.

I hope there are those who read the book as if it happened to a loved one so the events were more real. I would like to make this very clear, yes, Brandi stole my wallet then lied about sexual assault to cover the theft but I do not hate Brandi. Neither Brandi, nor my jury, put me in prison for life. The blame for my false imprisonment falls solely on the injustice system.

There is a secrete that only Sally and I knew yet to be revealed and I have some new information to be covered but first I need to reiterate some points from the book.

July 9, 2012 Brandi stole my wallet, a pack of cigarettes and she lied about sexual assault. She then stated I stole sunglasses at Walmart. I was arrested, held without bail, on four charges that included contributing for cigarettes and I was issued a Summons for shoplifting.

December 19, 2012 I went to court where plead and was found not guilty of shoplifting the sunglasses.

In January 2013 I was indicted on four charges and I had a March jury trial date set. In February my lawyer told me I would accept a plea deal, three years on one charge, or I would further be charged with abduction that carried life in prison. I accepted but I wrote on the plea deal that I was threatened with life in prison if refused. The plea deal was thrown out and in March I was reindicted to add the abduction charge, I faced life plus 22 years, not for a crime committed but due to malicious prosecution for refusing a plea deal.

In the police report Brandi said on Ray road her shirt and bra had been removed. In May 2014 Brandi violated probation and she was locked in a detention center where my lawyer made a video of Brandi in which she stated on Ray Road none of her clothes were ever removed, she forgot, "shirt-bra removed?" In the video Brandi then claimed on Ray Road that a naked man slammed her to the ground then jumped on top of for over two minutes but at trial, by her testimony, Brandi stated that never happened either. She then stated on Ray Road only her shirt had been removed, she forgot, "naked man on top of her?" The end result was that Brandi told three separate lies about sexual assault to irrefutable sources and my lawyer became a witness for the defense due to Brandi lying about sexual assault.

Amendment VI covers that assistance of counsel must be meaningful and effective. For a claim of ineffective assistance of counsel one must show that a lawyer did, or failed to do, something and it caused the defendant prejudice; some examples can be failure to impeach, failure to object or failure to perform a pretrial investigation and many others.

In my trial transcript there are patterns like, every motion by the prosecution the jury is in but every motion by the defense the jury is out. And the only time my lawyer argued for the defense the jury was out, when the jury was in he just mimicked the prosecutor on every point.

At trial Brandi lied about only having minor trespassing, counsel failed to object to known perjury, I was denied a fair trial. (wait for it)

Brandi lied about her siblings cleaning house, counsel failed to obtain a running objection to Brandi's contradictory hearsay and counsel failed to impeach even when the officer testified the house was never cleaned. I was prejudiced when it was repeatedly falsely bolstered as a grooming technique.

Brandi lied about driving to the bank in Richlands, counsel failed to object to known perjury. Further counsel failed to impeach when Brandi then stated I drove to the Valero. Counsel failed to show the VHS Tape proving Brandi neither drove to or from the Valero. I was prejudiced when it was repeatedly falsely bolstered I allowed-forced Brandi to drive in a grooming technique.

Brandi lied about sunglasses being shoplifted. Both my lawyer who held the Summons showing I was found not guilty and co-counsel who had defended me on the shoplifting failed to object. I was prejudiced when it repeatedly falsely bolstered I was a shoplifter and that I had shoplifted in a grooming technique. Counsel failed to present Walmart video one that showed Brandi entering Walmart with the sunglasses on her hat and counsel failed to present the Summons.

Brandi lied about being held inside Walmart. Counsel failed to present Walmart video two that shows Brandi alone, not held, before she runs left to the posters.

Counsel failed to object to fabricated evidence, Exiting Walmart Photo, as no one can drive 8.8 miles, 13 minutes, in under 4 minutes as proven by my bank statement. Therefore counsel failed to object to the entire Walmart photo series also proven to be, not me.

Counsel failed to object to what Walmart security footage showed, violation, Conclusory Allegation is not enough, code (8.01-254(B)(2)) because NO video was ever shown or entered into trial exhibits.

Brandi lied about the route driven from Walmart or ever going to Ray Road, no one could be at the ATM, spend any time inside Walmart then make a 12.1 mile, 22 minute, drive with any stop on Ray Road and still be inside Doran Grocery in under 22 minutes as proven by my bank statement.

In the first jury recess, in a trial of alleged sexual assault of a young girl a FEMALE juror literally left the jury when the juror realized she knew Brandi had threatened to lie about sexual assault numerous times.

Counsel failed to confront Brandi with her three separate lies about sexual assault by entering both the police report and lawyer video to confront Brandi with her own words when she said she did not remember. (wait for it) Counsel failed to state the lawyer, Jim Shortt, was a witness for the defense due to Brandi lying about sexual assault and counsel failed to introduce the actions and words of the female juror who left due to Brandi threatening to lie about sexual assault when there were clear grounds to do so. (wait for it.)

Brandi, in cross examination, made a comment, "he stretched my neck." Minutes after she said it, minutes before he testified the officer created a brand new, 3rd, page 5 to the police report in which at 2:17 pm the day of trial he suddenly recalled he observed a stretched shirt three years ago. The records show at no point prior to cross examination was a stretched shirt ever mentioned. Counsel failed to impeach the questionable observance and the police report alterations. Counsel failed to introduce reasonable doubt to the stretched shirt. (wait for it.)

There is no milk or milk carton. One has three kids and a dog, who drank the milk? Was there any milk to begin with? At this point one can say, "there is no milk," but anything beyond that is Conclusory Allegation. (I didn't do it! x3 it was the dog!) (woof - not me!)

Counsel failed to object to cans repeatedly falsely bolstered as beer cans (were they, where's the proof?) and, "he drank HIS," "he finished HIS," "he tossed HIS," or, "the cans corroborate," when Conclusory Allegation is not enough code (8.01-254(B)(2)) because...there are no cans...duh!

Officers stated they had failed to collect the cans, "because Brandi became HYSTERICAL." (wait for it)

Counsel failed to object on the whole when 20 photos were entered after jury selection the day of trial in violation of codes, (19.2-187) and, (19.2-187.01) Counsel failed to object individually to the photos as irrelevant, house, random asphalt road no one was ever on, a store and a gas station.

Counsel failed to object to evidence fabricated to bolster known perjury, the photo of a bank no one ever went to, the exiting Walmart photo and Walmart photo series proven are not me.

Counsel failed to impeach when the officer testified he was unsure what road the, "road," photos were taken on Ray or Daw road.

Counsel failed to object to perjury by detective Layne when he testified on July 9, 2012 he took photos of clothes at the jail or made stills at Walmart when no photos were on the police evidence sheet nor did any photos exist on the 2013 Motion For Discovery, proven by the prosecutor's response to the discovery.

Counsel failed to impeach when defectively Layne testified, "he followed on Walmart security footage," since he presented photos that are proven not me, whoever he followed on video was therefore, also, not me.

Any person who stated or wrote that I stole sunglasses is guilty of slander, First Amendment libel and defamation of character.

In early 2015 I had a trial date set, the prosecution, having no evidence, created a new, 2nd, page 5 to the police report to add J. Ray

Smith.

Counsel failed to call a mistrial on prosecutorial misconduct, the use of staged testimony to enter inadmissible evidence, the observance of an irrelevant computer in a house 20 miles away. I was prejudiced in that it implied a, "computer crime," element into my trial that had no computer element. Further the use of staged testimony to repeatedly refer to the irrelevant condition of a house being remodeled in a derogatory manner just to cast negative disparagements upon me.

Counsel failed to object to a surprise witness, Crystal Owens, and when Crystal had every single detail wrong counsel failed to object to prosecutorial misconduct, falsely bolstering Crystal's testimony in trial and in closing arguments as corroborating.

I put subpoenas on Robbie Davis and Brad Goff, Brandi's probation officers. My subpoenas were removed then the prosecution usurped my witness, Robbie Davis, who was allowed to testify in a secrete proceeding without either myself or the jury present. This violates Article III, Amendments V, VI, VII and XIV as a jury trial by definition would require a jury when a witness testifies. It further violates Amendment VI and code (19.2-256) that both protect the right to be personally present at every stage from arraignment to sentencing. The presence of a jury or defendant is not contingent upon the context or content of a witness's testimony.

I messed up concerning day two of trial, I was working between what is in my transcript and what really happened so some parts are confusing. At trial the jury was in recess when I tried to enter my bank statement the prosecutor made three separate objections and the last one was, he did not know what a bank statement is, "some kind of bank record, maybe?" One side argued bank statement, one side argued bank record and the judge ruled, "without agreement as to the type of record, I don't think it can be admitted," which is a judge saying, "I don't know what a bank statement is either." (if he knew what it was he'd have to allow it...that's kinda his fucking job!)

When I wrote no one said bank record, by that I meant, in my trial transcript the prosecutor never speaks, my lawyer moved to enter the bank statement for the defense, he then objects to the bank statement for the prosecution, but when they altered every instance of bank statement to bank record, there is no disagreement so the judge"s ruling is out of place, but then my lawyer objects to the ruling on the objection he made to the motion he made, can you say...Liar Liar.

Counsel failed to argue the prosecution had already entered the Corner Mart receipt that shows my name, debit card use, store, location, date, time and amount 11.77 that are ALL reflected in my bank statement along with completed checks. A bank record is still a record a business would rely on and therefore free from hearsay and to not admit the bank statement was abuse of discretion if not outright misconduct. May I please take this opportunity to politely interject, COME ON PEOPLE! IT'S A FUCKING BANK STATEMENT! (am I really arguing this point?)

I tried to enter my stolen wallet but the judge ruled there were no grounds to enter that. (wait for it) But the real point is, the jury had no idea my bank statement or my stolen wallet were ever mentioned.

Counsel failed to call a mistrial on prosecutorial misconduct when it was discovered the prosecution had sneaked a 16 year police report into the jury room which had been ruled could not be used. I requested a copy which my lawyer took from a juror and handed to me, my possession of said complete file proves the misconduct and the claim.

I knew the court was set to call a mistrial because my lawyer told me at the holding cell they were considering a point of mistrial after barely one hour of deliberations. Immediately after that it was discovered that the prosecution had appointed the female police dispatcher as jury foreperson who acted as an outside influence and she acted in collusion to illegally poll the jury, this is proven in the trial transcript when it shows, on two charges they had agreed to not guilty but on three - a majority - they were not yet decided. It was that action which prompted the judge to employ the Allen Charge where the judge said it was their duty to reach a verdict and he said, "establish guilt." The actions of the judge were so reprehensible the female assistant prosecutor objected, the jury were not gridlocked they had been illegally polled, then her objection caused a one hour time jump in the transcript to make the Allen Charge appear justified.

I still have a big secrete but it requires we step back in time, pay attention. In early 2015 we were set to walk into trial when my lawyer told me the court had just found in 2015 a medical record in which was found two little statements where Brandi had threatened to lie about sexual assault but to use those we had to postpone to subpoena witnesses.

Then we go forward to July 20, 2015 at the motions hearing. I am sorry it is confusing in my transcript and in my book. I will try to even it out. The prosecution acting on behalf of Brandi's mother moved to block the medical record, the judge ruled anything exculpatory would be able to come out for the defense. The rest is confusing because my transcript is altered. In the hearing it was the court who said Brandi's mother would be a witness for the Commonwealth and the prosecutor said yes she is a witness. When they doctored the transcript they tried to make it appear that Brandi's mother had been requested at trial by the defense but she was not present at the hearing.

Then come forward to the morning of trial and the judge ruled, having reviewed the medical record in its entirety he provided the two redacted statements and he said that nothing else pertained to my trial. If anyone is reading this I pray the two redacted statements, and probation report, have been put in the book's documents.

Now we must bounce far forward to 2020 when my appeal ended I sought my case file but at some point Carla claimed a Covid exception then she absconded to Vancouver, WA with my case file. There were many State Bar complaints and motions to compel attorney filed but it was a brick wall. At that time Covid exploded and millions were sick or dying.

Many people have asked me where did the probation report on Brandi come from? That's the big secret only Sally and I knew. I was in pursuit of my case file when I received some documents from the courts with a letter that basically stated, "here are all the unsealed documents we are able to provide to you at this time." And there it was.

Only then did I see the whole truth. What had been misrepresented as a medical record at trial, and in multiple legal proceedings, was in fact a Juvenile and Domestic Relations Court Progress Report, a probation report on Brandi, a legal court document that is free from hearsay so there had been no reason to postpone or subpoena anyone in early 2015. The probation report had not been just found in 2015, it had been filed July 17, 2012, only 8 days after my arrest, it had been withheld from the 2013 Motion For Discovery and it had been concealed for three years proven by it was only added to my case file the morning of trial.

Does everyone recall every (wait for it) in this chapter...the wait is over.

In closing arguments the prosecution made the exclamation that if Brandi wanted to lie she'd have made a better lie like, "he said he was going to kill me."

The probation report shows that (2011) a year prior to my arrest Brandi made a false allegation of sexual assault against another person at the therapist's office where she, in fact, did say, "he said he was going to kill me." The prosecutor was fully cognizant of the probation report's contents. That the prior allegation was false is proven when Brandi's therapist testified that Brandi, in early 2012, denied anyone have ever sexually assaulted her.

The probation report shows, multiple times at multiple locations Brandi had thrown, "hysterical," fits to the extent the police had to be called. Had this, and Brandi's prior false allegation, not been concealed it could have been argued on Ray Road, in light of my bank statement, Brandi knew the beer cans, if collected, would only prove she was lying again so she became hysterical as she was very prone to do.

The probation report shows that for a year Brandi had thrown psychotic fits, demanding cigarettes, and threatening to lie about sexual assault multiple times against multiple people to the extent the police had been called on Brandi numerous times by neighbors and a therapist had to discuss the seriousness of lying about sexual assault. Had that not been concealed it was grounds to enter the corroborating words and actions of the female juror who left the trial due to knowing Brandi threatened to lie about sexual assault numerous times and the neighbors could have been subpoenaed had anyone known to do so.

The probation report shows that Brandi had threatened to lie about actual rape, "calling him bald and a rapist," when she had been asked not to roll down a car window because it was cold. Had all of these not been concealed it could have been argued that lying about, and threatening to lie about, sexual assault was habitual behavior and when combined with my stolen wallet she more than had motive and willingness to lie about sexual assault.

The probation report reiterates multiple times that Brandi lies, Brandi steals and Brandi often says things she pretends she doesn't remember. All of which is exculpatory especially when Brandi often said she did not remember throughout her testimony at trial.

I had a contributing charge for cigarettes, cigarettes were referenced over 30 times in my trial an the only actual evidence presented at my trial were 20 irrelevant photos, the NOT stolen sunglasses and a pack of cigarettes meaning the only real evidence ever presented was a pack of cigarettes. And I had a stolen wallet in contention.

The probation report shows that the very month of my arrest, July 2012, Brandi had a court date for breaking entering, destruction of private property (not trespassing) she literally broke into houses to steal cigarettes and money multiple times.

Brandi's theft of cigarettes was directly exculpatory to my contributing charge and it was exculpatory to every stage of my trial, including the only trial evidence, had it not been concealed.

Brandi's theft of money, multiple times, meant that I'd had grounds to enter my stolen wallet had those grounds not been concealed. The probation report shows Brandi often fights with her sister to the point of bruises. Had my stolen wallet been entered and had the full content of the probation report been known it could have been argued, Brandi's sister was present when Brandi stole my wallet," they fought over the money," is reasonable doubt to the questionably observed stretched shirt.

The probation report proves that a plethora of exculpatory evidence that had ramifications to every stage of my trial had been concealed. Any person who had knowledge of the probation report's contents but chose to conceal them violated my due process rights, Amendment VI and XIV.

Redacted statement one was cut out in a manner to conceal that Brandi lies, Brandi steals and Brandi was charged with breaking and entering. Redacted statement to was cut out in a manner to conceal it was, "the police that had been called on Brandi numerous times by neighbors," thus proving the concealment was intentional.

When the court ruled anything exculpatory would be able to come out for the defense then stated no other information pertained to my case then he chose to conceal the exculpatory evidence that was abuse of discretion if not outright misconduct.

To add to the mess, I filed a State Habeas (160484) and in that Habeas the office of the Attorney General further misrepresented the probation report as a medical record and further argue that counsel called Brandi's therapist, and Brandi's mother, thus Brandi's prior history was fully presented to the jury.

The record actually shows that counsel acted in collusion and conspiracy by telling Brandi's therapist to limit her testimony to just the two redacted statements not the full probation report, then calling the prosecution's witness, Brandi's mother, to discredit just the two redacted statements proven because she was not asked about the contents of the full report and counsel allowed Brandi's probation officer to testify in a secret proceeding to insure the fact Brandi was on probation and the contents of the full probation report remain concealed...thus Brandi's prior history was NOT presented to the jury at all.

I need to further point out that when I filed my Habeas I had not seen my bank statement or the probation report, I did include the shoplifting Summons which they just removed and argued perjury, fabricated evidence and Conclusory Allegation on the shoplifting but all other points made in that Habeas it was argued that the evidentiary issues, rulings (like my bank statement to prove perjury) and prosecutorial methods should be raised in regular appeal.

It wasn't until 2017 that I saw my bank statement and only then did I see the 4.92 pizza bought at Doran Grocery that proves me innocent. Had Carla visited me in 2017 long before any appeal was filed she would have seen the bank statement, shoplifting summons and the points in my Habeas but Carla chose to lie, in writing, then she filed an appeal on only one item, the prior conviction. It was argued in the appeal that the prior conviction was not abuse of discretion, "because the jury not been shown any inflammatory fact specific aspects of the prior conviction." Had Carla fixed the transcript she'd have seen the jury had the 16 year old police report that constituted abuse of discretion, she lost due to her gross negligence and she failed to file on any of the points herein listed even when she'd been instructed to do so by the arguments of the Attorney General in the Habeas.

Had the jury been shown ALL of the points raised in this chapter alone the outcome of my trial would have been very different.

YOUR LYING PIECE OF CRAP HONOR, SIR, THE ONLY REAL DEFENSE EVER MADE RESTS!

Now let's see who REALLY paid attention. No one just wakes up one day on probation!

Throughout my trial Brandi was repeatedly falsely bolstered as a barely fourteen year old innocent who never done no wrong, did I not say it took six years to get the punchline.

The court document is not a good Samaritan award it's a probation report... GET IT! Brandi was on probation in 2012...why? The police had been called on Brandi numerous times in multiple locations. Brandi violated probation in 2014 to be locked up in the detention center... why was she violated? WHERE are the police reports, court records, the other probation reports, where are the actual psychological reports where the therapist had to discuss with Brandi the seriousness of lying about sexual assault. The probation report proves not only was a plethora of exculpatory evidence concealed but also that a multitude is yet still concealed (can you say Brady v. Maryland violations)...what else is in my case file? The probation report proves that either trial counsel acted in conspiracy to conceal exculpatory evidence or he failed to perform any pretrial investigation. (you decide) And, of course, Carla failed the raise the concealed exculpatory evidence on appeal. I prove ineffective assistance of counsel to a degree I was tried without representation.

People have asked me why I never spoke up especially about the sunglasses. I did, once. When the prosecutor said I stole sunglasses I told Mike Dennis that it was a lie but the judge called me down, I was told if I said one more word I'd be ejected and tried in my absence. That was the purpose for repeatedly falsely bolstering that I stole sunglasses, they expected I'd blow up, I'd have been ejected, I'd have been portrayed as a raving lunatic and the 16 year police report would have been, "lawfully (he says jokingly) entered." I never spoke but it didn't matter since they sneaked in the police report any way.

But no one sees the point. I NEVER SPOKE!...get it?

Had I testified and had I said I never left the house then the prosecution would have had grounds to enter the Corner Mart receipt to prove I did leave the house. My entire trial was NOT about an assault on Ray Road it was proving hearsay of what someone said, that someone said...that I said...I never left the house...but...I NEVER SPOKE!

But even more amusing, there are some sharp legal minds in prison and many have read my book but no one has seen it yet.

In early 2015 the court (judge) found in a medical record two redacted statements where Brandi threatened to lie about sexual assault. In the motions hearing, and start of trial, the court reviewed the file and made it available for both sides to review.

THAT'S NOT HOW COURT WORKS!

When a prosecutor or lawyer intends to enter evidence he makes a motion to which the other side objects, or not, then the judge rules according to the law.

Show of hands, how many people really believe ye' ole judge went out to rummage through doctors offices to find exculpatory evidence he then presented to the defense? If a judge pulled that crap the prosecution would still be filing complaints. The ONLY way that file was in my trial was because it was introduced by one side or the other. POP QUIZ : If we need a medical record do we, A.) go to the hospital, or, B.) go to the court house? The court does not store medical records... should have stood out from the get go.

Look at the motions hearing, the prosecution asked what is being requested from the file. Uh...if the defense had the file he would not need to make any request he'd have made a motion to enter said file. Maybe if the prosecutor had have said, "what is being requested from MY file that I've kept concealed for three years," it would have been more obvious.

To answer another question I've been asked several times, no, I was not singled out due to a prior conviction. Read the book, look at the documents, I was offered a three year plea deal on one charge long before the abduction was added. I was treated exactly the same as anyone else was, or will be in the future...and that is the whole point to the book. I was treated exactly like you, your child, would be if falsely accused. I understand the fear felt, trying to justify it by saying because it was me or some other non self relatable factor, but nope, one false accusation and you are me, (congratulations) and that should scare the hell out of people.

Upon discovery of the concealed exculpatory evidence I filed a motion to reconsider the previous Habeas the court declined to consider. I filed a motion to vacate the court also declined to consider. I have a letter dated January 2023 on the Motion To Vacate where the court said it could provide no relief. The probation report proves that a multitude of exculpatory evidence is yet still concealed but Carla adamantly refuses to relinquish my case file. Fearing to move forward on an incomplete record but having no other choice I filed a Federal Habeas (7:23cv00174) in the U.S. District Court for the Western District of Virginia.

I received an opinion on my Federal Habeas which states that I failed to show why I had not obtained the appellate counsel's case file at an earlier date even though I clearly stated on page 35 of the Habeas that appellate counsel refuses to relinquish my case file. The court afforded me a discovery date on the probation report of December 2021, had the Habeas been filed by December 2022 it would have been timely filed but the motion to vacate was not answered until 2023.

The opinion states that the merits of my claim would be considered if I showed my delayed filing was due to circumstances external to my actions, equitable tolling of the time limitation is available in instances where it would be unconscionable to enforce the time limitation (Rouse v. Lee 339 F. 3d. 238, 246 (4th Cir. 2003)) it goes on to say that I'd be entitled to equitable tolling if I could show, "1.) that I had diligently pursued my rights, and, 2.) that some circumstance stood in my way."

And just exactly how much time was I afforded to show I was entitled to equitable tolling, you ask?

ABSOLUTELY FUCKING NONE!

The judge who wrote the opinion just assumed I could not respond in a positive manner so he wrote the dismissal the same day. And this is where people get lost and most people in prison only find out about it years to late.

When a Federal Habeas is dismissed one cannot just file and appeal one must obtain a COA. What the fuck is that? The COA is a certificate of appealability. Uh, okay, what the fuck is that! The COA is a jurisdictional prerequisite so until it's issued the courts of appeals lacks jurisdiction to rule on the merits of appeals from a Federal Habeas. This is tricky to understand for the courts and for the petitioner. One does not have to show that an appeal would prevail only that it would be debatable among reasonable jurists. (that hopefully won't contain female police dispatchers) While the bar to obtain a COA is very low it is important to stay within the time limits. The time limitations can vary from 60 days to just 21 days depending on how unscrupulous that district is. The main thing is if a loved one is working on Federal Habeas get them the information on the time limitations well ahead of time because a majority of cases are rejected on technicality not grounds.

So, how is my COA going, you ask. IT'S NOT FUCKING GOING AT ALL!

Yep, ye' ole judge denied the COA in the dismissal before the COA was filed. How the hell does one deny a motion before it is even filed, talk about fuck due process! Why even have a process?

Okay. What does a person do when the COA, applied for or not, is denied? There are two chances of obtaining the COA left. First ask the district court who denied the COA to reconsider, which is asking the ass hole who violated due process to maybe NOT deny due process, little hope there. Mine was shot down within two weeks. So the second is to file a motion to reconsider the denial of COA in the Appeals Court

And that, ladies and gentleman, concludes our saga. My motion to reconsider the denial of COA is sitting in the Appeals Court. By god, any day now brothers and sisters I will find a judge with just enough intelligence to know what a bank statement is and one who can at least read the numbers on a Google Map then see...Hey! this dude's innocent so let him out!

Under Federal Habeas rule 11(a) first ask the District Court to reconsider denial of COA then the Appeals Court.

That brings me to the denial of COA without an opportunity to respond when, "movant (me) must be given opportunity to respond," (Rizzo v. United States 821 F. 2d. 1271, 1273 (7th Cir. 1987)). And what would I have shown had I been given opportunity to respond?

I have requested three letters be added to the book's documents. Throughout 2020 to 2023 multiple Virginia State Bar complaints were filed and at one time Carla claimed it was trial counsel who held my case file, why would the prosecutor hold my case file on an appeal filed two years later? Then Carla claimed her old firm, Ms. Gonzalez, had the file but Gonzalez stated the old firm was Faletti-Gonzalez, Carla was the old firm, I was told by Mike Dennis, Joey Stiltner and Ms. Gonzalez that Carla has the case file.

I refer to one letter from the State Bar to carla dated July 12, 2022, long before the time limitation to file my Federal Habeas, in which it states, "...please respond to Mr. Blankenship's request for his file or explain why you cannot provide it...," Carla refused to communicate and she refused to relinquish my case file. At the same time when I filed the motion to reconsider the previous Habeas, the motion to vacate and the Federal Habeas itself all contained a motion to compel attorney to relinquish my case file. So the courts failed to process my motions then rule they don't see why I could not obtain the case file at an earlier date. "Because your moronic ass didn't process my motion to compel attorney would be a pretty good reason...fuckhead!"

So I have three years of multiple State Bar complaints, multiple motions to compel attorney to relinquish my case file, Carla refuses to communicate, refuses to relinquish my case file, the State Bar refuses to investigate, the courts refuse to process motions, I believe I more than show I have pursued my rights diligently and that the failure of Carla, the State Bar and the courts stand in my way.

To go full circle there is a second Virginia State Bar letter to Carla dated June 5, 2023, "...please communicate with Mr. Blankenship regarding his CONTINUED requests for his case file. We note that you previously responded to an earlier complaint by Mr. Blankenship you stated you did not have access to Mr. Blankenship's physical paper file, please include in your response information that might help Mr. Blankenship contact the person or entity that might have access to Mr. Blankenship's file..." we're now in November, still no answer on who has my file, but any day now I'm sure.

Now this is just sad. At this point I received some documents from Carla, please see Carla Sample Letter 2023 in the book's documents. The papers I received are a disaster, the letters are illegible because all the words are different size fonts, it looks like it was done by a five year old, on crack, using MSword.

The rest of the papers Carla sent, she only had five out of 515 pages of my transcript all from the motions hearing, there are no filed motions, she did not have my bank statement, the shoplifting summons or the probation report on Brandi. If this is what was filed on my appeal no wonder she lost. Kinda hard to do an appeal when one is fucking clueless!

Carla contends she doesn't have my case file, she lied, again. Carla sent a scrambled version of the lawyer video transcript, THAT was never entered into exhibits or the digital records it only existed in my physical paper case file which Carla obviously has. Give me my case file... AND STOP FUCKING LYING TO ME! Hey! State Bar ass holes, Carla has the file, proven...FETCH BITCHES.

Oh, look at the June 5th State Bar letter, Carla is back in the area in the office of none other than Jim Shortt who made the Brandi video. So, Carla, pop open ole Jim's laptop and YOU watch the Brandi video then you tell everyone, is it 100 percent video or mostly audio as stated by Mike Dennis? Please don't answer that you'd only lie and make my head hurt, post it online so everyone can see the truth.

And does everyone recall how poor little Carla would only be paid less than 900 dollars? Uh, Carla, care to explain this invoice where you were paid 2,582.55 on my appeal. I ain't one of them gen-eus math-ah-muh-ti-tion types but I do believe 2,500 is greater than, not less than, 900. (wanna hear some shit...squeeze a lawyer.)

So. Along with my motion to reconsider the denial of COA in the Appeals Court, I am working with an exoneration project, I've filed an Actual Innocence and I have applied for an absolute pardon. And those are the cliff hangers, or fodder for future books. But I hope I have given a glimpse of, one false allegation and this could be anyone's future. I hope I was able to show the system is a hydra or a Gordian Knot...and there is no sword!

I have solid claims of violations of Article III, Amendment V, VI, VII and XIV along with codes, (19.2-187,) (19.2-187-01,) (19.2-256) and (8.01-254(B)(2)), there's abuse of discretion, Judicial and Prosecutorial misconduct, ineffective assistance of counsel both at trial and on appeal all of which have never been ruled on by the courts, blocked on technicality not grounds. But that's the cliff hangers, what will they do next on any of my filings?

And now a brief interlude with a bit of sophisticated poetry.

"You show and tell with the greatest of ease

Raving im-pos-i-bil-i-ties

But when the story takes a twist

It folds like a con-tor-tion-ist

Engaged in legalities, I grasp my throat

Enraged my mind, starts to smoke

Enforced men-tal overload

Angry Again! Angry Again! ANGRY!"

(modified lyrics from the song Angry Again, by Megadeth)

Sally and I received the probation report in 2021. Way back in 2012-13 we had started working on the book. The plan was simple as it grew, here is my bank statement that proves me innocent, here is the probation report proving intentional concealment of exculpatory evidence, publish my book, file with courts…NOW LET ME THE FUCK OUT. Sometime around December 2020 Sally contracted Covid, she was 69 when they'd just started vaccinations on 70 year olds and up. By February Sally was very sick and she was in the hospital. I spoke to Sally on her cell phone on the 10th and her last words to me were, "but I'm feeling much better," she did an impression from the, "bring out your dead," skit in Monty Python's, "The Life of Brian," which was a good exit line between us. Sally died February 13, 2021.

Covid exploded, millions were sick or dying, my wife, my sole contact with the outside world died, my goddamned lawyer refused to relinquish my case file, my book was a scattered mess, Sally had backed the book and documents up somewhere online but I've no idea where. I was not in the best of mental states. It took a flat year of writing and I managed to replace all the documents except the 3rd page 5 to the police report. I received Covid stimulus money, and a small insurance from Sally, I literally wiped out my prison account to publish my book. After months of nerve shredding stress that included removing some back story, reworking documents and writing 8,600 words of corrections my book finally published in February 2023.

I received my author's copy of my book which was promptly confiscated by prison officials on the grounds the police report depicts an act that breaks a law. (huh?) How the hell do you ban a police report...IN FUCKING PRISON!

Before I'm asked the same questions 3,247 times, the Supreme Court ruled that the First Amendment protects the rights of prisoners to tell their stories because it's told from their point of view. The right to send and receive mail, the right to write to news media, the right to conduct legitimate business, the right to write for publication and the right to create - possess manuscripts are all protected by the Constitution ruled on in numerous cases.

Anyone in prison who has ordered, or anyone who has ordered for a prisoner, publications knows once any publication is sent to a Publication Review Committee there is an 80 percent chance it will be banned and there is a 99.8 percent chance it will be lost, never to be seen again. I call it the, "Great Library of Never Was," when a missing publication is inquired after the person is told, "never was delivered," even when they hold a tracking number. Having lost dozens of publications over the years to the Great Library of Never Was I requested that the publisher return my original hand written book, my legal documents and a manuscript made after the 8,600 words of corrections were made.

Around May 9, 2023 I was informed my book was banned on the grounds that the police report depicts an act that breaks a law and that the book has depictions and photos of nude children. That claim constitutes manufacturing of child pornography. The claim is based on the police report in which Brandi said her shirt and bra had been removed but my book also has the lawyer video transcript where Brandi said none of her clothes were ever removed. Proving that a person lied on a police report is not sexually explicit in any way and I never state anyone's clothes were ever removed therefore the claim of depicting nude children is both slander and libel.

The false claim puts my life at risk, in my prison file it only states contains depictions and photos of nude children, the person reading that has no idea of the details or that it only refers to a falsified police report.

LOOK in the books documents, do YOU see any photos of children, nude or otherwise? NO! Those white things are American Eskimo dogs (in case anyone is as stupid as the moron who banned my book... confusing dogs for kids!) and all my dogs are properly dressed in their hair!

It was not until May 12th I was informed (sort of) that back on the 9th in direct violation of both Cadmus Publishing's and my Constitutional Rights they had also confiscated 8 manila envelopes the publisher had mailed that contained my hand written book, legal documents and manuscript. They just stapled a second confiscation form to the back of the first one. (like I wouldn't notice)

Common misconception. When a publication is confiscated or banned there is a grievance procedure, one has 7 days to file a written complaint. That is, a written complaint is filled out and put in the grievance box, there is no proof it was filed, then at some point one receives a receipt for proof of filing. More often than not they simply wait past 7 days, toss the grievance in the trash and claim never received and that kills any grievance procedure since it's past the 7 days deadline. My filed grievance may turn up any day now...after ten or so months.

A lawsuit was filed on the banned book and confiscated mail, (7:23cv00183) and weeks later my mail was delivered. No one can rob a bank then weeks later return the money to negate the crime, the delivery of the manila envelopes does not negate the Constitutional Rights violations...BUT, I could finally read my book.

This, however, creates a very ironic situation. Every prisoner not only has a right to possess his or her case file, police report, transcript and so on but also they are required to do so to file legal proceedings. All the documents in my book I am allowed, even required, to possess, so they are in my cell. The First Amendment protects my right to my manuscript so that too is in my cell. But, somehow, put the documents and manuscript into an actual book and I can't have that because I may read something I, who wrote it, don't know.

"Depicts an act that breaks a law" is both a very broad and commonly used description to ban publications second only to sexual content.

Every prison has some type of access to a law library, thousands of documents, entire sets of encyclopedia books that depict, describe and define acts that break a law. The entire Judicial Branch of the United States Government is built upon, and for, documents that depicts acts that break laws, kinda the whole goddamned purpose! To ban any publication on the grounds it depicts an act that breaks a law in an institution designed to house documents that depict acts that breaks laws is discrimination. (or raw fucking stupidity) Oh look what the law library sent me, (Velázquez v. Commonwealth 292 VA 603, 791 S. E. 2d. 556, 557 (2016 VA)), "computer solicitation of a child," which I do believe is a document that depicts an act that breaks a law given to me by the same people who ban publications because they depict acts that breaks laws...go figure.

I am not alone on the banned publication lists, the book, "It," by Stephen King and at least one of the, "Game of Thrones," books, and thousands of others, are banned under the same claims as my book. In the case of Mr. Martin and Mr. King they may want to look at, (Lewis v. State 2023 Ark 12 (Ark 2023)), the claim of manufacturing child pornography must contain a child defined as a person therefore the claims cannot be made on fictional or even CGI characters.

For all the avid photo collectors in prison, when required to pay for an, "over 18," stamp on a fictional or anima character that is discrimination. Can someone else take up the photo stamp war, I kinda got my hands full.

At the same time the regular prison library holds hundreds, if not thousands, of both fiction and nonfiction books that depict acts that break laws including every manner of sex crime. In my cell from the library are books like, "Our Little Secret," by Kevin Flynn and Rebecca Lavoie, "the true story of a teenage killer and the silence of a small town." Or, I have, "The Girl with the Dragon Tattoo," series by Stieg Larson that has bondage, pedophilia and rape while under custodial care. I also have Ian Rakin's book, "Dead Souls." There are way more books in the prison library that depict acts that breaks laws or that contain sex than books that do not. And at any time one can find many publications on the prison library that are on the banned publication list. The banning of publications is arbitrary with no real of adhered to guidelines, someone doesn't like Stephen King so he's banned but they love Ian Rakin so he's not banned, which is the very definition of discrimination.

What bout dictionaries? They define words like arson, murder an so on which are depicting an act that breaks a law, do we ban dictionaries.

Someone could, but I wouldn't since I own one, cite the bible which has murder, prostitution, mutilation and the wine drunken orgy of rape and incest on not one but two innocent, age unspecified, daughters by the person named Lot.

I KNOW! I KNOW! But if ye' ole Lot turned up in Virginia with a missing wife and two knocked up daughters after chillin' in a cave with a jug of wine, that whole, "pillar uh salt," and, "they raped me," defense ain't gonna fly, prosecutors would eat him alive.

Turn on any TV and almost 24-7 there is some news cast or True Crime where every manner or crime is depicted and described, even re-inacted, down to every little masochistic detail.

And, also almost 24-7, there is law and order SVU where every manner of sex crime is not only depicted but also narcissistically described in intense orgasmic detail to dramatic music, over, and over, and over. And millions are just so disgusted by child porn they can't wait to tune in to see what the pervert touched this hour...which, by the way, "was only watchin' to see how bad it is," is the same excuse used by those who collect child porn; law and order - child porn for the masses!

As a final kick in the nuts, the prison has two movie channels on which prison officials play DVDs and they played the uncut HBO, "Game of Thrones," series that has full nudity and sex by what is portrayed as underage persons.

YET MY BOOK IS BANNED BECAUSE ONE GIRL SAID NONE OF HER CLOTHES WERE EVER REMOVED!

The Federal Bureau of Prisons (BOP) regulations state that a publication can only be rejected if it found to be detrimental to the security, good order or discipline of the institution or of it might facilitate criminal activity. Can be rejected if the POSSESSION of the material is likely have an adverse effect on the prisoners physical or mental condition. Hmmmm...my book is literally my trial transcript written into a book, I do not believe anyone can claim with any validity that the police report and trial transcript that I've, "possessed," for over ten years is now detrimental to anything or anyone simply because its written into a book. Not to mention...I WROTE THE DAMN BOOK!

To date over 200 people in prison have either read my book or they have seen the actual documents without one security issue. In fact, the general opinion of those who have read my book was best summed up by OG...Quon, at Keen Mountain Prison when he said I was fucked over by the system worse than a drunk chick on prom night last seen entering the locker room with the football team...and a donkey!

While I cannot emphatically state that every person at the prison watched, "Game of Thrones," I'd damn sure bet a majority did and there was not one security issue, if anything it cut down on violence because everyone was watching TV. (full nudity and sex...whoo-hoo!)

As books are always better than any series and doubly so with, "Game of Thrones," how many people after seeing the series and being told about the books would buy the books but cannot because they are banned? How many hundreds of thousands of dollars has Mr. Martin lost, one can bet he is unaware while he loses money because his book is banned the same people who banned the book played his series on TV, which is blatant discrimination.

I had a list of over 200 people who would buy my book just to have some of the simplified legal crap in it. I sent the list to the ACLU to prove that I, like Mr. Martin and thousands of others suffer the loss of property, royalties is money and money is property.

Expand on that idea, there are no definitive databases of banned publications but there are low estimates from groups like The Marshall Project and many others. At best guess there are around 7,000 banned publications in Virginia alone, 10,000 in Texas and Florida leads at over 22,000 banned publications; most of which are banned on sex or simple nudity.

Think about all the regular books like, "It," or, art books, tattoo books, magazines, newspapers, newsletters, anime like,"'InuYasha," or graphic novels that can be banned for one exposed breast on a cartoon character. (it's a cartoon get over it) And, yes, there are companies that sale nude photos and magazines which, though I'm not sure why, I'm told are very popular in prison but they are limited to non-nude and sales of five photos a month per person.

"No one is an island!" Think of every person from the workers at the lumber-paper mills, to the authors, journalists, artists, book binders, to publishers, sellers from Amazon to the local used book store to the delivery person. All of those people buy materials, they all rely on the sale of each publication to make money. Every person who would create at any stage a publication banned on sex or simple nudity was discriminated against when prison officials chose to play, "Game of Thrones," on TV.

It's also been stated a warden may not reject a publication solely because its content is religious, philosophical, political, social or SEXUAL or because its content is unpopular or repugnant...but MUST review each issue, publication, separately. I only point out this out because when a publication is banned the practice is to simply use the description, but it's not defined. They don't show, "how," a publication is detrimental.

And correct me if I'm wrong, but when a prison sets requirements, like new books only or makes an approved vender list, that is in fact creating a rejected publication list, "all publications from a used book store," is not considering each publication separately. And an approved vender? That means a DOC little tin god has become I KING OF SHIT OF COMMERCE DECREE YE MAY SELL IN MY KINGDOM...BUT YE OTHERS MAY NOT! So every used book store or unapproved vender in America loses money daily just to appease the ego a little tin god who decrees them unworthy...just because he can. In a recent Prison Legal News it was opinionated that what effects prisoners effects everyone not just prisoners. The only way a publication can be banned is, someone bought it then no one else can. That means billions of dollars in manufacturing and sales will be lost which equates to billions in tax revenue dollars also lost. The person at the paper mill buys food, fuel, clothes and all the things that allow that person to do their job, and each item is taxed.

While everyone's taxes are raised yearly and used to support the ever growing mass incarceration prison systems they in turn cause the needless loss of billions in manufacturing, sales and, yes, tax revenue dollars simply because some librarian, or other little tin god, gets a stick up their ass and decides, "oh, god! a nipple on a cartoon character, they can't have that, they will just have to go watch, 'True blood,' or, 'Game of Thrones,' DVDs, or law and order a.k.a Rape TV for sex and nudity as God intended!" Another publication is banned just to feed the superiority complex of yet another little tin god who bans publications simply because they can.

Can't we use just a little common sense and ask ourselves, WHAT THE FUCK AM I GOING TO READ IN ANY GODDAMNED PUBLICATION I CANNOT TURN ON A TV AND WATCH SHIT THAT'S EVEN WORSE! I can watch, "Sons of Anarchy," "True blood," "Game of Thrones," I can see war, murder, rape, the mutilation of pregnant women, the slaughter of children, gang violence, mass robbery, mass shooters, and True Crime, but I cannot sit quietly and read a book, even one I wrote. I can trade for drugs, overdose on fentanyl and maybe die but I cannot sit quietly and read a book, even one I wrote.

ROBERT BLANKENSHIP

I can trade for knives and just stab someone for the hell of it, but I cannot sit quietly and read a book, even one I wrote. I believe a priority check is in serious order, the banning of publications many of which contain no violence at all in a world where ALL of the content, and worse, is available daily on mass media (have you seen Paradise Island, naked asses getting in the shower and when people get laid a red light let's everyone know, them folks be fuckin') means the loss of sales and tax revenue dollars is truly needles, while the prisons take money from the pockets of those who create publications and food from their children's mouths, those same people pay more taxes to pay the ass holes who banned the publication. That's hardly reasonable, sensible or fair. Corruption always gets worse, never better, and every day the banned publications lists grow longer. The next time YOUR taxes are raised ask yourself, how many more publications were banned today, how many more billions in manufacturing, sales and tax revenue dollars were lost? In fact I recently received a letter showing the ACLU has filed motions in District Courts on places like the Berkeley Detention Center in Monck's Corner, SC. that have banned all publications except the Bible from prisoners. Gee, wonder what their tax rates are like? Talk about an out of control little tin god.

While not totally unrelated, prisoners can buy music at a Kiosk for a JP6 tablet and recently some super genius has decided to censor any song with profanity. Yet, turn on any TV and there is Bob's Burgers, most animation, the Big Bang Theory, I could cite ESPN's The Pat McAfee Show, "there may be some cuss words used because that's how humans in the real world talk." AND IT'S PRISON! where one is going to hear, fuck, 30 times before breakfast and 300 times at breakfast as in, "what the fuck is that!" "It's boiled elephant semen," "how the fuck do you know what boiled elephant semen tastes like," "I don't, I've never had boiled elephant semen and I've never had whatever the fuck that is either...so the odds are 50-50." (Robert promises not to state outloud colorful creative writing food descriptions while people are eating the boiled semen regardless of the animal that secreted it) Trying to ban profanity in prison when almost every TV show, and real life, is covered in profanity is like trying to censor water from fish in the ocean. But that's a few more billion in sales and tax revenue dollars lost just to feed the ego of yet another little tin god. (or, again, just raw fucking stupidity.)

Here I must exit the banned publication arena but for more information, or anyone who has had experience with banned and or lost publications in prisons please contact Pen America (pen.org) and see the report (pen.org/report/reading-between-the-bars) I am on page 12 of said report. I am an honorary lifetime member of Pen America for my essay, "What If...breathe."

So how did I write about the book that was banned in the book that was published then banned, you ask. Well, my publisher closed but I was accepted by a new publisher, Prison Living Press, who then bought my old publisher so my new publisher that's also my old one (can't I ever do just one thing that's simple) afforded me an extremely rare opportunity to rewrite the last chapter to add some very up to date information. And they have worked most diligently to make this book a reality. See Cadmuspublishing.com for all the details, books and information.

I have to say a huge thank you to Mr. George Kayer, look him up at Goodreads. And a huge thank you to Barbra at A Book You Want, please look her up at Amazon under Barbra Jean Nagle. Thanks to both George and Barbara for the much needed, invaluable, advice.

Barbara, I love the :

"wizards of the coast,"

Magic Spell for protection against unwanted opinions.

Take a deep cleansing breath then say the words..."Did I Fucking Ask You!"

Keep up the good work.

Also a thank you to Cherie at Cherie's Gifts and to Kathy Scarborough in Crimora, VA for all your help.

I would also say thank you to the newspapers, The Buzzards Roost, in Rising Star, Texas, and, The Voice in Whitewood, Virginia.

I would encourage prisoners to write to, Prison Letters Project, at Yale Law School, 127 Wall Street, New Haven, CT. 06511. Put your story online. And a huge thank you for the books to, Prison Book Program, c/o Lucy Parsons Bookstore, 1306 Hancock St., Suite 100, Quincy, MA. 02169, request a book today before they all banned.

Several who read my book have sent me a lot of information on exoneration projects, or groups that look into cases, and I do thank you for trying. The average person has no idea, once a person gets to prison there are thousands of people already in line, "your expected hold time is 7 to 20 years, please stay on the line and our next available operator will assist you...if you're still alive." There are hundreds of groups but there are thousands already waiting, the odds of finding one group to even consider a case, then actually getting the case into court...think snowball and hell. Want to help, I filed an absolute pardon, call the Governor of Virginia and say, hey, y'all know that innocent dude ya' got locked up...let him the fuck out!

If anyone truly wished to help me, I humbly request any one reading, please go online and look for message boards or chatrooms in the Richlands, Raven and Tazewell areas of Virginia to post my book on. I'd like to blow up my book in those areas so that, just maybe, someday, some of my jury members may read it. Help promote my book online in any way possible. This could help others because the first step in justice reform cannot be changing the system that's already a run away train of raw corruption. Only by showing people, when they sit on a jury, are they seeing what's really there for what it is and are they doing what's right or are they doing what's popular? Are they truly aware they hold a person's life, a person's entire future in their hands and decide accordingly.

And if anyone who will, at Yahoo or Facebook, look for American Eskimo dog groups and send them a message, "Vorgoth wrote a book, it has Sally and Eskies in it." I am better known as Vorgoth online. Anyone else wanting to write to me, look me up, state number, (1484429), at Inmatefinder.com, Virginia, for my current location.

And while I am loathe to do so, I must say that not all lawyers are, "encrustalated specks of globular de-feceses," as Beavis would say, just the ones that have represented me. Any lawyer who takes my case, 70-30 on any settlement, or 80-20 on any tort claim on Carla... your way. "Can't find and honest one, I'd settle for a greedy one.

The most excellent author, Ian Rakin, in his book, "Dead Souls," wrote along the lines that everyday we all do injustices without the slightest evil intent and we need to more closely examine our duty and our obligations to our earthly service. I wonder then how Mr. Rakin would feel if he sat in a court room where his falsely accused loved one was on trial only to hear, "they will only do it again," "castrate 'em" and, "time to play hang the pervert, from his own books. And from the sour looks on the jury members faces he knows those are the sentiments of the jury as well, "time to play hang the pervert," no trial needed. Writing popular public opinion is awesome for news cast sensationalism, or book sales, but when it convicts an innocent loved one before trial even starts, not so awesome. AND Mr. Piers Anthony in knowing those are popular public opinions shouldn't we make goddamned sure of guilt before a conviction and that there is NO reasonable doubt and each person is given a fair and unbiased trial! (Firefly opinions.)

In 1692 we had, "time to play hang the witch." In 1970s we had, "time to play hang the vile Kingpin," and any drug charge was convicted by mass media before trial ever started. Today we have, "time to play hang the pervert," and any sex crime allegation is an automatic conviction if not a death sentence. Most would be burned at the steak without a trial. No one ever stops to think what group will be targeted next, "vile J-walkers," "freeway nose pickers," "vile milk drinkers," and y'all think I'm joking. "Law and Order: M.I.L.K." and suddenly milk is 200 dollars a gallon on the black market and possession is 20 to life in prison. Law and order is not bringing attention to a problem, they are using propaganda to program hate prosecutors use to strip away Constitutional

Rights from select groups and convict or force plea deals before trial even starts.

Our Village has grown, our intelligence has not. It's a witch...get a rope, this man sold one joint...an obvious Kingpin...life in prison, a sex charge, "time to play hang the pervert," no trial required. We are still at the mercy of corrupt prosecutors and unscrupulous judges that use popular public opinion to change laws like indecent exposure, a misdemeanor to indecent liberties a felony, they blow up mandatory minimum's and hand out exorbitant prison sentences and write statutes to eliminate Constitutional Rights protections.

There are groups like N.A.R.S.O.L, F.A.M.M and M.A.M.M and many others who battle the hydra of the injustice system working for justice reform that need support but every day, absolute power corrupts...even more absolutely!

When Mr. Rakin wrote we need to more closely examine our duty and our obligations to our earthly service, should not the first priority in that service, and the complete protection of our loved ones, be to insure anyone accused of any crime is given a fair and an unbiased trial free from charge stacking to force plea deals simply because conviction rates equals bigger budgets, free from mass media convictions before trial even starts, free from any unscrupulous influence, where all evidence is presented without grandiose stage show performances and no misconduct is excused or covered up. And to begin with, any person held in prison should be free from all time restrictions on filings and all grounds must be ruled on not rejected on some obscure statute or time limitation technicality bullshit.

The way I view my book is, I am done, I will most likely die in prison but my book will not. There is only one of me and I am irrelevant but there are thousands of under-agers out there, any one of which could steal anyone's money then lie about sexual assault to walk away. It could have happened already, the next car door, the next knock at the door, it's the police. That person, in ten seconds, will go from an everyday normal life to the most vile, despised and hated person this week...and next week there will be another.

Anyone, at any second, can be arrested on a false allegation, my book cannot prevent false allegations but I hope it warns of what comes next and what to watch out for.

When you are falsely accused of a sex crime, you will not believe it. When you are arrested, tried and convicted, you will not believe it. When the verdict, life in prison, is read, in that eternity of seconds between the sentence being read and full comprehension, at that moment you are looking through the eyes of Sarah Good, make no mistake, your life is just as over as hers. You look at the spectators, some with grins, watching your innocent life end and you wonder if even one of them thinks...What if I...or my child, is the next to be falsely accused... breathe. If you tried to warn them, would they listen. Are you listening to me now. Sarah Good 1692, Robert Blankenship 2015, You????

Wow.

When I wrote in my prologue that if I could step back to the 1690s and write book to warn the people of Salem of the impending witch trials, what could I say, or how could I present my book to people who have no interest in it or its topic...well, how did I do?

And as I was cruise writing, I recalled God's final message in "The Hitchhikers Guide to the Galaxy," and the books ending came to me. Sorry if I offended.

The End

Documents

Sally and Kobi

Robert and Kobi

Actual Inncocence

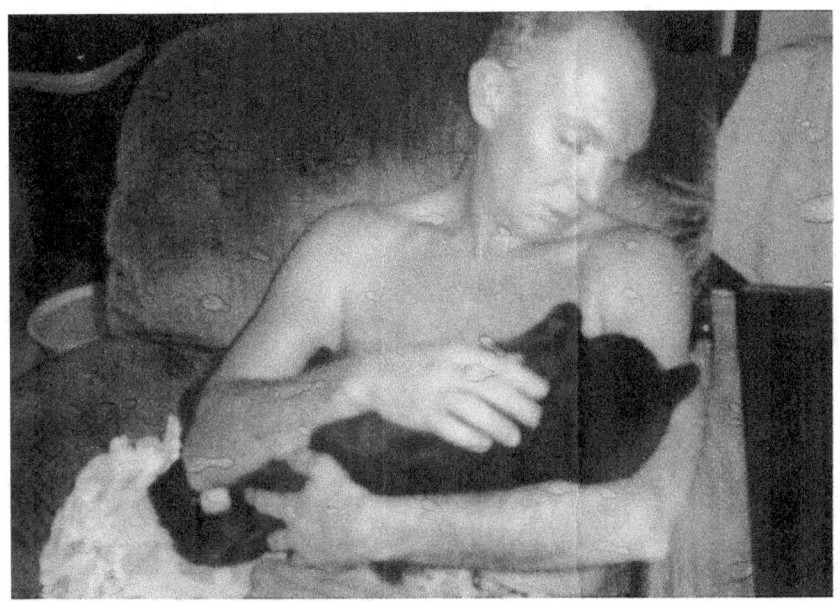

Robert and Itty-Bitty

Robert and Eskies

Lily

Jake

Kobi

Hardway

Robert's House

Sentencing Order

DEFENDANT IDENTIFICATION

Name: **ROBERT MCKINLEY BLANKENSHIP**
AKA:

SSN: 236-04-5848   DOB: 11/17/1963

SENTENCE SUMMARY:

Total Incarceration Sentence Imposed: **32 YEARS**

Total Sentence Suspended:

Total Sentence to Serve: **32 YEARS**

Total Post-Release of Term (Imposed and Suspended):   **3 YEARS**

Entry/Completion of Special Program: **SOAP**

Total Fines Imposed: **$5000.00**   Total Fines Suspended: **$5000.00**

ROBERT BLANKENSHIP

Statement Period:
06/18/12 - 07/15/12
Account 1320008160
Page   1 of 4
Enclosures   2

***************AUTO**3-DIGIT 246
1607 0.9890 AT 0.374   7 1 233

Robert M Blankenship
PO Box 532
Raven VA 24639-0532

FREE CHECKING

Statement Summary

Ending Balance on June 17, 2012		$	652.58
Total Deposits / Credits:	4		792.00
Total Checks / Debits:	48		1,567.28
Service Charge			.00
Ending Balance on July 15, 2012		$	122.70-

Deposits and Descriptive Items

Date	Amount	Description	Date	Amount	Description
6/20	198.00 CR	UI BENEFIT VEC - VIRGINIA 1546001795 06/20/12 ID #-012842933 TRACE #-061000107217368	6/20	32.00	2761 WAL-SAMS POUNDING MILLVA POS DEB 12:21 06/20/12 869227 SHELL Service Station
6/27	198.00 CR	UI BENEFIT VEC - VIRGINIA 1546001795 06/27/12 ID #-012842933 TRACE #-061000108176355	6/21	11.08	SHELL KINGSPORT TN POS DEB 18:12 06/20/12 913218 FOOD CITY #657
7/05	198.00 CR	UI BENEFIT VEC - VIRGINIA 1546001795 07/05/12 ID #-012842933 TRACE #-061000102382598	6/25	23.28	300 CLINCHFIELD STREET KINGSPORT TN POS DEB 12:42 06/24/12 425394 FOOD LION #0730
7/11	199.00 CR	UI BENEFIT VEC - VIRGINIA 1546001795 07/11/12 ID #-012842933 TRACE #-061000103482308	6/25	24.60	124 KENT RIDGE RD RICHLANDS VA DBT CRD 21:20 06/24/12 2206000 CLINTWOOD DISCOUNT TOBA
6/18	13.64	DBT CRD 12:32 06/17/12 7900014 DORAN GROCERY RAVEN VA	6/25	29.80	RICHLANDS VA DBT CRD 13:19 06/25/12 2401062 PIZZA PLUS CLAYPOOL HIL
6/18	24.26	POS DEB 19:44 06/17/12 0002190 GRANT'S SUPERMARKE 5943 SUITE 2 GOV. RAVEN VA	6/26	125.84	CEDAR BLUFF VA DBT CRD 09:11 06/26/12 9121786 TAZEWELL GENERAL DISTR. 276-9885962 VA
6/18	8.39	DBT CRD 14:27 06/16/12 1000268 NETFLIX.COM NETFLIX.COM CA	6/27	12.38	POS DEB 21:05 06/26/12 0942886 EXXONMOBIL 3 WAY FAST BR
6/20	10.07	DBT CRD 15:36 06/19/12 5900014 DORAN GROCERY RAVEN VA	6/27	12.52	DORAN VA DBT CRD 16:01 06/26/12 4900015 DORAN GROCERY
6/20	29.12	POS DEB 17:02 06/19/12 1068657 Wal-Mart Super Center	6/28	10.07	RAVEN VA DBT CRD 15:47 06/27/12 0900015

260

Actual Inncocence

Statement Period:
06/18/12 - 07/15/12
Account 1320008160
Page 2 of 4
Enclosures 2

Deposits and Descriptive Items

Date	Amount	Description	Date	Amount	Description
6/28	19.91	DORAN GROCERY RAVEN VA POS DEB 16:20 06/27/12 0001091	7/06	69.65	KINGSPORT TN CHECKPAYMT GEICO 1530075853 07/06/12 CHECK#-353 TRACE #-091000011834778
6/29	13.54	GRANT'S SUPERMARKE 5943 SUITE 2 GOV. RAVEN VA POS DEB 17:35 06/28/12 0001176	7/09	5.11	DBT CRD 15:57 07/06/12 8900016 DORAN GROCERY RAVEN VA
7/02	10.07	GRANT'S SUPERMARKE 5943 SUITE 2 GOV. RAVEN VA DBT CRD 12:40 07/01/12 3900015 DORAN GROCERY RAVEN VA	7/09	5.99	DBT CRD 04:16 07/08/12 2206000 CLINTWOOD DISCOUNT TOBA RICHLANDS VA
7/02	16.54	POS DEB 13:29 07/01/12 505087 FOOD LION #0730 124 KENT RIDGE RD RICHLANDS VA	7/09	6.23	POS DEB 14:29 07/07/12 0002542 GRANT'S SUPERMARKE 5943 SUITE 2 GOV. RAVEN VA
7/02	18.31	DBT CRD 21:19 07/01/12 8206000 CLINTWOOD DISCOUNT TOBA RICHLANDS VA	7/09	10.07	DBT CRD 12:35 07/08/12 9900016 DORAN GROCERY RAVEN VA
7/02	23.05	POS DEB 16:17 06/30/12 0001337 GRANT'S SUPERMARKE 5943 SUITE 2 GOV. RAVEN VA	7/09	10.07	DBT CRD 13:01 07/08/12 2900016 DORAN GROCERY RAVEN VA
7/02	24.29	POS DEB 13:11 07/02/12 627771 FOOD LION #0730 124 KENT RIDGE RD RICHLANDS VA	7/09	11.77	POS DEB 15:06 07/09/12 625428 CORNER MART 2 2659 FRONT STREET RICHLAND VA
7/03	5.11	DBT CRD 16:13 07/02/12 2900015 DORAN GROCERY RAVEN VA	7/09	17.37	POS DEB 14:14 07/07/12 374610 FOOD LION #0730 124 KENT RIDGE RD RICHLANDS VA
7/03	6.49	DBT CRD 16:13 07/02/12 7900015 DORAN GROCERY RAVEN VA	7/09	18.23	DBT CRD 19:08 07/06/12 7900016 DORAN GROCERY RAVEN VA
7/05	7.34	POS DEB 12:17 07/05/12 0379388 EXXONMOBIL 3408 KINGSPOR TN	7/09	18.78	POS DEB 17:53 07/08/12 0001060 GRANT'S SUPERMARKE 5943 SUITE 2 GOV. RAVEN VA
7/05	7.65	POS DEB 13:36 07/05/12 0393303 EXXONMOBIL 3408 KINGSPOR TN	7/09	21.99	POS DEB 16:28 07/08/12 543468 FOOD LION #0730 124 KENT RIDGE RD RICHLANDS VA
7/05	8.82	POS DEB 07:48 07/04/12 0189519 EXXONMOBIL 3 WAY FAST BR DORAN VA	7/10	200.00	ATM W/D 15:47 07/09/12 1617 13250 GOV PEERY HWY POUNDING MILLVA
7/05	12.52	DBT CRD 15:42 07/04/12 5900016 DORAN GROCERY RAVEN VA	7/10	4.92	DBT CRD 16:09 07/09/12 0900016 DORAN GROCERY RAVEN VA
7/05	21.55	POS DEB 12:43 07/04/12 946145 FOOD CITY #657 300 CLINCHFIELD STREET KINGSPORT TN	7/10	50.00	BOUNCE PAID ITEM(S) CHARGE
			7/11	10.07	DBT CRD 15:52 07/10/12 1900016 DORAN GROCERY RAVEN VA
7/06	44.05	DBT CRD 00:06 07/06/12 4980040 KINGSPORT VETERINARY HO	7/11	34.05	DBT CRD 22:10 07/10/12 9120004 FASMART 434 CEDAR BLUFF VA
			7/11	50.00	BOUNCE PAID ITEM(S) CHARGE

Check Detail

07/09/2012 354 $384.69

07/06/2012 355 $32.00

TruPoint Proof ①

Robert Blankenship 1484429
K.M.C.C.
P.O. Box 860
Oakwood, VA 24631

ROBERT BLANKENSHIP

TruPoint Proof (2)

TruPoint

13250 Gov. G.C. Peery Hwy
Pounding Mill, Virginia 24637

(276) 964-7445

Dear Mr. Blankenship,

As I read your letter, I believe that I know what you are looking for and will provide it with this letter. I did not print off any statements for we charge three dollars a statement. This will show how those overdraft fees were paid for.

Thank You,

Andrew Baker

Actual Inncocence

Current Date: May 06, 2022

Account Number: 1320008160
Capture Date: July 22, 2015
Item Number: 13010001063553
Posted Date: July 22, 2015
Posted Item Number: 203003483
Amount: 154.49
Record Type: Credit

Robert M Blankenship

ROBERT BLANKENSHIP

Current Date:	May 06, 2022
Account Number:	10010800
Capture Date:	July 22, 2015
Item Number:	13010001063555
Posted Date:	July 22, 2015
Posted Item Number:	203003485
Amount:	156.09
Record Type:	Debit

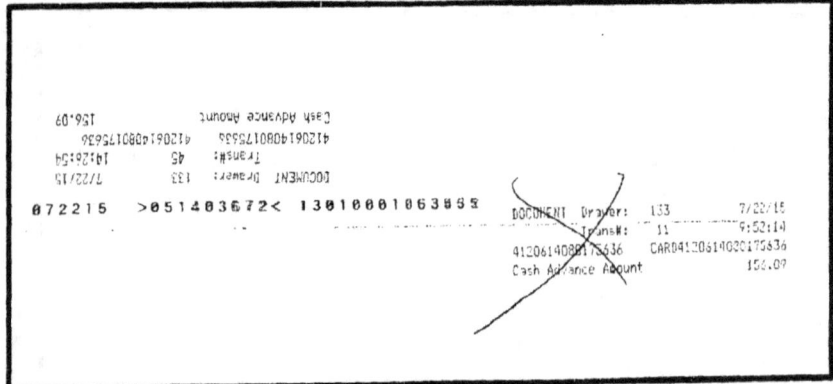

ORIGINAL

COMMONWEALTH

VS.

ROBERT MCKINLEY BLANKENSHIP

IN THE CIRCUIT COURT OF TAZEWELL COUNTY, VIRGINIA

Filed in open Court this
Feb. 8th, 2016
Time: 10:10 A.M.
Testo: Susie O. Vance
Chief Deputy Clerk

APPEARANCES:

DENNIS H. LEE, ESQ., Tazewell, Virginia

MELANIE B. MENEFEE, ESQ., Tazewell, Virginia

Commonwealth's Attorneys

MICHAEL L. DENNIS, ESQ., Tazewell, Virginia

MICHAEL LETSEN, ESQ., Tazewell, Virginia

Counsel for the Defendant

PROCEEDINGS OF JURY TRIAL OF JULY 21ST, 2015

EXHIBITS:

COMMONWEALTH'S EXHIBIT NO. 1 – Order of conviction

COMMONWEALTH'S EXHIBIT NOS. 2 – 20 – Photographs

COMMONWEALTH'S EXHIBIT NO. 21 – Cigarette package

COMMONWEALTH'S EXHIBIT NO. 22 – Energy drink

COMMONWEALTH'S EXHIBIT NO. 23 – Sunglasses

COMMONWEALTH'S EXHIBIT NO. 24 – Sign-in sheet for Detention Center

DEFENDANT'S EXHIBIT NO. 1 - Cumberland Mountain Community Services record (marked for identification only and not admitted)

DEFENDANT'S EXHIBIT NO. 2 – Cumberland Mountain Community Services record (marked for identification only and not admitted)

DEFENDANT'S EXHIBIT NO. 3 – CD (marked for identification only and not admitted)

COLLECTIVE DEFENDANT'S EXHIBIT NO. 4 – Bank records (marked for identification only and not admitted)

ACTUAL INNCOCENCE

Sipoena Rcst

COOKE, SHORTT & KEENE, PLLC
P.O. Drawer 749
Cedar Bluff, VA 24609

H. Shannon Cooke, Esq.
Jim Terry Shortt, II, Esq. (VA & WV)
John O. Keene, Esq.

Phone (276) 963-4381
Fax (276) 963-4297

May 22, 2014

VIA FACSIMILE 988-7501
Dawn Cole, Deputy Clerk
Tazewell County Circuit Court
101 East Main Street, Suite 202
Tazewell, Virginia 24651

Re: *Commonwealth of Virginia vs. Robert McKinley Blankenship*
Case Nos.: CR13-000003-04, to-wit: (ATTEMPTED RAPE);
CR13-000003-05, to-wit: (INDECENT LIBERTIES UNDER 15 YEARS OF AGE);
CR13-000003-06, to-wit: (ABDUCTION WITH INTENT TO DEFILE);
CR13-000003-07, to-wit: (ASSAULT & BATTERY); and
CR13-000003-08, to-wit: (CONTRIBUTING TO DELINQUENCY OF A MINOR).

Dear Dawn:

I hereby request subpoenas to be issued demanding the presence of the following individuals in your Honorable Court on the 4th day of June, 2014 at 9:00 o'clock a.m. in relation to the above-captioned matters, to-wit:

Robbie Davis, Juvenile Probation Officer
315 School Street
Tazewell, Virginia 24651

Brad Goff, Juvenile Probation Officer
54 West Main Street
Lebanon, Virginia 24266

Should you have any questions or anything further be required, please do not hesitate to contact me.

Thank you for your assistance in this matter.

As always,

Respectfully,

Jim Terry Shortt, II

cc: **Dennis Lee, Esquire** (Commonwealth's Attorney)
—**Robert Blankenship** (client) (hand-delivered)

blankenship - robert mckinley letter to clerk cc requesting subpoenas 5-22-14", J-13-140

CRIMINAL COMPLAINT
Commonwealth of Virginia

RULES 3A:3 AND 7C:3

Exhibit one, Page A1-5

of TAZEWELL CITY OR COUNTY

[ ] General District Court
[X] Juvenile and Domestic Relations District Court

Under penalty of perjury, I, the undersigned Complainant swear or affirm that I have reason to believe that the Accused committed a criminal offense, on or about

07/09/2012 DATE OFFENSE OCCURRED

in the [ ] City [X] County [ ] Town of TAZEWELL.

I base my belief on the following facts: (Print ALL information clearly)

RESPONDED TO 247 KEFY RD FOR DISPATCH. I MADE SUSPECT WAS UPSET BECAUSE ACCUSED ATTEMPTED TO RAPE HIS 14/yo DAUGHTER BRANDI SHORETT. I SPOKE with VICTIM SHE ADVISED THAT ACCUSED BROUGHT WITH HIM GOING TO COOK. THAT IN RICHARDS AND BOUGHT HER A DRINK AND A PACK OF CIGARS. AFTER WHICH SHE PROVIDED TO AT TRIP THAT SHE HAD TO DELIVER AND THEY WENT TO DAW RD. ON RAY RD WHERE ACCUSED PULLED OFF THE ROAD WALKED VICTIM 195 FEET ON A DIRT RD WHERE HE TOOK OFF HER SHIRT AND BRA. EXPOSED HIMSELF BY PULLING ALL HIS PANTS AND THEN TRIED TO FORCE HIS HANDS AT VICTIM. BEGAN TO SCREAM AND CRY AND ACCUSED STATED TAKING HER BACK TO THE CAR AND AT BACK HOME.

The statements above are true and accurate to the best of my knowledge and belief.

In making this complaint, I have read and fully understand the following:
- By swearing to these facts, I agree to appear in court and testify if a warrant or summons is issued.
- The charge in this warrant cannot be dismissed except by the court, even at my request.

[signature] Deputy J. M. ICS 3503
NAME OF COMPLAINANT (LAST, FIRST, MIDDLE)
(PRINT CLEARLY)

[signature]
SIGNATURE OF COMPLAINANT

Subscribed and sworn to before me this day,
07/09/2012 10:27 PM
DATE AND TIME

Zackary Alan Shook
[ ] CLERK [X] MAGISTRATE [ ] JUDGE

FORM DC-311 REVISED 07/11 (A12)(E) 08/11

JA010501-01-00

CRIMINAL COMPLAINT

ACCUSED: Name, Description, Address/Location
BLANKENSHIP ROBERT MCKINLEY
LAST NAME, FIRST NAME, MIDDLE NAME

247 Kefy Rd
DORAN, VA

RACE	SEX	MO	DAY	YR	FT	IN	WGT	EYES	HAIR
W	M	11	17	63	5	09	150	Blu	Brn

SSN 286-94-5848

COMPLETE DATA BELOW IF KNOWN

[ ] Complainant is not a law-enforcement officer or animal control officer. Authorization prior to issuance of felony arrest warrant given by
[ ] Commonwealth's attorney
[ ] Law-enforcement agency having jurisdiction over alleged offense

NAME OF PERSON AUTHORIZING ISSUANCE OF WARRANT

DATE AND TIME AUTHORIZATION GIVEN

ATTEMPTED RAPE VICTIM 14/yo
INDECENT LIBERTIES w/ CHILD 14 y/o
CONTRIBUTE TO DELINQUENCY
ASSAULT & BATTERY

ACTUAL INNCOCENCE

INCIDENT REPORT
COMMONWEALTH OF VIRGINIA

173-PAGE #	174-DATE	1754-INCIDENT #	176-REPORTING OFFICER			177-CODE #	178-VICTIM NAME	
3	07/10/2012	2012019958	Jonathan Caldwell			c035	Shortt, Brandi Lee	

VEHICLE/VEHICLE/AD

179-YEAR	180-MAKE	181-MODEL	182-STYLE	183-VIN		184-LICENSE NUMBER	185-STATE
186-OWNER'S NAME				187-ADDRESS			
188-TOP/SOLID COLOR		189-SECOND COLOR		190-DISPOSITION OF RECOVERY: ☐ (I) Impounded ☐ (R) Rel. To Owner	192-SUSP. VEHICLE? ☐ Y ☐ N	193-TELETYPE NUMBER	
179-YEAR	180-MAKE	181-MODEL	182-STYLE	183-VIN		184-LICENSE NUMBER	185-STATE
186-OWNER'S NAME				187-ADDRESS			
188-TOP/SOLID COLOR		189-SECOND COLOR		190-DISPOSITION OF RECOVERY: ☐ (I) Impounded ☐ (R) Rel. To Owner	192-SUSP. VEHICLE? ☐ Y ☐ N	193-TELETYPE NUMBER	

PROPERTY

209-OF. CODE	210-P. LOSS	211-P. DES.	212-QTY.	213-DESCRIPTION (include serial number, size, color, etc.)	214-OWNER	215-ITEM VALUE	216-RECOV. DATE
90Z	6	08	1	EVIDENCE-Camel Cigarettes	V1	4.00	
90Z	6	77	1	EVIDENCE-Energy Drink	V1	2.49	
90Z	5	48	2	Evidence-2 Reciepts	O1	1.00	
23C	7	19	1	EVIDENCE-Sunglasses	V2	10.00	
11A	8	77	2	discs of video surveillance from Walmart Item #4		2.00	
11A	8	77	1	VHS tape of video surveillance from Valero/ Item #5		2.00	

217-TOTAL NUMBER VEHICLES STOLEN:	218-TOTAL NUMBER VEHICLES RECOVERED:	219-TOTAL VALUE STOLEN: $10.00	220-TOTAL VALUE RECOVERED:

PROPERTY CODES

219-PROPERTY LOSS: (1) None (2) Burned (3) Counterfeited/Forged (4) Damaged/Destroyed/Vandalized (5) Recovered (6) Seized (7) Stolen, etc. (8) Unk

211-PROPERTY DESCRIPTION:
- (01) Aircraft
- (02) Alcohol
- (03) Automobiles
- (04) Bicycles
- (05) Buses
- (06) Clothes/Furs
- (07) Computer Hardware/Software
- (08) Consumable Goods
- (09) Credit Cards/Debit Cards
- (10) Drugs/Narcotics
- (11) Drug/Narc. Equipment
- (12) Farm Equipment
- (13) Firearms
- (14) Gambling Equipment
- (15) Heavy Equipment-Construction/Industry
- (16) Household Goods
- (17) Jewelry/Precious Metals
- (18) Livestock
- (19) Merchandise
- (20) Money
- (21) Negotiable Instruments
- (22) Nonnegotiable Instruments
- (23) Office-Type Equipment
- (24) Other Motor Vehicles
- (25) Purses/Handbags/Wallets
- (26) Radios/TVs/VCRs
- (27) Recordings-Audio/Visual
- (28) Recreational Vehicles
- (29) Structures-Single Occupancy
- (30) Structures-Other Dwellings
- (31) Structures-Commercial/Business
- (32) Structures-Industrial/Manufacture
- (33) Structures-Public/Community
- (34) Structures-Storage
- (35) Structures-Other
- (36) Tools-Power/Hand
- (37) Trucks
- (38) Vehicle Parts/Accessories
- (39) Watercraft
- (77) Other
- (88) Pending Inventory (of Property)
- (99) Special Category

DRUG INFO.

222-DRUG TYPE	223-WHOLE DRUG QUANTITY	224-FRACTIONAL DRUG QUANTITY	225-DRUG MEASUREMENT	226-TYPE DRUG MEASUREMENT:
				WEIGHT (GM) Gram (KG) Kilogram (OZ) Ounce (LB) Pound
				CAPACITY (ML) Milliliter (LT) Liter (FO) Fluid Ounce (GL) Gallon
				UNITS (DU) Dosage Unit (Pills, etc.) (NP) Number of Plants

222-DRUG TYPE:
- (A) "Crack" Cocaine
- (B) Cocaine
- (C) Hashish
- (D) Heroin
- (E) Marijuana
- (F) Morphine
- (G) Opium
- (H) Other Narcotics
- (I) LSD
- (J) PCP
- (K) Other Hallucinogens
- (L) Amphetamines/Methamphetamines
- (M) Other Stimulants
- (N) Barbiturates
- (O) Other Depressants
- (P) Other Drugs
- (U) Unknown Type Drug
- (X) Over 3 Drug Types

COMPLNT.

NAME:	Last, Caldwell, Jonathan M	First,	Middle	SEX: ☐ (M) Male ☐ (F) Female ☐ (U) Unk.	AGE: ☐ (00) Unknown	RACE: ☐ (W) White ☐ (B) Black ☐ (I) American Indian ☐ (A) Asian/Pacific Islander ☐ (U) Unknown
RESIDENT ADDRESS:	Street C/O Tazewell CO Sheriff's Office	City	State Zip	RESIDENT PHONE	EMPLOY'T. PHONE	

271

ROBERT BLANKENSHIP

CONFIDENTIAL SUPPLEMENT

226-PAGE #	227-DATE	228-INCIDENT NUMBER	229-REPORTING OFFICER	230-CODE #	231-VICTIM NAME
4	07/10/2012	2012019958	Jonathan Caldwell	c035	Shortt, Brandi Lee

234-SCENE PROCESSED BY: c035-Jonathan Caldwell
236-PRINTS FOUND? ☐ Yes ☐ No 238-EVIDENCE ☐ Yes
237-PHOTOGRAPHED? ☐ Yes ☐ No OBTAINED? ☐ No

239-APPROVING SUPERVISOR 240-CODE # 241-DATE APPROVED

WITNESSES

243-NAME: Last, First, Middle
244-SEX: ☐ (U) Unk. ☐ (M) Male ☐ (F) Female
245-AGE: ☐ (O) Unknown
246-RACE: ☐ (U) Unk. ☐ (W) White ☐ (B) Black ☐ (I) American Indian ☐ (A) Asian/Pacific Islander
247-RESIDENT ADDRESS: Street, City, State, 248-Zip
249-RESIDENT PHONE 250-EMPL. PHONE

243-NAME: Last, First, Middle
244-SEX: ☐ (U) Unk. ☐ (M) Male ☐ (F) Female
245-AGE: ☐ (O) Unknown
246-RACE: ☐ (U) Unk. ☐ (W) White ☐ (B) Black ☐ (I) American Indian ☐ (A) Asian/Pacific Islander
247-RESIDENT ADDRESS: Street, City, State, 248-Zip
249-RESIDENT PHONE 250-EMPL. PHONE

NARRATIVE:

I responded to 247 Kirby Rd for a report of a several subjects attempting to gain entry into a house. I was close in the area and responded to the house and found several white males screaming. I got out and spoke with a female, Tina Reedy, who advised that the male that lives there, Robert Blakenship, had attempted to rape their daughter. I then spoke to the victim, Brandi Shortt, age 14, she advised that her mom allowed her to go to the bank with Blankenship. She and Blankenship left Kirby Rd to go to the bank to get money and they stopped at the Corner Mart in Richlands, and he bought her a pack of Camel cigarettes, an energy drink, and himself a case of Budweiser beer. She advised that they then went to Valero in Cedar Bluff and bought gas, then to Tru Point bank and got money, then to Walmart. They both walked into Walmart where she advised that they went in the grocery side and Blankenship made her hold his hand. She went on to state that while in Walmart he found a pair of sunglasses and placed them on his head, see video, they then walked out without paying for the glasses.

The two left Walmart and headed back to Raven where she states he made her drive to Daw Rd, where he took off her shirt and bra, and he took off his pants, was not wearing underwear, she turned her head and he then tried to take off her pants but she began to scream for help. He then grabbed her around the neck and started to choke her until she began to cry when he then quit. He then made her get into the car and drive them home. She then went back home and was crying and told her mother what had happened.

I then went in to speak with Blankenship who advised that the subjects came to his home and tried to get in yelling at him. He advised that he did not know what was going on. Blankenship then told us that he had been at home all day and has not left the house. Blankenship gave permission to search the house and we did. I then went outside and asked Reedy if she had any other information and she advised that her sister Janet Lester had seen the two at Walmart holding hands. I confimed this from Lester via phone at 276-345-4374, and she gave a perfect description of the suspect.

I went back into the house and asked Blankenship if he was wearing any underwear and he advised no. At this point I began to Mirandise him when he told us to leave and I explained that he was being detained and was not under arrest. I then completed miranda and he never acknowledged if he would speak to us or not. I asked if he had anything in his pockets and he provided a 2 receipts to me. Both receipts confimed the purchases the victim had explained to us. Detective Greg Layne was notified and came out to assist.

ACTUAL INNCOCENCE

CONFIDENTIAL SUPPLEMENT NARRATIVE CONTINUATION

226-PAGE #	227-DATE	228-INCIDENT NUMBER	229-REPORTING OFFICER	230-CODE #	231-VICTIM NAME
5	07/10/2012	2012019958	Jonathan Caldwell	c035	Shortt, Brandi Lee

NARRATIVE:
The victim provided me with a statement and the items purchased for her. I then took all of the items into evidence and put Blankenship into my vehicle. Blankenship told us that he was a olent sex offender from Tennessee and was also registered in Virginia. The victim then took us to the place where the incident happened which was approx. 195 yards off of the road on Ray Rd at a posted gate, off of Daw Rd. She explained that there were going to be 2 Budweiser cans that are red and white. We arrived in the area and found the cans. I then conferred with Dennis Lee, Commonwealth Atty, who advised to place him under arrest for attemped rape. I then did this and Blankenship advised that his lawyer explained to him to say no to all of our answers. I then spoke with Detective Layne who advised that he would obtain video of the places they went.

I transported Blankenship to the regional jail in Tazewell where warrants for Attempted Rape, Indecent Liberties, Contributing, Assault and Battery, and an EPO were issued and served to Blankenship. Magistrate Stoots out of Washington Co held him without Bond. Detective Layne arrived and advised that he found video of the shoplifting at Walmart and showed me two still photos of Blankenship selecting the glasses and walking out. I then issued a summons to Blankenship for shoplifting.

Detective Layne is still assisting me with this investigation.

ROBERT BLANKENSHIP

CONFIDENTIAL SUPPLEMENT NARRATIVE CONTINUATION

224-PAGE #	227-DATE	228-INCIDENT NUMBER	229-REPORTING OFFICER	230-CODE #	231-VICTIM NAME
5	07/10/2012	2012019958	Jonathan Caldwell	c035	Shortt, Brandi Lee

NARRATIVE:
The victim provided me with a statement and the items purchased for her. I then took all of the items into evidence and put Blankenship into my vehicle. Blankenship told us that he was a violent sex offender from Tennessee and was also registered in Virginia. The victim then took us to the place where the incident happened which was approx 195 yards off of the road on Ray Rd at a posted gate, off of Daw Rd. She explained that there were going to be 2 Budweiser cans that are red and white. We arrived in the area and found the cans. I then conferred with Dennis Lee, Commonwealth Atty, who advised to place him under arrest for attempted rape. I then did this and Blankenship advised that his lawyer explained to him to say no to all of our answers. I then spoke with Detective Layne who advised that he would obtain video of the places they went.

I transported Blankenship to the regional jail in Tazewell where warrants for Attempted Rape, Indecent Liberties, Contributing, Assault and Batter, and an EPO were issued and served to Blankenship. Magistrate Stoots out of Washington Co held him without Bond. Detective Layne arrived and advised that he found video of the shoplifting at Walmart and showed me two still photos of Blankenship selecting the glasses and walking out. I then issued a summons to Blankenship for shoplifting.

I went back to the victims house and served the other half of the EPO and explained the victim witness pamphlet and asked if she needed any assistance tonight and she declined. I also provided a business card with my name and told her to call if she needed anything at all.

Detective Layne is still assisting me with this investigation.

SUPPLEMENT #4   Ray Smith - s0201   03/05/2015   10:34

On 7-10-12 I responded to 297 kirby rd to assist dep. Caldwell. Upon arrival I was present when Mr. blankership stated that he had not left the residance all day. He did state that he knew the victim, that her step-father had been working for him, he also stated that when he heard them beating on his door he was online with his girlfriend who lived out-of-state, he stated that he ask her to call 911 for him to which she stated that it wouldn't help due to her being out-of-state. I aslo witnessed him with the reciptes from in question.

ACTUAL INNOCENCE

VIRGINIA: IN THE CIRCUIT COURT OF TAZEWELL COUNTY

COMMONWEALTH OF VIRGINIA,   PLAINTIFF,

VS.   **PLEA AGREEMENT**

(Case Nos.:   **CR13-000003-00, to-wit: (ATTEMPTED RAPE)** On or about July 9, 2012, did unlawfully and feloniously attempt to rape a child, in violation of Sections 18.2-61;18.2-26; 18.2-10 of the Code of Virginia (1950) as amended. {**FELONY**}

CR13-000003-01, to-wit: (INDECENT LIBERTIES UNDER 15 YEARS OF AGE) On or about July 9, 2012, being eighteen years of age or order, did unlawfully, feloniously, knowingly and intentionally with lascivious intent, expose his sexual or genital parts to a child under the age of fifteen years, in violation of §§ 18.2-370(A)(1); 18.2-10 of the Code of Virginia (1950) as amended. {**FELONY**}

CR13-000003-02, to-wit: (ASSAULT & BATTERY) On or about July 9, 2012, did unlawfully assault or assault and batter a child, in violation §§ 18.2-57; 18.2-11 of the Code of Virginia (1950) as amended. {**MISDEMEANOR**}

CR13-000003-03, to-wit: (CONTRIBUTING TO DELINQUENCY OF A MINOR) On or about July 9, 2012, being 18 years of age or older, did unlawfully and willfully contribute to, encourage, or cause any act, omission, or condition which rendered a child, a minor less than 18 years of age, delinquent, in need of services, in need of supervision, or abused or neglected, in violation of §§ 18.2-371, 18.2-11 of the Code of Virginia (1950) as amended. {**MISDEMEANOR**})

ROBERT MCKINLEY BLANKENSHIP   DEFENDANT.
DOB: 11/17/63
SS#: 236-94-5848,

Actual Inncocence

AP 33

The following Plea Agreement has been entered into between the Defendant, Robert McKinley Blankenship, his Counsel, Jim Terry Shortt II, and the Commonwealth for the County of Tazewell, in accord with Rule 3A:8(C)(1)(c) of the Rules of Supreme Court of Virginia:

EMB 1. The Defendant, Robert McKinley Blankenship, stands charged in this Court with the following offenses by way of a **Grand Jury Indictment** returned as a true bill on the 8th day of January, 2013, to-wit:

Case Number	Count	Charge (Felony [F]/Misdemeanor [M])
CR13-000003-00	1	(ATTEMPTED RAPE) On or about July 9, 2012, did unlawfully and feloniously attempt to rape a child, in violation of Sections 18.2-61; 18.2-26; 18.2-10 of the Code of Virginia (1950) as amended. {FELONY}
CR13-000003-01	2	(INDECENT LIBERTIES UNDER 15 YEARS OF AGE) On or about July 9, 2012, being eighteen years of age or order, did unlawfully, feloniously, knowingly and intentionally with lascivious intent, expose his sexual or genital parts to a child under the age of fifteen years, in violation of §§ 18.2-370(A)(1); 18.2-10 of the Code of Virginia (1950) as amended. {FELONY}
CR13-000003-02	3	(ASSAULT & BATTERY) On or about July 9, 2012, did unlawfully assault or assault and batter a child, in violation §§ 18.2-57; 18.2-11 of the Code of Virginia (1950) as amended. {MISDEMEANOR}

ROBERT BLANKENSHIP

Case Number	Count	Charge
CR13-000003-03	4	(CONTRIBUTING TO DELINQUENCY OF A MINOR) On or about July 9, 2012, being 18 years of age or older, did unlawfully and willfully contribute to, encourage, or cause any act, omission, or condition which rendered a child, a minor less than 18 years of age, delinquent, in need of services, in need of supervision, or abused or neglected, in violation of §§ 18.2-371, 18.2-11 of the Code of Virginia (1950) as amended. {MISDEMEANOR}

2. The Defendant will enter a plea of no contest to the following charge, to-wit:

Case Number	Count	Charge (Felony [F]/Misdemeanor [M])
CR13-000003-00	1	(ATTEMPTED RAPE) On or about July 9, 2012, did unlawfully and feloniously attempt to rape a child, in violation of Sections 18.2-61; 18.2-26; 18.2-10 of the Code of Virginia (1950) as amended. {FELONY}

3. The Attorney for the Commonwealth shall move to nolle prosequi and not further prosecute the following charges, to-wit:

Case Number	Count	Charge (Felony [F]/Misdemeanor [M])
CR13-000003-01	2	(INDECENT LIBERTIES UNDER 15 YEARS OF AGE) On or about July 9, 2012, being eighteen years of age or order, did unlawfully, feloniously, knowingly and intentionally with lascivious intent, expose his sexual or genital parts to a child under the age of fifteen years, in violation of §§ 18.2-370(A)(1); 18.2-10 of the Code of Virginia (1950) as amended. {FELONY}

Commonwealth of Virginia vs. Robert McKinley Blankenship
Plea Agreement
Page - 3
J-13-140

Defendant's Initial _RMB_

CR13-000003-02	3	(ASSAULT & BATTERY) On or about July 9, 2012, did unlawfully assault or assault and batter a child, in violation §§ 18.2-57; 18.2-11 of the Code of Virginia (1950) as amended. {MISDEMEANOR}
CR13-000003-03	4	(CONTRIBUTING TO DELINQUENCY OF A MINOR) On or about July 9, 2012, being 18 years of age or older, did unlawfully and willfully contribute to, encourage, or cause any act, omission, or condition which rendered a child, a minor less than 18 years of age, delinquent, in need of services, in need of supervision, or abused or neglected, in violation of §§ 18.2-371, 18.2-11 of the Code of Virginia (1950) as amended. {MISDEMEANOR}

4. Upon the Defendant's above noted plea, the Attorney for the Commonwealth, the Defendant, and the Attorney for the Defendant agree the Defendant shall be found guilty as to the charge for which he has entered a plea of no contest to and the Attorney for the Commonwealth shall not file any further charges against the Defendant in relation to this incident herein.

5. Upon the Defendant's motion for a Presentence Investigation Report on the matters set forth in this agreement, the Court will order the same and sentencing will be postponed until the said report is prepared. At such time as this case is set for sentencing, the Defendant and the Attorney for the Commonwealth will present any relevant evidence they desire and upon the conclusion of the evidence and argument

from any source, and the Defendant respectfully requests that the Court accept this agreement.

RMB 10. That no Judge of the Circuit Court participated in any discussion leading to this agreement under Rule 3A:8(C)(1)(c).

In support of said agreement, the Defendant, his attorney and the Attorney for the Commonwealth hereto affix their signatures.

Given under our hands on this the __11__ day of February, 2013.

_____ Defendant

_____ Attorney for the Defendant

_____ Attorney for the Commonwealth

Accepted this __11th__ day of February, 2013.

Rejected this ____ day of February, 2013.

_____
Judge

Commonwealth of Virginia vs. Robert McKinley Blankenship
Plea Agreement
Page - 6
J-13-140

Defendant's Initial _RMB_

ACTUAL INNCOCENCE

si' 27 Plea Agreement
2-11-13

for a finding of guilt beyond a reasonable doubt? __yes__.

RMB 14. Do you understand that by pleading no contest, you waive your right to a trial by jury? __yes__

RMB 15. Do you understand that by pleading no contest you waive your right not to incriminate yourself? __yes__.

RMB 16. Do you understand that by pleading no contest you waive your right to confront and cross-examine the witnesses? __yes__.

RMB 17. Do you understand that by pleading no contest you waive your right to defend yourself? __yes__

RMB 18. Do you understand that by pleading no contest you waive your right to appeal the Decision of this court except for certain very limited matters? __yes__.

RMB 19. Are you in prison or on parole or probation? __no__.

RMB 20. Do you understand that conviction on any of these charges may affect your right to parole or result in a probation violation? __yes__.

RMB 21. Has anyone connected with your arrest and prosecution, such as the police or the Commonwealth's Attorney, or any other person, threatened or in any manner *in the sen* attempted to force you to enter this plea of no contest? __yes__. *w/ather I have* ~~yes, rel force abduction and life in prison~~ *advised not to prongd wt Abduction*

RMB 22. Has anyone made any promises concerning your plea of no contest? __no__. *RMB*

RMB 23. Do you understand that the maximum punishment for these crimes is TEN (10) YEARS in the Virginia Department of Corrections, plus fines and costs? __yes__

RMB 24. Have you discussed the sentencing guidelines with your attorney? __yes__.

RMB 25. Do you understand that the Court is not required to follow these sentencing Guidelines? __yes__.

RMB 26. Are you entirely satisfied with the services of your attorney in this matter this charge? __yes__.

RMB 27. Have you entered into a Plea Agreement with the Commonwealth's Attorney in this

Defendant's Initial *RMB*

CUMBERLAND MOUNTAIN COMMUNITY

SERVICES INTENSIVE IN-HOME SERVICES
DAILY REVIEW
CONTINUED

Name: Brandi Lee Short   Date: 6/7/12   Pg. 2

Notes:
family members. Goal 3:3-6 Mom reports things going o.k. at home, reports Brandi has an attitude and wants her way, getting mad when mom won't let her hang out in the neighborhood but has stayed home most of the time. Mom feels Brandi is beginning to understand why mom has safety concerns. Brandi continues to have difficulty getting along w/ others in the neighborhood, the people mom was allowing her to visit got mad at Brandi for no apparent reason. Reviewed progress towards ts goals and objectives, no self harmful behaviors or assaultive behaviors towards others reported, mom reports incidents where Brandi has walked off when in the past she would have become aggressive. Mom and siblings reports enjoying family time at the river, mom reports Brandi and siblings played together and did not argue as much. siblings seemed excited about outing. Mom reports continued problems w/ rule compliance, verbal aggression when not allowed to do what she wants, arguing, cursing, yelling, causing disturbances in the neighborhood, threatening to say they abuse her and accusing stepfather of sexual abuse, biting things. Brandi remained neutral did not engage in the conversation w/o being asked specific questions, reports she has not threatened lately, denies being abused admits she and her mom disagree on where she should be allowed to go, feels she is safe, plans on going where she wants to, reports she is not concerned about upcoming court date for breaking and entering, consumer participated very little when talking about the need to continue working on problematic areas. Mom feels Brandi will be sent off when she goes to court if she does not start obeying. Brandi seemed to not care or not understand how her behaviors may affect the court's decision. Commended Brandi on progress reported and encouraged her to keep working on problematic areas. Clinician continues to encourage consistent parenting, improved family relationships and communications, to provide encouragement and reassurance to consumer and family.
Goal 4: consumer is out of school for the summer plans to attend FPSHDI summer program.
Goal 5: discussed step down from IIH services, consumer to resume CM w/ former care manager, Eve Coleman, to continue w/ psychiatric services as sch, and consumer encouraged to attend therapy appt.'s at Healing Waters.

CONFIDENTIAL

_____D'\-\)_____   6-,-\"&-
IIH Clinician Signatur   Date

07/09 S-123a

Actual Inncocence

q,J1:) W!ff'«+
fh fo

4:05:19 P.M.

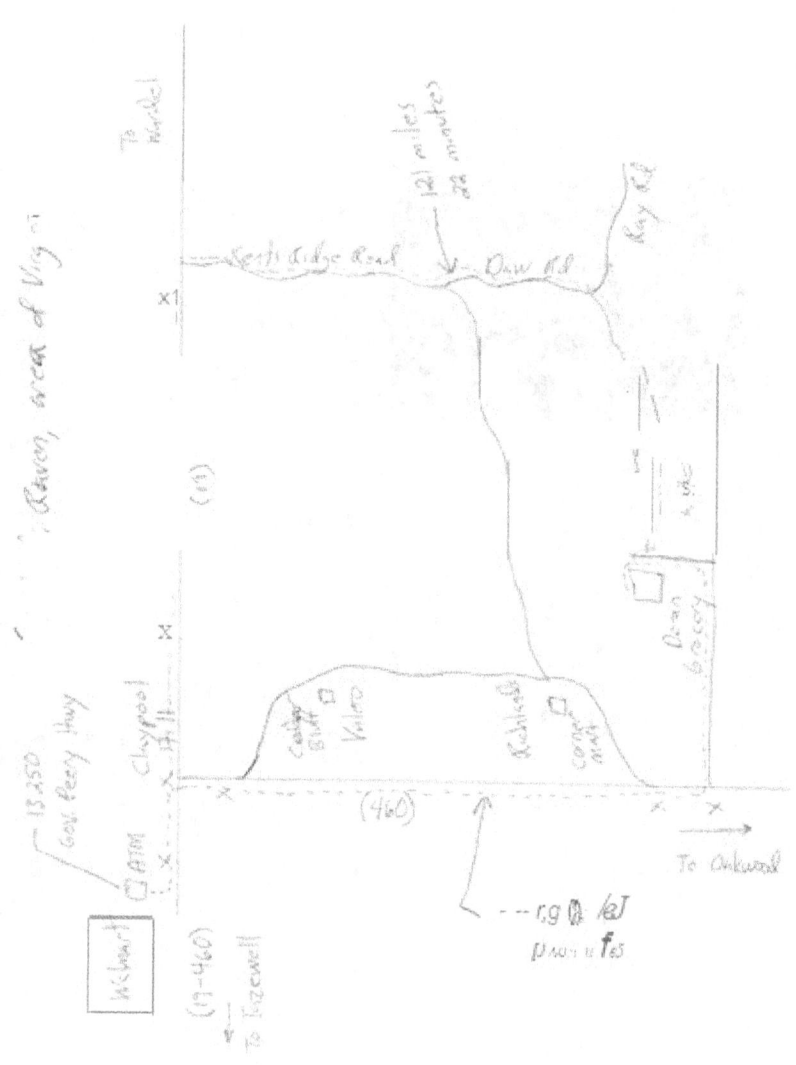

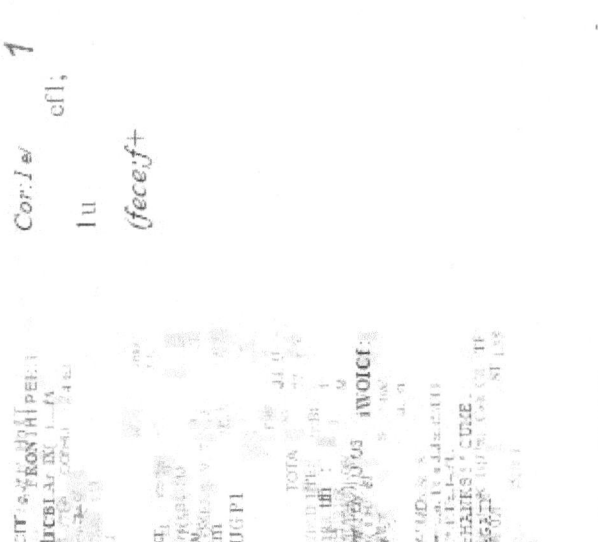

ROBERT BLANKENSHIP

exhibit text, 2 pages (?)

rec'd w/ b/e mom
Sexual Abuse

Redacted Statement 1

mom suspects drug use. Brandi curses, screams, threatens to say she is sexually, physically, sacred kicks and hits things when she doesn't get her way, per mom's report. Recently Brandi was charged

```
*********************
***  TX REPORT   ***
*********************

TRANSMISSION COMPLETED

TX/RX NO.              1812
DESTINATION NUMBER             9885165
DESTINATION ID
ST. TIME               07/20 11:59
COMMUNICATION TIME     00'48
PAGES SENT             4
RESULT                 OK
```

72-19

(!)

(k,J g1.s1 (

Cumberland Mountain C d r n c e s
Approval/Denial of Request to Disclose Protected Health Information to a Third Party

Consumer Name: Brandi Lee Sharp   Case#: j'tb3   Date: 7-17-13

Cont sent. File Location: ☒ O Oneida O Lebanon ☐ Jacewell O Other

Portion of Information disclosed:

Juv. & Domestic Relations Court Progress Report
Psych. Eval. 6-4-13

Disclosure ☒ approved as requested   O Approval in   O Disapproval

Description of financial information attached to disclosure statement for attach:

Signature of Person Approving/Disapproving Request
Signature: Darlee Butler   Date: 7-17-13

ACTUAL INNOCENCE

Name: SHORT, BRANDI LEE
Type: Quarterly Review MHSA

Cumberland Mountain Community Services
QUARTERLY REVIEW OF THE INDIVIDUAL SERVICES PLAN

Period of Review: 02/25/2012 To: 05/25/2012

DURING THIS PERIOD, THE CLIENT WAS SEEN FOR THE FOLLOWING SERVICES:
- ☐ Case Management
- ☒ Doctor visit
- ☐ Counseling
- ☐ Crisis Services
- ☐ Medication Disbursement/Lab work
- ☐ Psychosocial Rehabilitation
- ☐ Psychiatric Evaluation
- ☒ Intensive In-Home Services
- ☒ Other: IOP at school/therapy private provider

AT PRESENT, THE CLIENT'S PARTICIPATION IN THE ISP OF 02/15/2012
☒ Active   ☐ Marginally Active   ☐ Inactive

CLIENT STATUS:
- ☐ No change, but psychiatrically stable
- ☐ Has accomplished goals/objectives
- ☒ Is making progress toward treatment goals/objectives
- ☐ Is not making progress toward treatment goals/objectives
- ☐ Is non-compliant with treatment goals/objectives

REQUIRED SUMMARY STATEMENT REGARDING ISP:

During this quarter, Brandi was seen for MH services, seen for psychiatric services on 2/2/6, failed kept service appt on 5/22, participated in therapeutic day treatment at the school and was seen for therapy by Healing Waters Counseling Center. CPS complaint made by clinician and therapist currently involved w/ court services.

Goal 1 Brandi remains in the home with her family, cooperation and participation in services varies despite current level of services consumer remains at risk of out of home placement due to her defiant, impulsive, aggressive and illegal behaviors.

Goal 2: Brandi was seen once this quarter for psychiatric services, failed appt. on 5/22 for annual psychiatric eval, mom reports Brandi throws a fit and refused to attend, appt. rts for 6/4. Annual physical dental and eye check up completed per mom, records have been requested from PCP. Brandi wears glasses. Mom reports Brandi refuse take take meds at times, mom thinks meds are helpful at times then doesn't think they are at other times, reports she feels Brandi misbehaviors Non-Psych doesn't get her very. Consumer feels meds are helpful w/ concentration and hyperactivity / Michael Lewis physician aggression noted. Goal 3: Participation in services varies, at times consumer is in a good mood, seems motivated to work toward goals, other times is defiant, refuses to participate, sleeps, or leaves during services. Mom reports being unable to provide adequate supervision or enforce rules. Inconsistent parenting and consumers a lack of motivation towards services hinders progress. Mom reports being unable to find Brandi on several occasions, has unlocked her window, reports Brandi hangs out w/ older and negative peers, lies, steals continue to smoke, mom suspects drug use, curses, screams, threatens to say she is sexually and physically abused, yells and hits things when she doesn't get her way. Recently Brandi was charged with stealing and grandma and destruction of private property, court date set in July.

GOAL 4: Brandi's grades fluctuate, teacher reports motivation varies, inconsistent w/ doing work, sleeps in class and won't do her W/K at time, reports att 1) defiance and attitude improved. No school suspensions since 2/25. Brandi received therapeutic day treatment services at school, has consumer being able to handle her frustrations more appropriately, no physical altercations or outburst w/ school or on the bus. Brandi began therapy through Healing Waters Counseling, is greatly compliant. UM services are sch. to end on 6/30 Brandi will transition back to case management services to continue w/ psychiatric services, therapeutic day treatment plans to attend the summer program and to continue w/ therapy.

CON IDENTIAL

V-00 (1)

ROBERT BLANKENSHIP

CUMBERLAND MOUNTAIN COMMUNITY SERVICES
INTENSIVE IN-HOME SERVICES
DAILY REVIEW

Name: Brandi Lee Short Date: 6/7/12
Location: home Duration: 120 min
Participants: Clinician, Consumer, family

Summary (Mental Status, Concerns, etc):
Brandi was alert and oriented, mood/affect neutral, no SVHI, A HNH, no drug, alcohol or cigarette use reported. Sleep and appetite o.k.

Consumer's progress toward ISP Goals & Objectives and Staff Interventions:
Goal 1: Brandi lives with her mother, stepfather, and twin siblings. Brandi's older half brother is not living w/ the family. Family is home for most visits, participation and cooperation varies, left early today to pick up stepfather. Goal 2:1-4 Mom and consumer reports med. compliance, some drowsiness when sitting still, failed psych eval, appt. sch. for 5/22, was seen for psych eval. on 6/4/12. Overall fewer meltdowns and outburst, continues to be defiant and verbally aggressive, cursing, screaming, threatening. DX information reviewed, mom reports understanding dx information, and has a handbook on ADHD. Mom reports Brandi was seen for WCC, sees PCP when needed, takes allergy medicine, no physical complaints, has been seen for dental and eye checkup, wears glasses, no longer sees cardiologist. Reports failing therapy appt., because Brandi refused to go. Clinician continues to encourage compliance w/ meds., all appts. and recommendations for consumer and all.

CONFIDENTIAL

Next contact:

Actual Inncocence

Margaret A. Steffey

From: Darlene Bradley
Sent: Monday, May 21, 2012 10:58 AM
To: Crystal Mcglothlin, Margaret A. Steffey
Cc: Darlene Bradley
Subject: bs

Update on Brandi Lee Short. Brandi is set for a psych eval tomorrow. Brandi currently receives psychiatric services and intensive in-home services through CMCSB counseling through Healing Waters and therapeutic day treatment though Family Preservation services at the school. She plans to attend TDT program this summer, was participating in ROTC but is refusing to go.

She is taking Concerta as prescribed and the morning dose of Keppra, at times she refuses to take the evening dose. No SI/HI. AH/VH reports sleep and appetite as fine but they often report she is out in the neighborhood at 1 and 2 o'clock in the morning. She started her period last month for one day has not had any more periods. Brandi's moods varies, but lately is usually irritable, flat affect, doesn't seem to care, low motivation, says she is not concerned about legal charges, was actually in a better mood and more cooperative when I seen her after the breaking and entering incident and at court. Behaviors have steadily worsened since the family moved to a new neighborhood on March 18th. Mom is unable to supervise Brandi. Brandi leaves w/o permission, has been unable to find her on numerous occasions, lies about where she is, and who she is with, has been w/older boys on a few occasions, continues to smoke, has been involved in several conflicts in the neighborhood, and has been accused of bullying younger kids. Brandi and 2 other kids. In the neighborhood broke into Brandi's home, tore up the door. Brandi broke into her own home reportedly to get a cigarette, mom reports Brandi stole money on two occasions. Brandi refused to go with her family and was left unsupervised in the neighborhood. During the investigation Brandi was slurring her words and falling asleep, the officer recommend drug testing. Mom suspects Brandi is using something. On several occasion the police have been called by neighbors for disturbances at the home, mom reports Brandi is out yelling, screaming, cursing, demanding cigarettes, beating the mailbox, threatening to say stepdad raped her. at 1 and 2 o'clock in the morning. Mom has difficulty controlling her own anger, becomes involved in Brandi's conflicts w/ neighbors, the police has been called on the family. Mom reports slapping Brandi in the face when Brandi cursed her and whipping siblings W shoes and wood paddles. Clinician has filed a CPS complaint, the counseling center also has filed a complaint. Brandi threw a fit at counseling center, refusing to get out of the car, kicking the vehicle, screaming blowing the horn, refusing to mind mom, things escalated and the police were called. Brandi denies sexual abuse, denies her mother hit her when mom was saying she did, denies drug use.

Brandi went to court last week over the destruction of private property and breaking and entering, court date of a voi. drug test was completed and it was negative. The night before court she took off w/o permission, mom called the police when they couldn't find her, was with older boy and other kids, mom reports the office though Brandi's eyes were glassy and reports she was unsteady.

At school Brandi has not required office intervention since incident in Feb. Brandi reports problems getting along w/ kids on the bus but has not been in trouble lately, motivation and task completion varies, moods vary at school, seems to try hard then seems to not care., will do work for a while then won't, is drowsy in class on occasion, continues to receive TDT services at school. needs to improve organization and study habits, be consistent apse in doing work causes grades to drop and teachers concerned that it w cause problems later due to gaps in learning, has an F in English otherwise passing.

ROBERT BLANKENSHIP

CUMBERLAND MOUNTAIN COMMUNITY SERVICES

INTENSIVE IN-HOME SERVICES
DAILY REVIEW

Name: Brandi Lee Short Date: 5/15/12
Location: home 60 school 30 min office 30 min Duration: 120 min.
Participants: Clinician, Consumer, family, school personnel, therapist, DSS

Summary (Mental Status, Concerns, etc):
Brandi was alert and oriented, mood and affect neutral, at times seemed in a good mood, no SI/HI, AH/VH, consumer denies bullying, drug, alcohol use, admits to cigarette use, mom reports smoking and suspects drug use. Sleep and appetite o.k. Mom reports bullying, stealing, lying, threatening, disrespect and disobedience continues.

Consumer's progress toward ISP Goals & Objectives and Staff Interventions:
Goal 1: Brandi lives with her mother, stepfather, and twin siblings. Brandi's older half brother is not living w/ the family since they have moved, he is staying w/his uncle. Mom blames Brandi for this and for siblings negative behaviors. Home environment negative. Goal 2:1-4 Mom reduced Kapvay to 1 x a day beginning on 4/26 due to consumer falling asleep in class. Mom reports Brandi was refusing to take evening dose anyway but since reducing it she takes it sometimes, and being unsure if she takes/concerta as prescribed consistently, encouraged mom to monitor the meds. Brandi is compliant w/ med service appts. Brandi was sch. for therapy I'm spoke w/ Tara, consumer's therapist at Healing Waters Counseling Center. Tara reports Brandi came to the appointment but was belligerent, angry, refused to get out of the car, was kicking and screaming, blowing the horn, kicking the doors, cursing, screaming, saying she wasn't going to obey mom, didn't want to go home or be

CONFIDENTIAL

Next contact:

Darlene Bradley BSQ4
IIH Clinician
5-15-12

Actual Inncocence

CUMBERLAND MOUNTAIN COMMUNITY SERVICES
INTENSIVE IN-HOME SERVICES
DAILY REVIEW
CONTINUED

Name: Brandi Lee Short   Date: 5/15/12 Pg 2

Notes:

be around mom, saying she didn't have anything to eat but sandwiches. therapist had concerns about remarks and about remarks mom made about Brandi accusing stepdad of raping her. Things escalated the police were called. Tara did not feel that mental health crisis intervention was needed. Brandi was not suicidal, unsure what was going on at home, reports they did make a CPS complaint. Clinician called and completed CPS complaint as well, things escalating at home, mom previously reported getting angry and slapping Brandi in the face, being unable to supervise consumer, Brandi is leaving the home w/o permission and not being where she is supposed to be. Spoke w/ mom, things continuing to escalate, reports the police being called to the home mom reports incident last week when Brandi went for therapy, reports Brandi did not want to go. Mom reports when Brandi gets mad or doesn't get her way, she threatens to say her stepfather raped her, reports Brandi is hanging out with the wrong crowd, continues to smoke and mom suspects drug use, reports Brandi to leave the home w/o permission, does not seem to care. goal 4:1-4 Remains the same, spoke w/ Ms. crabtree and Mike/IIH worker; picked up discipline records, attendance and grades, turned in for scanning. Progress being made in behaviors, is getting along w/ others, no outburst that requires office intervention, none since Feb., consumer is struggling w/ math and english but does enough to get by, seems motivated at times other time doesn't care, inconsistent w/ completing assignments and motivation. The school is pleased w/ improvements. Brandi continues to receive IIH and this has helped. IIH worker reports participation and motivation varies but overall has made progress, is handling frustrations w/o aggression, some cursing. Updated family and consumer and commended consumer's progress. Goal 3:1-6 Met w/ consumer and her family, Brandi in a good mood today, mom reports she was in an irritable mood earlier, reports attitude problems continue when she doesn't get her way. Brandi does not seem concerned about court tomorrow, mostly did not respond here mom and clinician discussed the report being sent to the court, clinician has left a message w/ court services. Mom reports the police being called to the home several times by the neighbors for various disturbances and calling the police herself when unable to find Brandi. Reports Brandi is out at 1 or 2 o'clock in the morning, yelling, screaming, demanding cigarettes, hitting the mailbox w/ a board, cursing, threatening to say stepdad raped her if he corrects her or she doesn't get her way, calling him bald and ingest. Mom seemed various conflicts and times when consumer leaves w/o permission, is not where she is supposed to be, lying and stealing, reports they have been told by neighbors that Brandi is bullying younger kids. Mostly Brandi did not respond seemed unconcerned, denies bullying and has excuses and explanations reports trying to keep the kids from fighting. During one on one, Brandi reports saying things when mad but denies stepdad has ever raped her or having any concerns. Brandi also denied that her mom slapped her in the face, reminded Brandi that her mom was the one that said she did. Brandi then reports that the police said it was not abuse. Encouraged Brandi to report abuse if it occurs and reviewed who she can report abuse to. Clinician encouraged Brandi to work w/ her mom on resolving conflicts of the need for both to resolve conflicts peacefully. Clinician continues to work w/ family on I.S.T. on improving communications and resolving conflicts. Brandi did n't seem to a lot current home situation or legal difficulties, was non complicant w/ participating in IIH activities

ROBERT BLANKENSHIP

Name: SHORT BRANCH, LEE
Type: Doctor Progress Note

MEDICAL PROGRESS NOTE

Type of contact: ☒ Face to Face ☐ Telephone ☐ Telepsychiatry ☐ Family Contact
Service provided: ☐ Med Mgmt ☐ Psychotherapy ☒ Patient Education ☐ Emergency Assessment
☒ Psych Evaluation ☐ Other

Relationship of service to ISP:
☒ Pharmacotherapy ☐ Psychotherapy ☐ Crisis Intervention ☐ Other

Progress toward service objectives:
☒ Compliant w/ treatment/meds ☐ Improved ☐ Noncompliant w/ treatment/meds ☐ Unimproved
☐ Utilizes recommended services ☐ Drug levels therapeutic ☐ Other

NOTE:

Time: 30 minutes

Chief complaint: Here for psychiatric evaluation and follow up

HPI:
Patient is a 13 year old white female accompanied by her mother. Had previous report from Darlene or PH worker that says that Brandi sometimes refuses her evening medications. Brandi says sleep and appetite are good and sometimes is out in the neighborhood at 1 or 2 in the morning. Mood seems but she often is irritable, flat affect, doesn't seem to care, has low motivation and doesn't seem to be concerned about legal charges. She has a breaking and entering charge for breaking into her own home. During the incident she was slurring her words and falling asleep. Police have been called on several occasions due to disturbances at the home. CPS has also been notified, mom's will be out yelling screaming, cursing, demanding cigarettes, beating the mailbox, threatening to say her stepfather raped her even though she claims the abuse sexual abuse. Brandi and her mother have been involved in conflict with neighbors. Brandi's behavior has been better at school. Her grades have dropped but she did pass everything and will be moving onto the 5th grade. Her mother says Kapvay is helpful. She did cut it back to 0.1mg QAM, 0.2mg QHS for awhile because she felt the girls was too drowsy if she wasn't active. Teachers reported she did better with this dose. Mother has now started giving her 0.2mg BID again for summer. Brandi will be going to summer school through FPS. Mother feels the meds are helpful.

Current medications:
Concerta 36mg 1 po QAM; Kapvay 0.2mg BID

Takes Loratadine and Singulair

SEs: None

Old psychiatric history/medications:
No previous psychiatric hospitalizations. Was on Adderall in the past from PCP. Had problems with weight loss. Was changed to Vyvanse in 2008. Vyvanse was helpful with school and was maintained on it in combination with meds of other meds until it was changed in March 2011 to Concerta. She was tried on Focalin with Vyvanse and mother did not feel like it was helpful. She later tried on Abilify with Vyvanse which mother also did not feel like was helpful. Combination of Kapvay and Concerta seems to be somewhat helpful.

Medical history:
Born after 39 week pregnancy with no complications. No problems at birth. No developmental delays. Met goals on time. No previous surgeries. No seizures. Head injury with LOC. Has seasonal allergies on Singulair and Loratadine. NKDA. 2x with ophthalmic hypertension and wearing ambliopia.

CONFIDENTIAL

Actual Inncocence

CUMBERLAND MOUNTAIN COMMUNITY SERVICES
INTENSIVE IN-HOME SERVICES
DAILY REVIEW
CONTINUED

Name: Brandi Lee Short   Date: 1/19/12   Pg. 2

Notes:
Associated recently. Clinician contacted Associated, records should be sent out in a few weeks. Spoke w/ Mike, consumer's FPS worker, reports no physical aggression, is being more respectful to authority figures, getting along w/ a peer she once had a fight with, some hyperactivity. Clinician picked Brandi up after school, commended consumer on positive behaviors reported by the school and FPS, discussed ways to improve organization, study habits, concentration, and tutoring available at school, Brandi being homework with her today. Brandi was receptive to suggestions, seemed down, has limited insight to her emotions or feelings, shrugs when clinician mentioned that she seemed down. Met w/ mom, consumer and friend before siblings arrived home. mom reports Brandi and her sister got in trouble on the bus for fighting w/each other, then Brandi showed herself on the ride home from the bus stop. Mom reports they both have bruises. Brandi reports getting irritated at her siblings, reports she tries to entire them around, reports they won't leave her alone, reports her sister hit her first, Brandi gets hot and was screaming and yelling wanting the window down on the way home from the bus stop, got mad at her stepdad when he wouldn't let her roll her window down because it was cold, was screaming, using profanity, and threatened to say he sexually abused her when he attempted to correct her. Mom reports Brandi has also threatened to say he dad sexually abused her when he makes her mind. Brandi denies saying this.   Brandi reports she gets mad when Neil her stepdad tries to boss her, but feels they have a good relationship most of the time. Discussed ways to improve behaviors, to let the bus driver correct her siblings, ways to deal w/ irritation, considering others feelings, discussed ways to improve relationships w/ siblings, stepdad, obeying adults. Brandi has difficulty accepting correction from authority figures. Discussed ways to think before acting, to report if she is abused but discussed the seriousness of lying. Brandi continues to say she did not threaten this. Mom reports when Brandi gets so mad she often does not remember what she says or does. Mom reports giving Brandi Concerta yesterday evening due to her behaviors, to calm her down, Brandi reports she was still awake at 12 last night, got up and helped her mom clean. Brandi reports she tries but cannot go to sleep. Discussed that taking Concerta in the evening could be interfering w/ sleep, mom does not feel it affects her sleep, she does not sleep even when she does not take the Concerta. Brandi and her siblings are sch. for med. service appt, encouraged mom to discuss w/ Dr. Drevenhoer. Some positive behaviors reported. No smoking, has been doing homework. Updated mom on school report and ways to help Brandi w/ organization and study habits. Mom reports filling out papers to have consumer tested at Gate City, clinician explained that consumer already had testing completed by and that Medicaid does not pay to duplicate testing. Mom feels this is fo   ian offered assistance. Brandi sees PCP for allergy shots and takes meds a/ ordf, lt gets a feet, a specialist in the past when she was passing out, no problems found and no further problems with passing out. Mom reports Brandi has nose bleeds and stays hot all the time. Mom to let PCP know at next visit and check if WCC is current. Mom to sch. dental appt. Clinician has sent for updated records from PCP and from Associated. Consumer's stepfather brought the other kids home and then then had to leave. Clinician met w/ consumer, mom and younger siblings. Clinician assessed for positive family interactions since last visit, consumer's sister and brother reported Brandi played a game w/ them, mom reports they got along and had fun, Brandi readily participated in anger mgt., decision   m solving, activities. Her siblings were less

ROBERT BLANKENSHIP

Name: SHORT, BRANDI LEE	Case#: 34065	Page: 2? of 37
Type: Treatment Plan Case Manager:		Date: 10/06/2010-10/05/2011

Individual Progress Note (08/02/2011)

Form#:	65993	Date: 08/02/2011		Start		Durat
Unit:	MH CASE MANAGEMENT		service:			ion
SubUnit:	MH CASE MANAGEMENT CHILD/		Travel: Documenta tion			0.15 0.00 0.15
Server:	BRYANT, LISA		Partici pants:	0		
Supervisor:						
Service:	CASE MANAGEMENT- CUMH		Days:	0		

CONTACT: Consumer's mother called QMH today - unserved - phone contact

CM INTERVENTION: Assessed needs - continue on: 1) CM ongoing appt for CM services; and 2) continue therapy services. Maintained FOCUS - disclosed consumer's recent and ongoing situations. No interpersonal today. Reminded about appts next week. Supportive counseling provided. Contact Type: CONS, REL, TEL.

INCIDENT: Mother called today to request that consumer and her sister be seen by Husty Fiore from consumer's another to being referred to the for an evaluation. Mother stated that "since nothing is easy to AFFORD... CM NEEDS to do even too." CM educated mother on LIHEAP. Mother continued that consumer is another has reports of being inappropriately touched by someone and inappropriate physical acts toward others. Mother verbally expressed understanding of the TREATMENT. After seen not to discuss recent/ongoing inappropriate behaviors. reported that consumer "wets his way all the time and becomes verbally/physically aggressive when she does not get her way." reported that consumer takes her meds as prescribed but will continue to act out verbally. In the car ride to places. CM causes mother reported that consumer is being envious of her sister's friendships with another female child at the Cottage and is demanding that her sister not be allowed to interact with that particular child. Mother reported that consumer, along with her siblings, is scheduled to be evaluated by Dr. Shreand on 8/12/11. Mother continued to report that she "don't know what else to do with 'em." Mother agreed to come to the next scheduled therapy appt. or CM.

Concerta 15mg Kapvay 3mg - Dmycxhinex

PLAN: Continue to monitor. Therapy and CM face to face - $$00 @ 9am. Followup on Dr. Shreand appt. Staff case at next staffing on 8/3/11.

Obj: 1.1.2 Make good choices
Obj: 1.1.3 Take medication as directed
Obj: 1.1.1 Eliminate aggression

Name: BRYANT, LISA, QMHP	Date: 08/02/2011	Time: 1:30 p.m	Electronic:

Actual Inncocence

Individual Progress Note (07/25/2011)

Format:	657086	Date: 07/25/2011		Start	Duration
				1:00 p.m.	1:00
					0:10

Progress Note

Brandi and her "Daddy" (mom's boyfriend) report that things continue to get worse. Brandi recently stated that a boy at the 3-D program touched her inappropriately, and threatened to kill her if she told. She finally told and now family and 3-D supervisors have discussed this and are taking action. Talked with Brandi about importance of telling things such as this and trusting adults to keep her safe. Brandi talked about not feeling safe at her father's house due to his drinking and verbally abusive behavior toward her and her siblings. She sees him every-other-weekend and denies physical or sexual abuse. Brandi's anger has also increased over the past couple of months. She blames this on the boy at the 3-D program. Brandi did talk today about knowing it's wrong to curse, and tell her mother but to get so angry that she doesn't always remember. Used CBT to promote self-reflection and soothing and discussed ways to remove herself from the situation before it gets to that point. Also encouraged mother to not hesitate to call the police due to the risk of harm to self and others during these episodes.

Next session $\frac{1}{2}$ for f/u.

	MH OUTPATIENT		Documentation
Org 1.1 SUBURBAN Large MH OUTPATIENT – CHILD/ADOL			
Name:	CLERIC, AMY R (STEVENS)	07/26/2011 Time: 10:40 a.m.	Electronic
Clinician/by type		Participants: 0	
Supervisor:		Days: 0	
Service	THERAPY	Quantity: 0	
Lab			
Provided To:	CONSUMER (CLIENT)	Provided At:	OFFICE
Outside		Contact Type:	CONSUMER FTF
Facility:			
Appointment Type:	SCHEDULED	Billing Type	AUTHORIZED ON TREATMENT
Intensity	ROUTINE		
Type:			

CONFID N I

ROBERT BLANKENSHIP

Jim Shortt video transcript   SS 056

Jim Shortt: Okay, today is May 21, 2014. I am at the Highlands Detention Center with Brandi Short and Brandi um you understand that my name is Jim Shortt. I am an attorney and I have been appointed to represent Robert Blankenship in relation to the matters involving you.

Brandi Short: Umhum

Jim Shortt: You understand that you don't have to talk to me if you don't to, um but are you willing to talk to me?

Brandi Short: Yes.

Jim Shortt: Okay. Do you recall what happened between you and Mr. Blankenship back on uh July of 2012, July 9, 2012?

Brandi Short: Yes.

Jim Shortt: Okay. And and you're voluntarily speaking with me, right? I'm not forcing you or anything like that.

Brandi Short: No.

Jim Shortt: Okay. Um, you understand that I may have to cut this off at times because I think this only records in like three or four minute segments?

Brandi Short: Yes.

Jim Shortt: Okay. Make sure this is recording. Alright can uh, did did you know before this incident, how did you know Robert Blankenship?

Brandi Short: Well, where we lived down in Raven he would stop and he would be out with his dogs

Jim Shortt: Um hum

Brandi Short: and he would ask my brother and sister because where we walked down through there he would ask Shaina and Christopher if they wanted to walk them, he said the twins said I don't care because they loved dogs

Jim Shortt: Sure

Brandi Short: and after that the twins would go went down one day to help him clean his house and he said that he'd pay'em thirty bucks a piece and I went with him

Actual Inncocence

a(f-S-)

to the he asked me to go to the bank with him

Jim Shortt: um hum

Brandi Short: to get the money and I went in there and asked my mom and she said it was okay, she said I guess and I went with him. He went to the, I don't even think he went to the bank...I don't think so....no

Jim Shortt: but that's where you thought you all were going to go

Brandi Short: yeah, that's where I thought we were going to go and he stopped at Corner Mart, got cigarettes and I think that was it....then he drove to the high school....made me drive from there....went to Wal-Mart....stole a pair of sunglasses

Jim Shortt: Who who drove from the high school to Wal-Mart

Brandi Short: me

Jim Shortt: Okay. Did did he make you rr did you drive all the

Brandi Short: Yes he made me. He made me drive.

Jim Shortt: Okay. Had you drove a vehicle before that day?

Brandi Short: No

Jim Shortt: So, that was the first time you ever drove

Brandi Short: Yeah I'd did drove a vehicle before on backroads

Jim Shortt: Okay, who, okay, but not with him?

Brandi Short: No

Jim Shortt: Okay, so he, you drove from the high school, Richlands High School to Wal-Mart in Pounding Mill

Brandi Short: Yes

Jim Shortt: Okay, did he force you to do that?

Brandi Short: Yes.

Page 2 of 13

ROBERT BLANKENSHIP

RP 52

Jim Shortt: Okay. So pick it up from where you all went to Wal-Mart.

Brandi Short: When we got to Wal-Mart...he made me hold his hand...he walked to the sunglasses...he said, what do you want...I like I just want to go look at the sunglasses...I didn't ask him to buy them for me...he didn't buy them for me...he put them on his head and took, walked out with them.

Jim Shortt: Okay

Brandi Short: and when um we got out, he reached them to me...he said here you can have them...I was like but you didn't pay for them...he was like they don't know that.

Jim Shortt: Okay

Brandi Short: and um when we got out of Wal-Mart we went to the vehicle...he made me drive from there...we stopped at Taco Bell to get gas and then he made me drive back down to Ruu or on Daw Road to Ray Road...Ray Road, he said he was going to show me a chimney that his parents or something owned.

Jim Shortt: um hum

Brandi Short: and when we got there he walked... there was a piece of rock thing, chimney...so after that he started taking his clothes off and I told him no because I already knew what he w... to... to... held off...and he kept taking 'em off...he came after me picked's my feet up off the ground, put me on the ground, and was on top of me with his hand around my neck and he was trying to take my clothes off with his other hand and I started screaming telling him to stop, please and taking my hands moving him again. I Way from my clothes and finally stopped and put his clothes on and made me go back in the vehicle and drive from there to his house and then I went home...and do you need to know what my mom did?

Jim Shortt: When you got home, who was there?

Brandi Short: My mom, my little brother and Shania...Chris and Shania...

Jim Shortt: Okay. Now, did did you come to find out that someone saw you at Wal-Mart with him earlier?

Brandi Short: Yes, my aunt.

Jim Shortt: What's her name?

Actual Inncocence

rA?-S3

Brandi Short: Janet Lester

Jim Shortt: So, was mom a little bit mad at you when you got home?

Brandi Short: Yeah.

Jim Shortt: Did she already know that you had been to Wal-Mart and other places with, or at least Wal-Mart

Brandi Short: Wal-Mart, yeah

Jim Shortt: with Mr. Blankenship

Brandi Short: Yes

Jim Shortt: you didn't have permission to do that did ya?

Brandi Short: No

Jim Shortt: Okay. So how was mom? Was she upset? Was she screaming?

Brandi Short: She was worried and mad. She wasn't screaming at me but she was like why were you at Wal-Mart holding his hand? I was like he made me. I started crying and she walked out the door, went down his house, knocked on the door

Jim Shortt: Did you go down there with her?

Brandi Short: Yeah

Jim Shortt: um hum

Brandi Short: after she, I heard the door slam I came back out of my room and went out there

Jim Shortt: Alright, and what happened when your mom and you got down his house?

Brandi Short: She'd ugh told me and she told the cops that when she knocked on the door he opened it she'd punched him in the face, got him in the face, he shut it and locked it. She kept knocking it, he wouldn't open it. She tore his ugh onions out of his garden and ugh....she called um her husband Neal and told him to get down here. Brandi was almost rap d and

ROBERT BLANKENSHIP

RB 54

Jim Shortt: Whose Neal?

Brandi Short: My, he was my step-dad.

Jim Shortt: Neal

Brandi Short: Reedy

Jim Shortt: Where's he at?

Brandi Short: Jail, now

Jim Shortt: Okay, and um how do you spell his name? Do you know?

Brandi Short: N-E-A-L R-E-E-D-Y

Jim Shortt: and he was married to your mother?

Brandi Short: Yes

Jim Shortt: but there divorced now?

Brandi Short: Yes

Jim Shortt: Is, is your mother married to anybody now?

Brandi Short: No

Jim Shortt: Does she live with somebody?

Brandi Short: She is seeing Randall

Jim Shortt: Randall who?

Brandi Short: Justice

Jim Shortt: That's her boyfriend?

Brandi Short: um hum

Jim Shortt: Does he live there?

Brandi Short: Not now

Actual Inncocence

EP 55

Jim Shortt: no

Brandi Short: Not right now

Jim Shortt: Did they live together for a period of time? No, they never lived together?

Brandi Short: okay

Jim Shortt: Do you know Randall? Do you like Randall?

Brandi Short: um huh

Jim Shortt: Okay. Is he good to ya?

Brandi Short: yeap

Jim Shortt: he is? Okay. Um, when he got yo – did anything else happen between you and Mr. Blankenship?

Brandi Short: No.

Jim Shortt: Okay. Well, let me take you back to where um you are on Kay Road

Brandi Short: um hum

Jim Shortt: Did he take - you said he took his clothes off

Brandi Short: his clothes off

Jim Shortt: um huh, he did

Brandi Short: um hum

Jim Shortt: Did he take all of his clothes off?

Brandi Short: Yes

Jim Shortt: So, he w _fully nude_?

Brandi Short: um hum

Jim Shortt: Okay, when he was fully nude, did he run towards you or walk towards you

ROBERT BLANKENSHIP

RB-57

Brandi Short: walked towards me

Jim Shortt: and

Brandi Short: I didn't run because I didn't know if he had weapons or anything. I didn't want to get hurt.

Jim Shortt: Right, I understand. And did um, okay, did, after he got close to you, what did he do specifically?

Brandi Short: He knocked my feet out from under me, like picked me up off the h-ound and put me on the ground and he had his hand on my throat and he was trying to 'take my clothes off.

Jim Shortt: Okay, did he ever remove any of your clothing?

Brandi Short: No.

Jim Shortt: Did... were you scratching, hitting him and trying to get him off?

Brandi Short: No, I was pushing his hands away from my clothes.

Jim Shortt: his hands, you were pushing his hands away from your clothes?

Brandi Short: Yes

Jim Shortt: Okay...um...okay...and um, did, you said that he grabbed you around your throat?

Brandi Short: Yes.

Jim Shortt: Okay, how long did he, did he have both hands or one hand around your throat?

Brandi Short: One.

Jim Shortt: And how long did he have his hand around your throat?

Brandi Short: I'm not for sure... just a couple of minutes

Jim Shortt: Okay, seem like a life time?

Brandi Short: Yeah.

Jim Shortt: I'm sure. Did he um....did you, what kind of markings did you have from this

Actual Inncocence

ff-s7

ncident?

Brandi Shortt: It didn't leave no mark eye because he didn't push down enough

Jim Shortt: Okay

Brandi Short: He just had his hand there and I was afraid if I'd fight it he would've choked me.

Jim Shortt: Right. Did um. did you scratch him or anything like that?

Brandi Short: No.

Jim Shortt: Okay. So, after he got off of top of you, he was still fully nude, right and you had all of your clothes on?

Brandi Short: Yes.

Jim Shortt: Did he ugh, what happened next?

Brandi Short: He put his clothes on and told me to take him to his house and himself to the drive from there.

Jim Shortt: What were you doing while he was putting his clothes on?

Brandi Short: Walking to the vehicle.

Jim Shortt: Okay. And then he did he did you drive to his house Or did you

Brandi Short: Yeah. he made me

Jim Shortt: Okay. So every time you drove, he always made you?

Brandi Short: um hum

Jim Shortt: Okay. Alright. And you don't want to testify in court, right?

Brandi Short: No.

Jim Shortt: Okay, I understand. Now, um what what are you in detention for now?

Brandi Short: over knives. I think. I'm not for sure and over my sound where I have been in trouble so much.

Jim Shortt:	What, what have you been in trouble for, past?
Brandi Short:	school
Jim Shortt:	like
Brandi Short:	stuff like that
Jim Shortt:	Like what?
Brandi Short:	Fight, getting in trouble from violation of probation.
Jim Shortt:	What did you do to violate probation?
Brandi Short:	I don't remember
Jim Shortt:	Okay, that's fine. So, you right now you just in trouble for taking a knife to school?
Brandi Short:	Yeah
Jim Shortt:	Okay, um so once you, you plan on being released Sunday?
Brandi Short:	Yeah.
Jim Shortt:	Once you're released you gonna go back home with mom?
Brandi Short:	Yeah
Jim Shortt:	Who does mom live with?
Brandi Short:	Herself.
Jim Shortt:	Okay. Does she work?
Brandi Short:	No, she's disabled.
Jim Shortt:	Is she, okay. And what, and her name is?
Brandi Short:	Tina Lowe
Jim Shortt:	What is her telephone number?
Brandi Short:	276-701-3363

ACTUAL INNCOCENCE

f P. S

Jim Shortt: Okay, you have a pretty good relationship with mom?

Brandi Short: um hum

Jim Shortt: okay. Um, are you receiving any kind of counseling now?

Brandi Short: Anger Management Counseling with Rick Teague.

Jim Shortt: He's a nice guy isn't he?

Brandi Short: Yeah, he's funny

Jim Shortt: Yeah, really smart guy

Brandi Short: um hum

Jim Shortt: Really, really intelligent guy. Have you received counseling from anywhere else?

Brandi Short: Cumberland Mountain and stuff but I ain't in it no more. I did.

Jim Shortt: Okay, who was your counselor at Cumberland Mountain?

Brandi Short: God, I don't remember.

Jim Shortt: Don't remember? What did you go to counseling for?

Brandi Short: Anger problems.

Jim Shortt: Okay, okay. Um, what makes you angry?

Brandi Short: Little things.

Jim Shortt: Okay. Are you learning how to control your anger a little better?

Brandi Short: Yeah.

Jim Shortt: That what there trying to teach you through Anger Management and everything? Seem to be working? Okay, alright. Um, let's see, who, who is your mom seeing? Her boyfriend, what is his name?

Brandi Short: Randall Justice

Jim Shortt: Okay and you get along well with him?

ROBERT BLANKENSHIP

RP 60

Brandi Short: Um hum

Jim Shortt: Pretty honest guy?

Brandi Short: Yeap

Jim Shortt: Okay, good relationship?

Brandi Short: um hum

Jim Shortt: Does he live with your mom?

Brandi Short: Not right now.

Jim Shortt: Okay, but he's good to you?

Brandi Short: Yeah.

Jim Shortt: Good to your sister and little brother?

Brandi Short: um hum

Jim Shortt: Now, are your sister and your little...your sister and your little brother, are they both smaller than you?

Brandi Short: Yeah

Jim Shortt: Younger than you? Okay, um just a second. Whose your Probation Officer?

Brandi Short: Brad Goff

Jim Shortt: Oh, he's out of Russell County?

Brandi Short: Um hum

Jim Shortt: Okay. What's your mom's address?

Brandi Short: I don't know from where she's moving.

Jim Shortt: Oh, okay

Brandi Short: I don't know

Actual Inncocence

1-1-9/

Jim Shortt: She move around a lot?

Brandi Short: No, we got to move from this place becaus e of problems with her ex-boyfriend.

Jim Shortt: Oh, who is her ex-boyfriend?

Brandi Short: Chuck Justice.

Jim Shortt: Chuck Justice, okay. Um, did you like Chuck?

Brandi Short: No.

Jim Shortt: No, was he mean to you?

Brandi Short: He's sick. He's got cancer. He's grouchy sometimes. The medicine he takes chokes on him sometimes because he can't stand hollering and stuff.

Jim Shortt: Oh, okay. Alright. Have you ever been in trouble for not telling the truth?

Brandi Short: ught um

Jim Shortt: Have you ever told a lie before?

Brandi Short: When I was younger.

Jim Shortt: Okay, but nothing major?

Brandi Short: No.

Jim Shortt: Alright, we'll anything else you want to tell me? Okay. Now, just in conclusion, you, this was voluntarily on your part, right?

Brandi Short: Um hum

Jim Shortt: I didn't force you or anything like that?

Brandi Short: No.

Jim Shortt: You understand who I am?

Brandi Short: Yes.

Jim Shortt: You understand that I represent Robert Blankenship?

Brandi Short: Yes.

ROBERT BLANKENSHIP

RP-62

Jim Shortt: Okay, any questions for me?

Brandi Short: No.

Jim Shortt: Alright. I thank you very much for your time.

END OF MEETING

"blankenship - robert, transcript from interview with brandi short, 5-25-14"; J-13, 140

ACTUAL INNOCENCE

 Subpoena Proof

COOKE, SHORTT & KEENE, PLLC
P.O. Drawer 541
Cedar Bluff, VA 24609

H. Stewart Cooke, Esq.
Jim Terry Shortt, II, Esq. (VA & WV)
John O. Keene, Esq.

Phone (276) 963-4381
Fax (276) 963-4297

May 22, 2014

VIA FACSIMILE 988-7501

Dawn Cole, Deputy Clerk
Tazewell County Circuit Court
101 East Main Street, Suite 202
Tazewell, Virginia 24651

Re: *Commonwealth of Virginia vs. Robert McKinley Blankenship*
Case Nos.: CRJ 3-000003-04, to-wit: (ATTEMPTED RAPE);
CRJ 3-000003-05, to-wit: (INDECENT LIBERTIES UNDER 15 YEARS OF AGE);
CRJ3-000003-06, to-wit: (ABDUCTION WITH INTENT TO DEFILE);
CRB-000003-07, to-wit: (ASSAULT & BATTERY); and
CRJ 3-000003-08, to-wit: (CONTRIBUTING TO DELINQUENCY OF A MINOR)

Dear Dawn:

I hereby request subpoenas to be issued demanding the presence of the following individuals in your Honorable Court on the 4th day of June, 2014 at 9:00 o'clock a.m. in relation to the above captioned matter, to-wit:

Robbie Davis, Juvenile Probation Officer
315 School Street
Tazewell, Virginia 24651

Brad Goff, Juvenile Probation Officer
54 West Main Street
Lebanon, Virginia 24266

Should you have any questions or anything further be required, please do not hesitate to contact me.

Thank you for your assistance in this matter.

As always,

Respectfully,

Jim Terry Shortt, II

cc: Dennis Lee, Esquire (Commonwealth's Attorney)
—Robert Blankenship (client) (hand-delivered)

ROBERT BLANKENSHIP

FALETTI & GONZALEZ, PLLC
ATTORNEYS AT LAW

CARLETTA J. «CARLA» FALETTI   MONICA M. GONZALEZ

July 3, 2017

Carla letter 1

Robert Blankenship
1484429
Warren's
Ridge
State
Prison
D220 PO
Box 759
Big Stone Gap, VA 24219

Dear Mr. Blankenship:

I am in receipt of your letter of June 29.

I do understand your allegation that the trial transcript that was submitted by the Circuit Court clerk's office to the Court of Appeals is not a fair representation of what went on at trial. Following receipt of the record we have forty (40) days to request a copy of the audio recording of our trial and with that we should be able to [illegible handwriting] identify from transcript and compare it to audio recording. All trial procedures or legal errors that occurred both before the trial (e.g. motions granted or denied, etc.) and during the trial (e.g. objections sustained or over-ruled). There is little to do on your appeal until the entire record (not only the transcript) of the proceedings is transmitted to the Court of Appeals. An appeal must be based upon errors within the proceedings and cannot be based upon the facts of the case, the credibility of the witnesses, allegations of misconduct by the prosecutor or defense counsel, etc. It is a common misconception that an appeals court reviews the case for an incorrect verdict. The appeals court only reviews for errors that could have influenced the ultimate outcome of the trial.

1700 East Main Street   (276) 963-9226
Lebanon, Virginia 24266   fax (276) 345-4074

Actual Innocence

July 3, 2017
Page 12

Additionally, any procedural or legal errors that we identify in the trial or pre-trial proceedings must have been preserved for appeal in the record. That means that the error must have been identified at the time it was made and must have been objected to or challenged on the record. An error that was not objected to or challenged is not appealable. If an appeals court overturns a verdict it does not mean that the defendant is found "not guilty", it only allows for the matter to return to the jurisdiction for another proceeding to correct the error. The ultimate outcome may be the same.

You allege misconduct on the part of counsel during the trial. In general, issues such as errors in trial strategy, failing to call witnesses, failing to preserve issues for appeal, etc. would need to be addressed in a *habeas corpus* proceeding and not an appeal. As explained above, the only issues addressable to the Court of Appeals are procedural and legal issues arising within the litigation and preserved for appeal at the time the error occurred.

It is clear from your letter that you are understandably very upset about inconsistencies in the transcript that was initially submitted to the Court of Appeals. I will do everything possible to assure the transcript submitted to the appeals is accurate. It is an ~~~~~~~~~~~~~~ entity to file a motion with the Court to ~~~ that the transcript be typed anew by a court reporter unrelated to the initial OHL.

I believe it is important for you to know that based upon the Rules of the Supreme Court of Virginia I am required to follow certain protocols in filing your appeal. I can do everything reasonably possible to assure the transcript is correct but it is ultimately up to the court to make the determination as to which transcript is to be made a part of the record and submitted to the Court of Appeals.

I intend to visit you to discuss our appeal once I have been able to review the transcript and compare it to the audio recording. I understand your desire to also listen to the transcript and I will inquire of the DOC as to their policy with regard to bringing playback equipment into the facility. In my experience, all I have been able to take to DOC facilities is legal papers and a pen.

STATE OF NORTH CAROLINA

CATAWBA County — NEWTON

In The General Court Of Justice
Superior Court Division

STATE VERSUS

ROBERT McKINLEY BLANKENSHIP

WHITE — MALE — 11-17-1963

DAVID LEARNER — JOHNNY TURNER

JUDGMENT SUSPENDING SENTENCE - FELONY
☒ IMPOSING AN INTERMEDIATE PUNISHMENT
IMPOSING A COMMUNITY PUNISHMENT
(STRUCTURED SENTENCING)

The defendant ☒ pled guilty to: INDECENT LIBERTIES WITH A MINOR CHILD

Offense Date: 09-02-1997

$130.00	$503.00	$0.00	$700.00	$100.00		$1,430.00

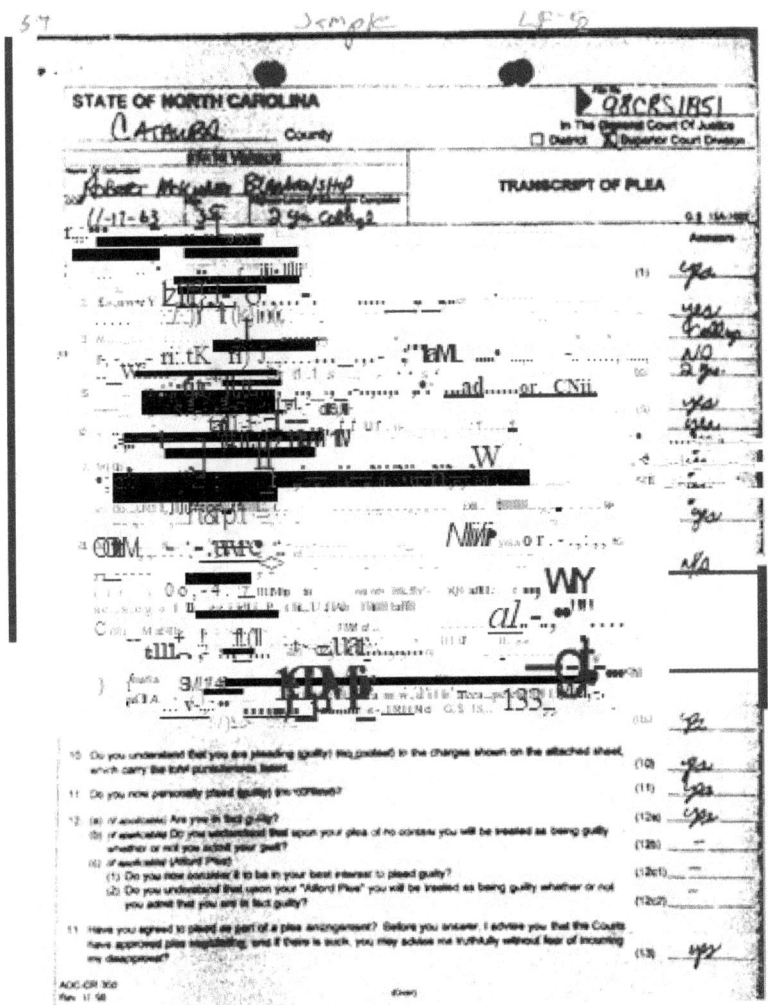

Hick Police Dept.   NC   010200   97-3613

Ashley Bradshaw responded: He's a friend of mama's who used to want her. R/O asked Ad... ee ... ster tee? Ashley Bradshaw FOSJ36ASee IIE Ae-tee me two times. I hate him. R/O asked: Why do you hate him? Ashley responded: Cause he was beating it in the middle. R/O asked: What do you mean, beating it? Ashley responded: You know. R/O asked: What? Ashley Bradshaw then made a motion with her hand in front of her penis area like the motions of male masturbation and she stated: He does it like that. R/O then used some anatomy drawings and asked Ashley Bradshaw to label the different parts of the body (see attached). R/O then asked Ashley Bradshaw to circle the part of the body on the drawing that Robert beat. She circled the penis on the drawing. R/O then pointed to different parts of the body on the drawing and asked Ashley Bradshaw to say whether that area would be a good touch or a bad touch if someone were to touch her there (see attached drawings). R/O then asked Ashley Bradshaw: Did he say anything when he did it? Ashley responded... esm... e goo... e a... me a oo... as e:... did ...e bo it? Ashley rest3eAEfee: last week of the... R/O asked: Where did A do it? Ashley responded: In the car. We were parked behind that place. The brick station near the train tracks. R/O asked: Was it just you and him? Ashley responded: "S-h" "OfUPd"dy" "the R/O asked: How many times did he de-... ey respoAEJed: On time. He told me to lean back and we can... o. R/O asked: Go where? Ashley responded: To my school. R/O asked: When he beat it, how long did he do it? Ashley responded: Two or three minutes. R/O asked: Did you tell anyone? Ashley responded: First I told my school teacher. Then I told Robin, then mama. Mama said I was never going to ride with him again. Mama wanted to kill him. R/O asked: What ... dark. I don't know if he had his pants unzipped or not. R/O asked: Did he ever do any bad touches on you? Ashley responded: He had his hands on me like that. (Ashley put her arm around R/O's neck and shoulders.) R/O then asked: What kind of car were you in? Ashley responded: A red car. R/O asked: Where were you sitting? Ashley responded: I was in back. He was in front. Then he hopped in back with me. R/O asked: Were there any other bad touches? Ashley responded: No, cause mama would beat him up.

Inv T. W. Vvhtsnon+   [signature]   1/22/97 1700

Actual Inncocence

tf,, May 17, 2015 12:54PM Hickory Police Department PAGE LF-53 No. 1044 P. 5

| Hickory Police Dept. | NC | 0180200 | | | 48 3 |

Ashley Bradshaw responded: He's a friend of mama's who use _____ WI _____ er. R/O asked _____ . _____ Ct _____ d? AsRley Bradshaw FOrxRent La5t vook As4ee me two times. I hate him. R/O asked: Why do you hate him? Ashley responded: Cause he was sticking it in the middle. R/O asked: What do you mean, sticking it? _____ R/O asked. What Ashley **Brodshow j-ien n,a** _____ swift her hand in front of her civis rea like the motion _____ ole masturbation and she stated: He does it like that. R/O then used some anatomy drawings and asked Ashley Bradshaw to label the different parts of the body (see attached). R/O then asked Ashley Bradshaw to circle the part of the body on the drawing that Rob beat. She circled the penis on the drawing. R/O then pointed to different parts of the body on the drawing and asked Ashley _____ a _____ say _____ e er a res a girl be a good touch or a bod touch if someone were to touch better. ye (see attached) drawings). R/O then asked Ashley Bradshaw: Did he say anything when he did it? And Ashley respon _____ ea _____ god _____ e a do _____ as t _____ en did +1 0 R? Ashley res F1999: besi v r < e e k e r f h G y s k G d: Why did he do it? Ashley responded: In the car. We were parked behind that place. The brick _____ station near the train tracks. R/O asked: Was it just you and _____ 'im! As _____ ey responded: _____ rdf-elle.-RI9-e9keel!: 1 kew **past'17 time, abv+e** deW filhiey responded: On time. He told me to lean back andwe cah a. R/O asked _____ responded: Tommy school. R/O asked: When he took it, how long did he do it? Ashley responded: Two or three mines. R/O asked: Did you tell anyone? Ashley responded: First I told my school teacher. Then I told Robin. Then mama. Ma a said I was never going to ride with him again. Mama wanted to kill him. R/O asked: What _____ dark. I don't know if he had his pants unzipped or not. R/O asked: Did he ever do any bad touches on you? Ashley responded: He had his hands on me like that. (Ashley put her arm around R/O's neck and shoulders.) R/O then asked: What kind of car were you in? Ashley responded: A red car. R/O asked: Where were you sitting? Ashley responded: I was in back. He was in front. Then he hopped in back with me. R/O asked: W ere there any other bad touches? Ashley responded: Not cause mama would beat him up

L _/ 7 W.Whisnqn-t 4-S8'7 [signature] 6/28/97 1700

11: Mar. 17, 2015 12:59PM   Hickory Police Department   No. 1044   P. 19
97-34813
77-65

KID CONNECTION
connecting children, families, and schools

⑥

SIGN-IN AND SIGN-OUT

Week# Name	Monday In	Monday Out	Tuesday In	Tuesday Out	Wednesday In	Wednesday Out	Thursday In	Thursday Out	Friday In	Friday Out
Breves Shayla	RS	RS	—	WSRS	—	—	RS	RS	RS	—
Smith Darrian	RS	RS	—	WSK	—	—	RS	RS	RS	—
Hodges Robbie										
Nelsen Ronnie										
Hart Shane		4:00		5:00		5:0				
Hildebran Cody	DH	—	DH	—	DH	—	—	—	DH	—
Haynes Brooke				VA						
Bradshaw Ashley			4:00	VA			(RB)			
Howell Kenika										
Howell Darien										
Ingle Caleb	DC	4:00	DS	4:12	OC	5:0	DC	10:50	OC	25
Jones Kaleb										
LeoHa Jordan	RE	5:15		5:17			RE	5:45		—
LeoHa Lacey	RE	5:15		5:0			RE	5:4		
Lackey Brandon	QU	5:35		5:15		TP	QU	5:36	QU	
McMahan David	SM			4:30	SM		SM	4:05	SA	
Morrison Crystal										
Moorpa Melissa										
Matucci Krista		RW	4:20	6:00	5:10		6:30	5:30	RW	
Williamson Daniel	RP	4:20		5:10			6:30	5:30	RW	
Williamson Robbie	RW	4:20		5:10			6:30	5:30	RW	
Nichols James		4:13		4:45				4:45	My	
Nichols Megan		/		/		/		/		/
Day Ashley		/		/		/		/		/
Nguyen Ngoc	4:15		4:00		3:		3:55			
Payne Christopher	Lott	JP		4:10	JP		4:12	JP	4:05	JP
Payne Damian	Lott	JP	JP	4:10	JP		4:12	JP	4:05	JP

Morris, Adam
Morrison, Ashley

Go gfe Maps 373 Bottom Rd, Raven, VA 24639 to Walmart Supercenter, 13320 Gov GC Peery Hwy, Pounding Mill, VA 24637 Drive 8.4 miles, 14 min

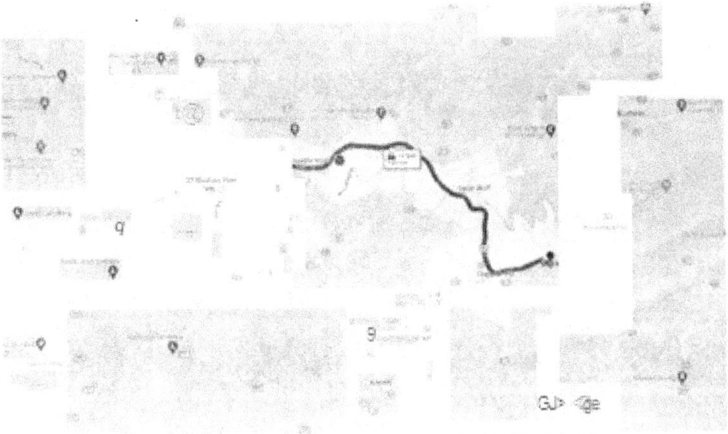

via U S-460 E 14 min
Fastest route now due to traffic conditions 8.4 miles

Explore Walmart Supercenter

1

ROBERT BLANKENSHIP

Evidence 
1 of 2

rhd HUMAN
Specialized Pediatric Services of Virginia
Address: PO Box 282/Abingdon, VA 24212
Phone: 276-206-8721 Fax: 276-206-8045

SEX OFFENDER RISK & NEEDS ASSESSMENT

IDENTIFYING INFORMATION:

Name: Robert McKinley Blankenship Sex: Male
DOB: 11/17/1963 Address: SWVA Regional Jail Authority, Tazewell Facility, Tazewell, VA 24650
Age: (Concealed)
Race: Caucasian/White
SSN: XXX-XX-5898

DATE OF OFFENSES: 07/09/2012
DATE OF EVALUATION: 08/12/2013
REFERRAL SOURCE: Phillip Ward, Probation & Parole District 43
EVALUATOR: Cheryl A. Claxton, L.C.S.W., C.S.O.T.P.

SOURCES OF INFORMATION:

Incident Report regarding 1997 Sexual Offense- Hickory, NC Police Department Incident
Report regarding Instant Offense (2012)- Tazewell County Sheriff's Department
Indictment on 1997 Sexual Offense - Catawba County North Carolina
Conviction Order on 1997 Sexual Offense - Catawba County North Carolina
Confidential Supplement regarding Instant Offense (2012)-Tazewell County Sheriff's Department
Incident Report regarding theft of Mr. Blankenship's wallet (2012)- Tazewell County Sheriff's Dept.
Grand Jury Indictment Tazewell County Circuit Court 2012
Tazewell County Circuit Court Jury Trial Conviction Order 2012
Client Criminal History
Intake Interview
Clinical Interview
Hanson Sex Attitude Questionnaire
Burley Cognitive Distortions Scale
Hare Psychopathy Checklist- Revised - 2 (PCL-R- 2)

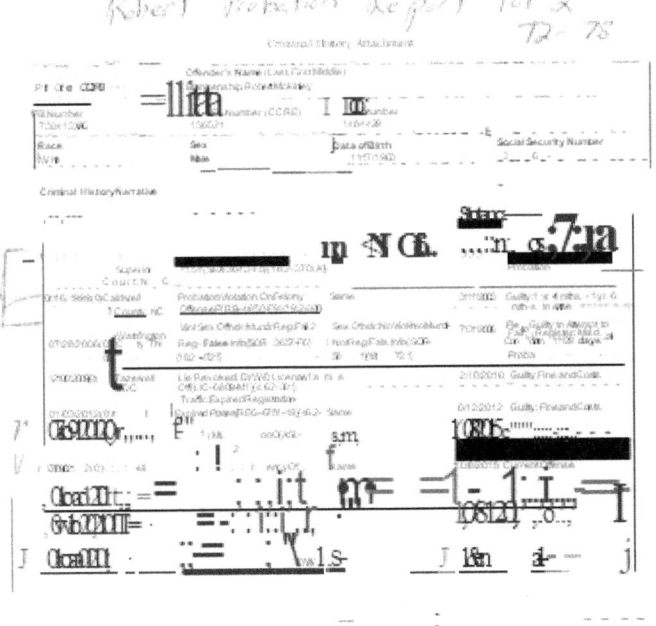

ROBERT BLANKENSHIP

TAZEWELL COUNTY SHERIFF'S OFFICE

Brian L. Hieatt, Sheriff
315 School Street, Suite 3
Tazewell, VA 24651
276-988-5966
Fax: 276-988-5790

Mr. Robert Blankenship

After checking with multiple deputies about contact being made with the female named Ms. Bourne. The incident that you are asking about can't be located in our jurisdiction with any information in which you have provided.

Thank You

Actual Inncocence

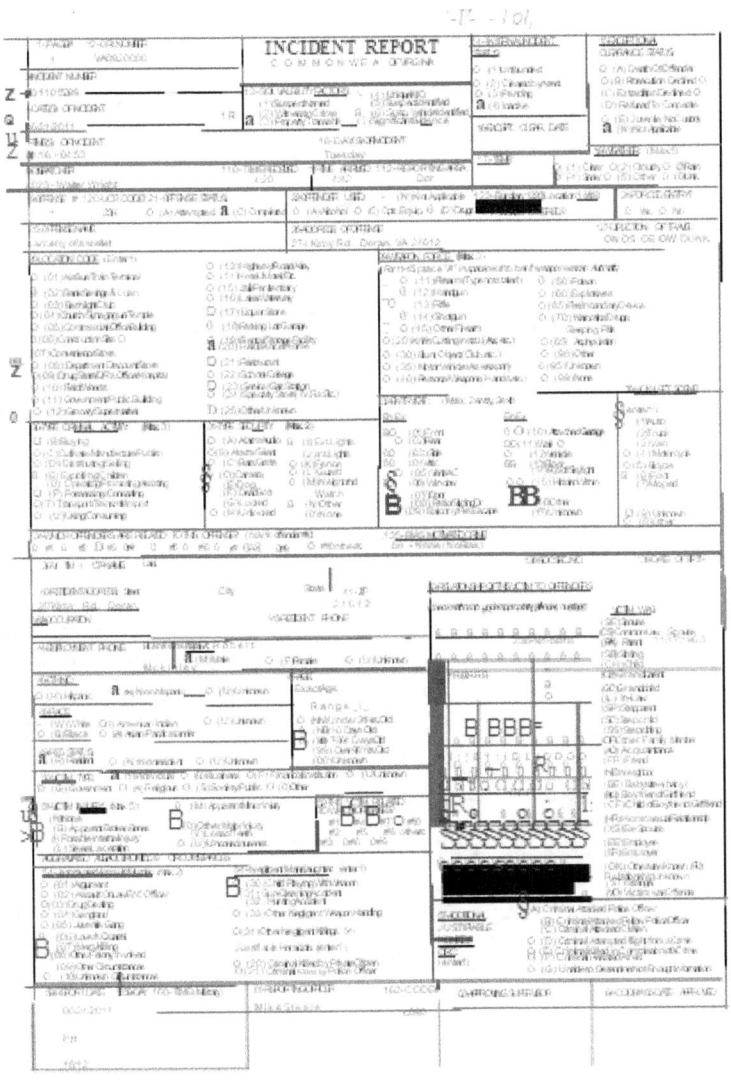

ROBERT BLANKENSHIP

Actual Inncocence

ROBERT BLANKENSHIP

Virginia State Bar

1111 East Main Street, Suite 700
Richmond, Virginia 23219-0026
Telephone: (804) 775-0500

Fax: (804) 775-0501 / TDD: (804) 775-0502

July 12, 2022

PERSONAL AND CONFIDENTIAL

Carletta Jean Faletti, Esquire   via email only
5311 NE 84th Loop
Vancouver, WA 98662

Re: Complaint from Robert McKinley Blankenship
      VSB Docket # 23-444-126319

Dear Ms. Faletti:

Attached please find a copy of a complaint concerning you that the Virginia State Bar received from the above referenced complainant. To resolve the problem(s) between you and the complainant and avoid our office initiating a formal ethics investigation into this matter, **please respond to Mr. Blankenship's request for his file or explain why you cannot provide it.** Please send me a copy of any written communication you send to the complainant. If you communicate orally with the complainant, please send me a written summary of your conversation.

Pursuant to Virginia Rule of Professional Conduct 8.1(c), you have a duty to comply with the bar's lawful demands for information not protected from disclosure by Rule 1.6 which governs confidentiality of information. This request constitutes a lawful demand for information from a disciplinary authority pursuant to Rule 8.1(c). The VSB requests that your response to this complaint **BE RECEIVED IN THIS OFFICE via regular mail or by email to intakereb@vsb.org by JULY 22, 2022.**

Very truly yours,

Mary W. Martolino

Mary W. Martolino
Assistant Intake Counsel

MWM/mu

Attachment(s): Complaint

cc: Robert McKinley Blankenship
      Keen Mountain Correctional Center
      P. O. Box 860
      Oakwood, VA 24631

Actual Inncocence

CoMMON WEALTH OF VIRGINIA

RICHARD C. PATTERSON
JACK S. HARLEY, JR.
Tazewell County Circuit Court
131? Court Sand North st/2
Tazewell, VA 24651
(276)988-1229
(276)988-1049 Fax

PATRICK W. JOHNSON
Buchanan County Circuit Court
P.O. Box 1975
Grundy, VA 24614
(276)935-6567
(276)935-8183 Fax

TWENTY - NINTH JUDICIAL CIRCUIT
SERVING BUCHANAN, DICKENSON, RUSSELL AND TAZEWELL

MICHAEL L. MOORE
Chief Judge
Russell County Circuit Court
P.O. Box 435
Lebanon, VA 24266
(276)889-8045
(276)889-8049 Fax

BRIAN K. PATTON
Dickenson County Circuit Court
P.O. Box 190
Clintwood, VA 24228
(276)926-1605
(276)926-6548 Fax

January 30, 2023

Robert M. Blankenship (K.M.C.C.)
Central Mail Distribution
1821 Woods Way
State Farm, VA 23160

RE: *Commonwealth of Virginia, v. Robert Mckinley Blankenship*
Supplemental Brief in Support of Motion to Vacate

Dear Mr. Blankenship,

The Court has received and reviewed your Supplemental Brief in Support of your Motion to Vacate.

As per my previous letter dated January 11, 2023, this Court is without jurisdiction to provide any relief in this matter.

Additionally, neither the Court nor any of its employees may provide you with legal advice. You may ask the Warden's office or seek legal counsel as to your questions.

Best Regards,

Garrett W. Patton
Law Clerk to the
Honorable Richard C. Patterson
Honorable Jack S. Harley, Jr.

cc: Clerk's Office

ROBERT BLANKENSHIP

VIRGINIA
DEPARTMENT OF CORRECTIONS — Notification to Publisher of Publication Disapproval

COMMONWEALTH of VIRGINIA

Department of Corrections

April 28, 2023

Cadmus Publishing
P.O. Box 2146
Port Angeles, WA 98362

To the Publisher:

You are hereby advised that the following item(s) of publication(s) sent to an inmate of the Virginia Department of Corrections have been disapproved for delivery to inmates of the Department.

Indecent Liberties: A True-Crime Modern-Day Witch Hunt by Robert Blankenship 3/22

for the following reasons:

8. Material that contains solicitations for or promotes activities that are in violation of state or federal law including the abuse or sexual exploitation of children or contains nude depictions of children in the context of sexual activity.

You may obtain an independent review of this decision by writing within fifteen calendar days, to the Chief of Corrections Operations, Virginia Department of Corrections, P.O. Box 26963, Richmond, Virginia 23261

Sincerely,

Wendy Brown
Chairwoman, Publication Review Committee

Should you not wish to receive such notification in the future, please sign below and return to the Publication Review Committee at the above address.

Signature: _____ Date: _____

Title: _____

✦ 328 ✦

ACTUAL INNCOCENCE

Virginia State Bar

1111 East Main Street, Suite 700
Richmond, Virginia 23219-0026
Telephone: (804) 775-0500
Fax: (804) 775-0501; TDD: (804) 775-0102

June 5, 2023

PERSONAL AND CONFIDENTIAL

Carletta Jean Faletti, Esquire *via email only*
Cooke, Shorts, Brewer and Falletti, PLLC
3148 Cedar Valley Drive
Richlands, VA 24641

Re: Complaint from Robert McKinley Blankenship #1484429
VSB Docket #23-444-128329

Dear Ms. Faletti:

Attached please find a copy of a complaint concerning you that the Virginia State Bar received from the above referenced complainant. To resolve the problem(s) between you and the complainant and avoid our office initiating a formal ethics investigation into this matter, please communicate with Mr. Blankenship regarding his continued request for his file materials. We note that you previously responded to an earlier complaint by Mr. Blankenship. You stated that you did not have access to Mr. Blankenship's paper file. Please include in your response information that might help Mr. Blankenship contact the person or entity that might have access to Mr. Blankenship's physical file. However, if you have digital copies of the file, as Mr. Blankenship's former attorney, you may have a duty to provide what documents you have. You should consult Rule of Professional Conduct 1.16(e) regarding such duties and govern yourself accordingly. Please send me a copy of any written communication you send to the complainant. If you communicate orally with the complainant, please send me a written summary of your conversation.

Pursuant to Virginia Rule of Professional Conduct 8.1(c), you have a duty to comply with the bar's lawful demands for information not protected from disclosure by Rule 1.6 which governs confidentiality of information. This request constitutes a lawful demand for information from a disciplinary authority pursuant to Rule 8.1(c). The VSB requests that your response to this complaint BE RECEIVED IN THIS OFFICE via regular mail or by email to intakerob@vsb.org by JUNE 15, 2023.

Very truly yours,

/s/ Jane A. Fletcher
Jane A. Fletcher
Deputy Intake Counsel

JAF/sam
Attachment: Complaint

cc: Robert McKinley Blankenship #1484429
VADOC Centralized Mail Distribution Center
3521 Woods Way
State Farm, VA 23160

ROBERT BLANKENSHIP

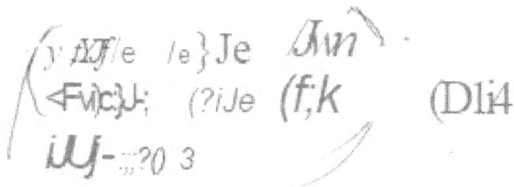

z
Tue- 23-Jul-2019

Dear Mrs. Faletti, r
understand **busy and** carry

a

you

probably very case

Toad.

Actual Inncocence

beavy

I can look at my appeal online and couple of questions, th being why did e commonwealth the
2 have s
not file an
answer to our

ROBERT BLANKENSHIP

(8 to 2 Pal.S) (3rizier 5.
$= W Le H$

Saturday, August 11, 2018

Hello Sweetie,

8:40 AM- Good morning! Waiting on you to call this morning. I wish I could have gotten in touch with Mr. Tiller yesterday, but I do have lawyer news for you. I didn't talk to Carla but I did talk with Jean Lee who is the same person that said they'd send me the audio recording.

Not much is going on this morning. It's a cloudy humid day out right now. I think the sun is supposed to come out this afternoon. I'm wearing the gray shirt with the regular tank top this **week** for pajamas. That's what I'm wearing. I need to go down to the pool at some point this morning and unlock the bathroom doors. Then I'm supposed to work from 2 to 9PM. I won't be able to write to you this afternoon, unless it starts storming. I've got a letter that needs to go to the mailbox this morning. The people who live under me are moving out. More new neighbors.

Oh yeah, I found out why we have so many gnats in this building. The dude who lives in the other downstairs apartment is a trash hoarder. They found out I guess when the bug man came, that the spare bedroom in his apartment was filled with trash. He's on a waiting list so it must be hard for him to get to the dumpster. I found out about it from the girl who lives next door to me. Their kitchen is right above his spare room. Yesterday, he had his van or SUV or whatever it is pulled up to the door of his apartment. Maybe he was putting trash in it to drive to the dumpster. At least, I hope he was.

I'm praying about writing to Suzy and Bobby. I know you said I should do. I'm not sure what to say to them. I suppose I could tell them my friends/news my job at the pool and the kiddos. I'm trying to think of something that I can ask them to see if they'll write back to me. It's hard, but I'm going to do it.

Notes from phone conversation with Carla: Only appeal til to do th appeal... did Mike Dennis cross examine Officer Hale and attempt to impeach him on the bicer cane evidence, frameless canes, best practice... the audio recording belong to the court... can't change the outcome of the trial... the transcripts we have today is in your brief... It doesn't want to hear the recordings... who did you file the habeas with? Supreme Court of VA? Can now file with Federal Courts... told her about them sending the clothes to me... she thinks your case has merit... really good shot... Sandy Sanders read the brief... told me way you won't get a new trial... premises for habeas if denial 1) admission of prior conviction... 2) counsel did not object to bicer cam testimony so ineffective counsel... Called clerk of court and was told, they still have the audio transcript... will file a motion to preserve the audio recording until all appeals have been exhausted... Thanks Jan Shrout doesn't fully believe the illegal victim... would be in most.

10: 20AM-OK. I just got off the phone with Carla, and she and I agree that you need to calm down!! OK here's the deal on the audio recording. She says they are NOT strarppropriety, they ARE the property of the court. She called the clerk of the court a **few** minutes back and at that time, the clerk of the court said that the recordings were **saur**. They were on a shelf above the sheriff with the rest of your trial documents. I will tell that you are old old that the recordings will be destroyed, and IF your appeal is denied, then you won't be able to get the in Seepid. she will file a motion with the court that the audio recording of your trial be preserved until such time as all appeals habeas etc., has been exhausted... We would have to pay the court clerk's office to get a copy of the audio recording.

Here's another part of why you need to calm down. Your trial is over. DON'T PANIC !! Remember? Carla is on your side, and she would like for you and her to get along. You don't have to be best friends with her, just try to be on the same page she is on. She's trying to find out what you're objecting to about the bicer pt. I talked to her about Office Hale's testimony about the bicer cam and that there **were** still told. If the judge overruled the objection to the best avery, then Mike Dennis should have on cross-examination, asked how bicer cam brought in.

ROBERT BLANKENSHIP

Actual Inncocence

3:30 PM until still be cold at 11:30 PM on a hot day in July. She agrees with us that there's no way he been cuts could have been cold after being outside for seven hours. But it was Mike Dennis' job to discredit the witness. He was your defense attorney — and he wasn't looking out for your best interests. If the transcript you have does not show him objecting to and cross-examining Officer Hale, then it shows ineffective counsel. So your trans- script can be good for that. I need to read the transcript again.

Then Sandy Sanders (that's her full read her brief — well, just let me be angry and gripe about him. "Elwood 'Sandy' Sanders is a Hanover attorney who is an Appellate Procedure Consultant for Lantagne Legal Printing, and has written ten scholarly legal articles. Sandy was also Virginia's first Appellate Defender." Lantagne Legal Printing is who printed her brief. Halfass. Anyway, she read the brief and his opinion was that he didn't see any reason why you should not get another trial. "No way" you should not get a new trial are the words she used. (see notes on previous page)

She wanted to know who you filed your habeas with? She said she hopes it was with the Supreme Court of VA because then you can go to Federal District Court with your next one. If the appeal is denied. She was shocked to find out that your clothes were sent to me. I told her a t-shirt, shoes, underwear, socks, belt, watch. I told her they only showed pictures of your clothes at your trial. She found that very interesting. I'm pretty sure that she's seen the picture. I think she started to say so but thought of something else to say. Anyway, she's your appellate attorney and I believe she is willing to become your trial attorney if your case is remanded back to the Circuit Court in Lunenburg. BUT! You need to quit sending her threatening letters!!! Very important! Try to get on she came page she saw for this appeal. She is not AGAINST you, she is your advocate. She wants to win this case, and I feel like she wants to win it bad. She's trying not to get excited about it, but she is.

She asked me about them offering your good "husband" you wanted to take it to trial. I told her yes, that was true because YOU DIDN'T DO IT!!! I told her that I know you very well and there's no way on God's green earth that you would get raped outside in daylight hours!!! I told her you wouldn't even piss off the back porch at home at night.

12:55 PM- Jetta came by. I ordered some stuff from my online drugstore for her, so she had a box of s stuff. Between her and April and myself, we ordered $99 worth of stuff. I think I've got about $99 to order this month or I lose whatever's left. I may have to get Christy since I meet her.

I've totally forgotten what all I was writing when Jetta got here. I did finish my sentence but kept talking to her when she came in. It seems like I was about finished with what I was saying. Jetta had to stay for a while because it started pouring down rain. I'm hoping the rain is finished for the day because I'm supposed to work the pool from 2 to 9 PM. That's not long. I need to get some things out before I go down there.

1:00 PM- OK, I ate a 1/2 piece of bread sandwich. Turkey and cheese. It was good. I guess I need to get back to answering your letter since there's another one on the way and up. Oh, Caella asked me what difference this new case were and I told her it was evidence state king. She got sort of quiet for a minute, then started talking about how we can use the transcript to accuse Mike Dennis of ineffective representation. That's not suing him, which of course, you can't do, but you can accuse him of ineffective representation.

Whew! What a busy day today has been. Now that I've talked to everyone else, Christy is nowhere to be seen. They were supposed to move into their new place last night, but the landlord is still putting down raw hardwood floors. So she and Eli are staying in a motel today and tomorrow. They're going swimming there. I'm not sure where they're staying. She said the pool is right outside their door. They're moving to Bluff City, which is 30 minutes away from here. Her Josh had to leave this morning for National Guard training. His brothers are going to unpack the U-Haul truck for her. I sure hope they get finished with her house on Monday. Staying at a hotel's own on Etowah-Lodge, to expensive. That certainly renting a double-wide trailer, not a house, but I think I told you that. He said, On 1.5 acres. Sounds like a good place to raise kids.

www.ingramcontent.com/pod-product-compliance
Lightning Source LLC
Chambersburg PA
CBHW072147070526
44585CB00015B/1027